SWORDS AND COVENANTS

Essays in Honour of the Centennial of

the Royal Military College of Canada

1876–1976

SWORDS AND COVENANTS

Edited by

ADRIAN PRESTON and PETER DENNIS

The Royal Military College of Canada

CROOM HELM

ROWMAN AND LITTLEFIELD

© 1976 Adrian Preston

Croom Helm Ltd, 2-10 St John's Road, London SW11

ISBN 0-85664-383-1

First published in the United States 1976
by ROWMAN AND LITTLEFIELD, Totowa, New Jersey

Copyright © 1976 A. W. Preston

Library of Congress Cataloging in Publication Data
Main entry under title:

Swords and covenants.

Includes index.
1. Militarism – History – Addresses, essays, lectures. 2. Military History – Addresses, essays, lectures. 3. Kingston, Ont. Royal Military College of Canada – Addresses, essays, lectures. I. Preston, Adrian W. UA10.S87 1976   355'.009   76-20716
ISBN 0-87471-862-7

Printed in Great Britain by offset lithography by
Billing & Sons Ltd, Guildford, London and Worcester

Contents

Acknowledgements

Without the generous support of the Commandant, Brigadier-General W. W. Turner, CD, AdeC, IDC, NDC, PSC, RMC, the Principal, Dr. J. R. Dacey and the Director of Administration, Commander P. C. Fortier, this book might never have been published and to them we are most grateful. We would also like to thank especially the Chairman of the RMC Centennial Committee, Dr. Jack Pike, whose enthusiastic commitment to the notion of a *festschrift* has never wavered and who has unfailingly placed at our disposal his time, advice and assistance. We would also like to thank Mrs Karen Brown, our Secretary, whose genial efficiency enabled us to meet our deadline. We would wish to acknowledge as warmly as we can the technical help supplied by Mr. Bill Reid of the College Book Stores which was so freely rendered over many years. Finally, we are much indebted to our publisher, David Croom.

A. W. P.
P. J. D.

TO

The Gentlemen Cadets of the Royal Military College of Canada,
1876–1976

that their Courage, Loyalty and Good Cheer may continue
to grace and favour the nation they serve

Introduction

This collection of essays is offered as a sort of *festschrift* to the centenary of The Royal Military College of Canada. It is a modest and very personal tribute to an institution which during the first hundred years of its existence has in its own unobtrusive way had a profoundly formative effect upon the tone and the temper of much of Canadian life. It is unrepentantly an historians'*festschrift*, appropriately inspired by a member of the College's history department. Neither in their authorship nor in their subject matter therefore do the essays reflect any of the pioneering work in mathematics, the physical sciences, engineering, political economy, linguistics and Canadian literature upon which the College has otherwise built a substantial reputation within the academic community. Still less do they pretend, as some might have hoped, to a full and faithful representation of the state of historical scholarship at RMC since 1948.

I had at first hoped to solicit a series of original papers on the general theme of civil-military relations in Canada from those defence specialists and military historians practising in the universities, the Services and elsewhere, both in Canada and abroad, who had been or still were either as staff or students in some way connected with RMC, especially since its re-opening in 1948. While honouring the Centenary as a whole, it seemed to me that here was also a fitting opportunity for paying particular tribute to the new post-war College, to the visions and ideals of the men who first moulded it and what it has since meant to the military and intellectual life of contemporary Canada. The official history of the College was largely a conventional treatment of its pre-war development and had been published on the occasion of the national cententary of 1967, some nine years before that of the College. I felt that it would be unfair to expect the official history to serve the purposes which I had in mind and that the academic aspects of the College centenary should be memorialised in a more distinct and separate fashion.

For when the College had re-opened its doors in 1948, it had done so in all important respects as a federal, tri-service. military university, the bulk of whose lecturers were civilian and the bulk

of whose graduates would pursue careers not in the permanent
military service of Canada but in the civilian professions which
lay beyond. It was from the start a unique experiment, unprecedented in the history of military education, which no great
power dared seriously to imitate and which in certain quarters in
Canada was criticised, and still is, as being wrongheaded, ex-
travagant and irresponsible. At the strictly military level this experiment was favoured by the belief, then current among most of
the armies of the Grand Alliance, that the techniques and attitudes of joint-service co-operation which had largely accounted
for the flawless planning of all the large-scale combined
operations of the Second World War should be deliberately inculcated from the very start of an officer's career. It was an experiment which was made possible by two advantages which no
great power could share: the lack of any vital and defensible
strategic interests which were not already taken care of by
Canada's membership of the Permanent Joint Board on Defence,
NORAD and NATO; and the absence of powerful academy
lobbies among the rival services.

But it was an experiment which depended as much for its
success upon the single-minded vision of its architects as upon its
capacity to adapt to the developing conditions and needs of
Canadian defence on the one hand and higher education on the
other. When in 1959 the Provincial government of Ontario conferred upon the College the right to grant its own degrees –
becoming thereby the first military college to compete effectively in the academic market-place – it was formally acknowledg-
ing its dual status as a university the core of whose curriculum, it
must be remembered, was the humanities, without which any
college, but especially a military college, must by definition remain a mere polytechnic, incapable of attracting the best minds
of the country or of putting the technical military knowledge it
imparted into some sort of social, political and historical perspec-
tive. What must strike anyone who stops to consider the matter,
as it struck me when I began scouting about for an appropriate
Centenary project, was the degree to which the humanities
programme, especially in historical studies, had been successful. It
is a fact that with one or two exceptions virtually every military
historian of consequence in Canada has at some time and in some
way been associated with RMC. Moreover, since those
Cinderella days in the early 1950s when George Stanley publish-

ed his pioneering history of the Canadian Army, members of the History Department have produced a steady flow of books on local, military, Imperial and naval history and biography. What was perhaps most remarkable of all, however, was the fact that the History Department, almost singlehandedly and always against heavy odds, had inspired a whole new generation of military and political historians in whose advance guard strode such men as A. M. J. Hyatt, Desmond Morton and Jack Granatstein.

No one who read the works of these historians could fail to notice how indelibly an appreciation of the incidence of war and the existence of armed forces had quickened their perceptions of the past or the degree to which social and economic factors had shaped the means and purposes to which they were to be put. By examining more dispassionately and persistently than had ever been done before the military 'fact' in Canadian society and politics, by clearing away the scrub and undergrowth of much myth and sentiment and indifference, these historians prepared the way for the phenomenal and trendy growth within the civilian universities of a new discipline of 'strategic studies' by which their own work, orthodox and revisionist though it had been as history, was ironically and popularly eclipsed. It was this achievement which suggested to me that a good case could be made for building a *festschrift* around the theme of civil-military relations which had been so marked a feature, though not always an explicit one, of their historical preoccupations.

There were other reasons why such a theme seemed appropriate to the Centenary. By virtue of its hybrid status as a military university, RMC was microcosmic of the larger dialectical problem of the relations between governments and soldiers with which its graduates at some stage of their career would probably have to grapple. Moreover, it seemed to me that here was a very real gap in Canadian military historiography which no one had attempted to fill in a systematic or comprehensive way and that a collection of essays might at least probe its dimensions and suggest some ways of getting to the bottom of it. I visualised a range of topics which dealt with the higher administration of defence, strategic planning, the politics of military assistance to developing countries, military government, international peace-keeping, disarmament and alliances, the influence of garrison towns and soldier settlements upon regional communities and problems of command, control and reconstruction.

It was a heady brew, which quickly evaporated in the chilling light of academic and military realities. The tone and substance of the book, it was clear, would pretty well be determined by the special research interests of those who were prepared to contribute to the *festschrift* in circumstances wherein there lay for many anxious months little hope of publication. It was after all, as with most matters of education, a voluntary act of faith. It was also a matter of editorial regret that no serving officer, especially among those officially employed in strategic analysis, intelligence and planning could be persuaded to spare the time to write an article on the basis of his personal experiences in NATO, Cyprus or Vietnam or be convinced that he might have something useful to say.

It is a commonplace, but one which bears re-stating, that Canadian officers are not so ready to take up the pen as their British or European counterparts. Canadian military autobiography, for instance, is a thin and unsustaining gruel. Time and again, in presenting their version of events, Canadian generals have allowed themselves to be out-written by their political masters by simply choosing to write nothing at all. Diaries kept by Canadian generals are virtually non-existent. Certainly there is nothing to compare with those of Mackenzie King or Charles Ritchie or with the autobiographies of Robert Borden, Lester Pearson, Vincent Massey or John Diefenbaker. One has to go back well into the nineteenth century, to Denison's *Soldiering in Canada* or Strange's *Gunner Jingo's Jubilee,* to find military memoirs which have the sparkle and punch of British ones. With the exception of Otter, MacNaughton, Pearkes and Vanier, Canadian generals have not as a rule attracted the interest of biographers and those have often done so largely because they went on to pursue other, political or viceregal careers. But if a nation's style and sense of purpose is explicit in its literature and the particular form – biography, fiction, poetry – which that literature takes, then military biography and memoirs must constitute the starting-point for any real understanding of the psychology of the officer corps, the manner in which policy is formulated and the nature of its relations with political and official society. For all practical purposes therefore the Canadian historian is in these matters faced with a closed book and the public understanding of war and defence in Canada is to that degree diminished. This impoverishment is also evident in the more conventional genres of trade journalism and strategic writing, and it raises disturbing questions – which it would be impolitic of me to address myself to here – about the kind of education which is most appropriate to the Canadian officer corps as it gropes its way into the last quarter of the twentieth century.

It is inherent in the historical evolution of modern standing armies and in the contract with the Crown which an officer's commission implies that the profession of arms cannot be indifferent or unaccountable to the social and political environment which provides the only rational legitimacy for its existence. Every technical military decision – whether to build a bridge or to mount a divisional attack – must be taken in the full knowledge of its probable social and political ramifications. In formulating its philosophy of military education, therefore, the High Command must take into account a wide range of variables: the chief of which are the official objectives of national security policy and the manner and means in which they are to be met; the nature of its alliance obligations; federal-provincial relations and the maintenance of internal order and unity; and the state of both military technology and higher education. If the profession of arms is to serve the social and political purposes for which it is recruited and maintained, its officer corps must be thoroughly instructed in those academic disciplines which bear directly upon three main areas: applied science and weapons technology, political and strategic studies, and economics and management.

It is axiomatic to professional students of the history of war and defence administration that too specialised or too technical a form of military education often conduces to a state of professional myopia in which the High Command may find itself dangerously ill-equipped on the battlefield to orchestrate the complex administrative, financial, strategic, diplomatic and political requirements of total coalition warfare or even in calmer times to stand up for its rights against its more powerful and more broadly – education ministerial or official colleagues in the Defence Council. This is not to say that the senior officer corps should become so politically indoctrinated as to be unable to voice the military point of view it is paid to provide. What is required, in the education of one's officer corps as in the composition of one's forces, is an awareness of the importance of balance, a sense of the fitness of things and a belief that all expert advice must be strongly diluted by an admixture of common sense and compassion. But it is precisely the nature of that balance, the right combination of academic ingredients appropriate to a bewildering and shifting range of variables and priorities – political, social, economic and strategic – which except in the most doctrinaire sense can never be definitively resolved. It is for this reason that official studies of the state and objectives of Canadian military education and professionalism are so frequently conducted and their reports as frequently shelved.

No other profession segregates its recruits quite so completely or at so early a stage in their calling as does the Armed Forces. Insulated behind the garrison walls of their barracks or academies, and largely immune from the social and political forces with which they must some day reckon, the novitiates are carefully indoctrinated in the *'servitudes et grandeurs'*, the mystique and techniques of their chosen profession. In these circumstances – and this is a point which most official historians and military pedagogues miss – a military college invariably develops a life--force of its own, with its own discrete moods, interests and purposes which may not always seem to correspond with those of official policy or be immediately relevant to the wider defence needs of the country. This is particularly true of RMC whose academic standards are regulated by Provincial, not Federal, law and by the professional societies and associations with which it is accredited. A military college is inherently unclassifiable: it has a life and soul apart from that granted to it by official authority. It is a tightly disciplined, self-contained community, properly jealous of its prerogatives and autonomy, more akin to a seminary than a business or law school, yet in its management not unlike them, and dedicated to its unique and distinctive function – the education of a professional military elite. It is here that the attempt is made to homogenise the diverse regional and ethnic backgrounds and outlooks of its recruits and transform them into the corporate loyalty and efficiency of a truly national, apolitical officer corps. On the other hand, it would be strange if the location of Canada's three military colleges – RMC in Ontario, Royal Roads in British Columbia and Collège Militaire Royale in Quebec – did not in some degree reflect the provincial and racial make-up of Canada or if each military college did not absorb and radiate something of the ethos and values of the community in which it was located.

There has always been to my mind a certain Britishness about RMC. Not the arrogant and frivolous Englishness normally associated with the Guards, the Cavalry or Bloomsbury, but the fierce and hardy Britishness of the Canada Firsters: men who, like the historian Gerald Graham, the publisher Lovat Dickson, or the diplomatist Charles Ritchie, felt that Canada was a larger and a better place because, rather than in spite of its membership of the British Empire. 'We of the Colonies stand present for the King', ran one of their regimental mottoes. Though few today would probably recognise it and most would deny it, it is a Britishness which still persists in every Graduation Parade, when every cadet is dressed in ceremonial scarlet, and which is still capable of working its old magic upon those who believe that tradition is the soul of an army. There is about this Britishness a permanent and primordial quality which derives in part from the location of the College on Point Frederick, dominated by the escarpments and low-sunk walls of Fort Henry above which floats the Union Jack, and in part and perhaps mainly from the high Victorian architecture of its original buildings. This architecture embodies the *zeitgeist* of an age when for all practical purposes, as the official history shows, the College was run as a British military college in Canada, complete with its British Commandant, instructors, textbooks and drills. It is at one with the architecture of City Hall, St George's Cathedral, Barriefield and the Empire Life Building and has therefore made RMC an integral part of Kingston without being centrally lodged within it.

Save only in the most superficial sense or where because of conditions of climate and recruitment it was unavoidable, it made no concessions to the North American model provided by West Point. In much the same way RMC has figured only as a shadowy and slightly sinister place somewhere in the Kingstonian background of Robertson Davies' early novels. It has never itself been the subject or the locale for a satire on academic or military intrigue of the kind made notorious by Auberon Waugh, G. K. Chesterton, David Garnett, C. P. Snow or Michael Innes. Unlike the military colleges of nineteenth-century Europe and America it has never in itself constituted a breeding ground or provided a permanent refuge for would-be Clausewitzes and Jominis, Mahans and Fochs, Uptons and

Hamleys whose strategic treatises, which were to change the face of warfare in the Industrial Age, innocently began as classroom textbooks. Unlike the military colleges of most continental powers, RMC has never been identified with any military politics of a particularly dangerous or chauvinistic kind. Its graduates, even when they became generals, have shown very little desire to act as schoolmasters to the nation or to rebel against the government. RMC, like the Regimental system to which it was once organically linked, can never be defended or justified on any grounds of its efficiency in producing officers alone or its relevance to the needs of the country which must extract the maximum contribution from the professional skill of every officer who serves beyond his initial four-year term.

A military college is a parochial and secretive institution, the guardian of the *virtú* of the Armed Forces and its reputation for courage. It instinctively bristles like a hedgehog at the intrusions of politicians and professional reformers alike. It has the infuriating habit of dragging its feet at the mere mention of internal reform. But if a military college is the starting point in the process whereby the officer corps is in some degree isolated from the society it serves, 'it also tames them, fixing their eyes on minutiae, limiting their ambitions, teaching them a gentle, parochial loyalty difficult to pervert to more dangerous ends. It may be an obstacle to full professional efficiency; but it is perhaps a barrier to much else as well'. [1]

Adrian Preston.

Notes

1. Michael Howard. 'Soldiers in Politics', *Encounter*, no. 108, September 1962, pp. 77-81. Michael Howard was here describing the regimental system but I believe that it also describes the military college system.

The American Invasion of Canada 1775-1776: A Strategic Overview

G. F. G. STANLEY

I

Nations go to war for the purpose of achieving some clearly defined political purpose – clearly defined, at least, in the minds of their political leaders. What we call strategy is simply the means used by a warring nation to achieve that political purpose. Strategy is therefore no more and no less than policy-in-execution. It co-ordinates and directs the national resources available for the attainment of its goals as defined by national policy. Thus, strategy is concerned with the political and economic, as well as with the military means available. All of these are woven together in what is generally referred to as grand strategy. Warfare on the grand scale includes propaganda, blockade, economic pressure and diplomacy, as well as military operations. That means that grand strategy is concerned with all the problems of time, space and force.

On the purely military plane, strategy has been defined by one authority as 'the art of distributing and applying military means to fulfil the ends of policy'. In essence this means that military strategy is primarily concerned with movement and communications; it means, too, that the aim of the military strategist is not so much to seek out the enemy and destroy him, or even to seek battle with him, as to 'seek a situation so advantageous that if it does not of itself produce the decision, its continuation by battle is sure to achieve this'.[1] That is the definition of strategy given by Captain Liddell Hart in 1929.

Interestingly enough, Liddell Hart's emphasis upon seeking an advantageous position reflects the emphasis upon manoeuvre so characteristic of eighteenth-century strategists. In 1766, Henry Humphrey Lloyd, the foremost English writer on strategy and tactics of his day, in the preface of his *Military Memoirs*, stated that there were two sides to the art of war; one, which was purely mechanical or scientific and could be learned, the other which was intuitive or a matter of inborn talent and could not be learned. Lloyd, while appreciating the importance of natural talent

that went into the making of a great commander, did not un-
derplay the importance of a military education, particularly in
topography and mathematics. A firm grasp of these disciplines,
he maintained, would give the commander the basic knowledge
necessary to manoeuvre his army so as to attain the results he
desired.[2] Only if manoeuvre failed should a battle be necessary.
Manoeuvre was the supreme test of generalship. Like the
Maréchal de Saxe before him, Lloyd considered that an able
general should be able to attain his objective without fighting.
The Chevalier Johnstone, the Scottish Jacobite who acted as
Montcalm's Aide de Camp in 1759, thought likewise. In his
Dialogue in Hades, he wrote, 'The gaining of a battle is very often
the effect of mere chance. But reducing the enemy without
fighting must be the result of well combined operations – is the
essence of military science, and was always the most radiant and
distinctive trait in the conduct and character of the great men
whom History has handed down to us.'[3]

The ability to manoeuvre could only be acquired with time
and training. Without long periods of drill and discipline, armies
could not move with the machine-like precision that manoeuvre
required. Manoeuvre might be the best way to win a campaign,
but there was another reason for placing emphasis upon it, and
that was the high cost of producing and equipping a well-trained
soldier. Eighteenth-century infantry tactics, relying as they did
upon the short-range musket, were based upon the devastating
effect of a shoulder to shoulder massed volley. Thus, when two
armies did meet in battle in the eighteenth century casualties
were considerable. Since the loss of a soldier meant the loss of an
investment, small and unnecessarily bloody encounters were
something to be avoided. That is why eighteenth-century armies
rarely went too far away from their fortified bases; and, when on
the offensive, armies should direct their operations against the
fortifications, supply depots and lines of communications of their
opponents, rather than against his well-equipped and equally
numerically strong armies. If stand-up battles were fought it was
because they were unavoidable or because one side had a decided
advantage of numbers or position. Eighteenth-century military
manners were as formal and artificial as eighteenth-century social
manners. And because all European armies came out of the same
mould, they thought alike and fought alike. It was the age of
classical art, classical architecture and classical warfare; the age of

great generals, notable sieges and grand manoeuvres; the age in which technological developments in weapons were limited largely to the artillery, with interchangeable parts, limber boxes, howitzers and horse-drawn field guns; and in which the only significant development in personal infantry weapons was the substitution of the iron for the wooden ramrod. [4]

II

It was in the third quarter of the eighteenth century, in June 1775, when the members of the Continental Congress, meeting in Philadelphia, decided upon an invasion of Canada. Their motivation was twofold; militarily, they hoped to deprive Great Britain of a base of operations from which a counter-movement might be launched to stifle the American rebellion and end the movement towards independence; politically, they hoped to bring Canada into a continental union with the American colonies. There always seems to be a powerful expansionist thrust in the minds of all revolutionaries and the Americans were no exception. Perhaps because it was in their own interests to do so, they saw themselves as liberators of an oppressed world, and particularly of Canada. [5]

In planning the strategy to be employed in an invasion of Canada, the first factor to be studied was, as Lloyd suggested, the topography of the country to be invaded. [6] What routes should be followed? What lines of attack would achieve success with the minimum expenditure of time and effort? Obviously the critical area of Canada was the Saint Lawrence valley. Here were located the principal centres of population and, in the region south and east of Montreal, the best agricultural land of the country. Barring easy access to the Saint Lawrence valley from the south, was a range of mountains extending from Gaspé in the east to the Alleghanies in the west, including the Shickshock and Notre Dame massif, the White and Green Mountains, the Adirondacks and the Catskills. To lead men over this mountain barrier in the absence of roads, with the long supply trains required by an eighteenth-century army, operating far from its fortified base, was not a feasible operation of war. Indians with no military impedimenta might do it, but not regular troops trained in eighteenth-century warfare. The wilderness of forests, hills and swamps which lay between Canada and the Thirteen

Colonies was not a European officer's idea of suitable campaigning country.

The mountains, however, had their passes. There were several clearly defined defiles through which an army might make its way from New England or New York to the Saint Lawrence Valley. The first and most obvious route was by way of the great river of Canada itself. This, however, meant an approach by sea and then a long sail up the river against the current, to Quebec, or even to Montreal. The British had done just that when Wolfe and Saunders led the offensive against Quebec in 1759. But such an entry into Canada necessitated a fleet of troop transports and escorting ships in numbers sufficient to fend off any hostile opposition. This was just what the American colonies did not have. Lacking a navy, they could not think in terms of a seaborne expedition. They had, therefore, to fall back upon the inland waterways which cut through the mountain barrier guarding Canada. There were four possibilities; the routes marked out by the Kennebec, Dead River and the Chaudière; the Connecticut River, Lake Magog, Lake Mephramagog and St Francis River; the Hudson River, Lake George, Lake Champlain-Richelieu River; and finally the Mohawk River, Oswego River, Lake Ontario route. Of these four, the best known and the most travelled was the third, the Hudson-Lake Champlain-Richelieu route, which emptied into the Saint Lawrence above Montreal and below Quebec. This route, incidentally, contained only three portages of any significance, between the Hudson River and Lake George; between Lake George and Lake Champlain and on the Richelieu River at Chambly. Over this route all the major overland expeditions, military and commercial, had made their way between Canada and New York during the seventeenth and eighteenth centuries. It was the highway used by the Iroquois, the British and the Americans. That explains why it was the most heavily defended route leading into Canada, with fortifications at Ticonderoga (Carillon), Crown Point (St Frédéric), Saint Jean and Chambly.

Important as were the natural hazards to the strategist planning a campaign, even more important were the enemy's manpower resources and above all, his will and determination to resist. Natural hazards present fixed conditions which are calculable; and because they are calculable, planning to overcome them presents fewer problems and worries than the incalculable factor of the enemy's psychology. Physical obstacles can be overcome pretty much to a time-schedule by careful planning and preparation in advance. Napoleon, who knew what he was speaking about (had he not led his army over the Alps according to a time-schedule?) said, 'the moral is to the physical as three is to one'.[7] Ignoring the arithmetic, the point to be made is that moral or psychological factors present the strategist with his most serious problems. Mountains or forts on the frontier would be of little use to Canada, if the people in them and behind them had no will to fight for their country. George Washington was well aware of the pre-eminence of the moral or psychological factor. Frequently he stressed the necessity of ensuring the support of the Canadian people in any invasion of Canada. In an outline plan sent to General Philip Schuyler in Albany on 20 August 1775, Washington pointed out that the success of any American invasion of Canada would, in large measure, depend upon the active collaboration of the Canadians themselves. Schuyler had much the same idea in mind when he wrote that 'If the American troops should experience a reverse in Canada it could only happen as a result of "foul play" on the part of the Canadians.'[8] He meant, of course, if the Canadians should turn against their self-styled liberators.

The Americans, indeed, saw no reason to suspect that there would ever be any such 'foul play'. As far as the English-speaking population in Canada was concerned, the Americans were convinced that it was generally hostile to the British Governor and to the military officers and civilian officials who supported him. Was it not true that, of the small English-speaking group in Canada, many of them came originally from the Thirteen Colonies? To these people the catch words 'Liberty' and 'Protestantism' (in the minds of the Americans they were always equated with each other) were bound to have a strong emotional appeal. And as for the French-speaking population, what reason had it to take up arms for the King? The Quebec Act, which Governor Guy Carleton believed would win him the support of the Canadians, appeared in American eyes only as an instrument of tyranny, something to satisfy the seigneurs and please the Roman Catholic clergy, but wholly abhorrent to all lovers of 'Freedom'. Even while admitting that Carleton might have a few under-strength British regiments (there were three of them, the 7th, 8th and 26th, scattered from the Ohio valley to Gaspé), a few French Canadian seigneurs and Scottish highlanders who were still prepared to follow the leader, to support him, the Americans felt that they had every reason to assume that the bulk of the civilian population in Canada would join them in any invasion of the country. After all, who could withstand the enthusiasm of men who had no other thought than to bring 'Liberty' to the downtrodden, priest-ridden Canadians? That the Canadians might *not* look upon them as friends and liberators was simply inconceivable. The invasion of Canada would be, therefore, a mere matter of marching. Certainly Washington never doubted that a bold advance would quickly overwhelm Carleton; Benedict Arnold declared that given 2,000 men he could overrun the whole country; and Ethan Allen, the leader of the Green Mountain Boys, went one better, boasting that 'with fifteen hundred men and a proper train of artillery' he would have no difficulty in taking Montreal. [9] And he nearly did!

The initial steps in the campaign against Canada were taken some months before George Washington was appointed Commander-in-chief of 'all the continental forces raised or to be raised for the defence of American Liberty.' [10] In February 1775, John Brown, a thirty-year-old lawyer from Boston, who rather fancied himself as both a spy and a soldier, slipped into Canada. Ostensibly he was there to buy horses for the American market, but in reality he went to Canada to learn what he could about Canada's defences and to establish useful contacts in Montreal. He passed each of Canada's principal defence works, Ticonderoga, Crown Point, Saint Jean and Chambly, noted their decrepit state and counted the number of troops and cannons in each. In Montreal he put himself in touch with Thomas Walker and other discontented Anglo-American merchants, persuaded them to form a Committee of Safety to correspond with Massachusetts, and then returned to Boston, thoroughly convinced that the time was ripe for revolt in Canada. A few months later he was back again, this time bearing a large bundle of propaganda sheets translated into French by the Continental Congress, for distribution in the French-language parishes of the province.

It was the colony of Massachusetts which sent Brown to spy the ground in Canada and to find collaborators in that country. It was also the colony of Massachusetts which provided Ethan Allen with the commission he carried when he led eighty-three

Green Mountain Boys to the western shore of Lake Champlain and seized the Fort Ticonderoga from a sleepy and surprised British commandant. This took place on 10 May 1775. Several days later it was followed by the occupation of Crown Point. Connecticut followed the example of its neighbour by giving Benedict Arnold the commission he carried when he seized Philip Skene's schooner on Lake Champlain and rushed off down the Richelieu River to Fort Saint Jean to take possession of a royal schooner and all the military supplies he could lay his hands on. [11] On the face of it, Allen and Arnold look like two irresponsible freebooters; but it should be remembered that both of them were sponsored by the duly elected legislatures of two New England states.

The Continental Congress was momentarily embarrassed that state legislatures should thus have taken the initiative in a field the Philadelphia Congress regarded as its own province. But not for long. The members of the Continental Congress were not prepared to return the forts and their contents to their British garrisons, particularly two forts which would be the first two hurdles to be overcome in the event of any expedition against Canada. Why not take advantage of these unexpected gifts, accept them as evidence of divine support and go for Broke? They did. On 27 June the Continental Congress formally authorised an invasion of Canada and appointed Philip Schuyler, a New York patroon, to take command of a force to proceed via the Richelieu River to seize Montreal and the Saint Lawrence valley.

Meanwhile, the new commander-in-chief of the Continental army, George Washington, had been giving some thought to the idea of invading Canada by another route. Sometime previous, he had learned of the existence of the Kennebec-Dead River-Chaudière route to Quebec, from Colonel Jonathan Brewer of Massachusetts, who had offered to make a demonstration with 500 men before Quebec. With the Schuyler operation approved, Washington began to think in terms of a two-pronged invasion, one by way of Lake Champlain, the other by way of the Kennebec. He reasoned that if an American force could reach Quebec by the Kennebec and the Chaudière, Governor Carleton would be forced to leave Montreal, where he had established his headquarters in anticipation of the Schuyler thrust, in order to save Quebec, 'or suffer that important place to fall into our hands, an event which would have a decisive effect and influence in the public interests'. [12] Admittedly General Thomas Gage would be on Washington's flank with British troops in Boston; but on 17 June Gage had taken quite a drubbing from the American militia at Bunker's Hill, and was in no mood to try conclusions with the Americans again. Gage could, therefore, be ignored, and Washington felt that he could safely detach say 1,000 men for the Quebec diversion. That is why, when Benedict Arnold presented himself personally to Washington after his exploits at Ticonderoga and Saint Jean, offering to lead a force against Quebec, Washington received him with open arms. Where would he find a better man to lead a swift-moving expedition through the wilderness than the energetic, aggressive, ambitious Arnold? Washington therefore gave Arnold a commission in the Continental Army, assigned him 1,200 men, including a strong contingent of riflemen, and sent him on his way with a bundle of printed proclamations to be scattered among the French Canadians, telling them that the Americans all looked forward 'with pleasure to that day not far remote, when all the inhabitants of America will have one sentiment and the full enjoyment of the blessings of a free government'. [13]

Washington's two-pronged invasion got under way at the beginning of September 1775. On 30 August Brigadier-General Robert Montgomery (who had replaced the ailing Schuyler as commander of the Northern Army) set out from Crown Point with 1,500 men; his objective was Montreal. Twelve days later, 11 September, Benedict Arnold left Cambridge, Massachusetts with 1,200 men; his objective was Quebec. Not that there was an overall plan for this interesting operation. The fact is that there was no serious attempt to co-ordinate the movements of the two armies. Communications between Washington and his two field commanders were slow and uncertain; those between the two commanders themselves were even more so, subject as they could not help but be, to interception by British Indians. As far as the troops of both armies were concerned they were, almost to a man, short-enlistment volunteers. As far as their military training was concerned, it was minimal, although most of the serving soldiers had had some experience with the rural militia or the urban train bands. In addition, they lacked funds, supplies and transport. What they did have in abundance, were confidence and courage. John Adams was proud of them. They might be short on training and military know-how, but they were, he said, 'filled with that spirit and confidence that so universally prevails throughout America, the best substitute for Discipline'. [14] If confidence could conquer, Canada was as good as won. Washington was not quite so exuberant; to Schuyler he wrote, 'I trust that you will have a feeble enemy to contend with, and a whole province on your side, two circumstances of great weight in the scale. [15]

Having started Montgomery and Arnold on their way to Canada, Washington then turned to watch General Gage in Boston. He wondered what the British officer was going to do. But 'blundering Tom', even though he had men sufficient for offensive action, did nothing, and in September he was replaced by Major-General William Howe. There were rumours circulating that the British were preparing to pull out of the city. [16] The question was, where would they go? Was it New York or Quebec? Should they choose Quebec, then they would bring so substantial a reinforcement to Carleton's assistance that the whole American project to conquer Canada would be imperilled. On the other hand, were the British to go to New York, they would be in a vitally strategic position along the line of the Hudson from which to threaten Washington. In the end, the British, after spending a miserable winter cooped up in Boston, went neither to Quebec nor to New York. They went, instead to Halifax, where they could neither help Carleton nor threaten Washington.

III

The initial phase of Montgomery's operation went as well as could have been expected. After a little shakiness on the part of his troops when, for the first time, they encountered musket balls fired in anger, they settled down in good eighteenth-century style to lay siege to Fort Saint Jean.

Now it was time for Montgomery to play the politician. With the help of several Americans who had previously lived in Canada, men like Moses Hazen, James Livingston and Jeremy Duggan, he endeavoured to recruit Canadians into the ranks of the American army. But instead of the enthusiastic response which he had been led to expect, Montgomery found Canadian recruits joined him only in dribbles. Subjected to pressures from

their seigneurs and clergy – even to the extent of being deprived
of the sacraments should they join the enemy [17] – the habitants
showed no disposition to throw in their lot whole-heartedly with
the invaders. Why take sides in a purely English contest? After
all, they had no particular quarrel with Great Britain; and there
was always the chance that the British might win the war. Then
where would they be? Perhaps the best policy would be to adopt
an attitude of benevolent neutrality: to sell the enemy a few
supplies, furnish him with labour and transport in return for
good, solid coin, but not to support him with arms.
Montgomery, convinced by the optimistic reports of John
Brown and others, attributed lack of a strong Canadian response
to his appeal, to the numerical weakness of his own forces. 'Our
feebleness', he confided to his friends, 'has intimidated the
Canadians from embarking on so uncertain an adventure.'
Interestingly enough, the British authorities in Quebec could
have said exactly the same thing, and did. They attributed the
French Canadian reluctance to show enthusiasm for militia service in the British cause to the apparent weakness of the British
regular troops. The fact is that neither the British nor the
Americans wholly trusted the habitants. 'They were', wrote one
American officer, 'a people by education averse to resistance to
the commands of their Sovereign, be they just or unjust.'
Benedict Arnold put it more bluntly. The Canadians, he said,
were 'too ignorant to put a just estimate on the value of
freedom' [18] – freedom American style, that is.

On 3 November, the commander of the British garrison at
Fort Saint Jean, Major Charles Preston, marched out of his
beleaguered fort at the head of his men. His drums were beating
and flags flying. But these were merely the trappings of an
honourable surrender. At least Preston had salvaged the honours
of war, giving up a position which had undergone a considerable
battering in the two months it had resisted a numerically superior
enemy. He had run out of rations, lost his ships, been outflanked
when Fort Chambly gave in with scarcely a shot being fired, and
been abandoned by his superior officer, Guy Carleton, who
made no real effort to come to his assistance. Preston had done all
that he had been expected to do – and more. For almost two
months he had held up the invaders and in so doing compelled
Montgomery to enter upon a winter campaign. 'A winter campaign in Canada, Posterity won't believe it!' Montgomery

exclaimed.[19] Yet that was exactly what Preston had forced upon his opponent; a winter campaign in temperatures well below freezing and in four and five feet of snow.[20].

Having reduced Saint Jean, Montgomery went on to Montreal, taking possession of the city on 13 November. Carleton, whose conduct during the autumn months had been a compound of caution, hesitation, distrust of his troops and even timidity, showed sufficient energy to escape by the river, guided by a French Canadian, Jean Baptiste Bouchette, 'the wild pigeon'. On the 19th he reached the safety of Quebec. The officers and troops of the Montreal garrison who attempted to escape with Carleton were talked into a blue funk by the ubiquitous John Brown, who convinced them that a non-existent battery of long 32-pounders at Sorel would blow them out of the water. Montgomery was disgusted. In a letter to his wife, he wrote, 'I blushed for His Majesty's troops [after all, Montgomery had once been one of them]. Such an instance of base poltroonery I have never met with....' [21] But there was another kind of poltroonery which caused Montgomery to blush with both shame and anger. Many of his troops had enlisted only for three months. Now it was time to pack up and go home. Montgomery had managed to keep them in the service after the capture of Saint Jean only by promising to let them go once Montreal had been occupied. Now they were determined to hold him to his promise. Some pleaded ill health as an excuse to leave; but it was all too clear that, after receiving their discharges, the invalids promptly recovered their health and happily set off on a two hundred mile hike with no apparent disabilities. Among the genuinely sick and wounded, one American officer discovered 'upwards of a hundred damned rascals crowded amongst them, fit for duty'. To Montgomery's annoyance, few of those whose terms of enlistment had expired were willing to re-engage, hence the sarcasm in his report that he was sending 'the lame, the blind, the halt, the lazy and the lads who are homesick, to the Mammies, the Daddies and Wives and pumpkin pies'. [22] There were times when Montgomery wished he could run his amateur army like the British professionals ran theirs, instead of having to conduct military business along the lines of a town meeting. Collecting what troops he could and leaving a small garrison at Montreal under Brigadier-General David Wooster, Montgomery sailed down the Saint Lawrence to join forces with Benedict Arnold at Quebec.

The story of Arnold's march over the Kennebec-Dead
River-Chaudière with his frontiersmen, his musketmen and his
riflemen, is one of the great stories of unshakable fortitude under
distressing circumstances. But such a march could not be kept a
secret and as soon as Arnold's approach became known, the
authorities at Quebec, the military commanders, Allan Maclean
in particular, set about strengthening the walls of the fort and the
morale of the garrison. When Carleton arrived he thrust the
traitorous and unreliable elements out of the city and mustered
his force of defenders. They numbered over 1,200 and included
regulars, Royal Highland Emigrants, French Canadian and
English militia, artificers and seamen, and a few New-
foundlanders. Thus, when Montgomery arrived to take over
command of the joint force from Arnold (he was senior to Arnold in rank) the defenders of Quebec were ready and waiting
for the assault everyone knew must come sooner or later. And it
had to be soon. Both the British and Americans alike knew that
Montgomery's army, numbering about 800 men, was not
equipped for a winter siege, that it lacked adequate quarters,
supplies and artillery. They knew, too, that Carelton had rations
to last the winter and that he did not need to poke his head outside the walls of Quebec until the spring came. In some way,
Montgomery would have to force a battle upon him, if only
because another large segment of the American army was due to
return home at the end of the year. Their term of enlistment
would end on 1 January 1776. Time was on Carleton's side; it
was running out for Montgomery.

Montgomery's plan of assault was uncomplicated and predic-
table: a feint against the walls of the Upper Town to cover the
attacks of two columns, one along the river's edge below Cape
Diamond, and the other through the suburb of St Roch into the
Sault au Matelot. Once firmly established in the Lower Town
the two forces would set fire to warehouses and other buildings
in the hope of persuading the English merchants who owned
them to bring pressure upon Carleton to surrender and thus
avoid further destruction of property. Montgomery also hoped
thereby to create sufficient confusion to enable his troops, with
the help of collaborators, to force their way into the Upper
Town, where they would engage Carleton's men in the decisive
battle Montgomery so desperately wanted.

The night chosen for the assault was 31 December. It was very dark, without a moon and with a stiff wind and driving snow. [23] The wind would be hard on the assaulting troops, who had to march several miles before reaching their objective: but at least it would muffle the sound of marching feet. Many of the Americans pinned slips of paper to their caps bearing the words 'Liberty or Death'. Their purpose in so doing was to identify themselves, since they were wearing warm British uniforms captured at Saint Jean. Montgomery never hoped for a strategic surprise – the chances of that had long since evaporated – but he did count on a tactical surprise.

When Montgomery pushed through the first barrier at Prés de Ville at the head of his men he was met by a blast of gunfire. He and several of his staff were mortally wounded. His troops, fearing to be caught between the river and the escarpment, were stricken with panic. They turned and fled. On the other flank, Arnold was fired upon from the wall as he approached through St Roch. He broke through the initial obstacle, but was wounded, and before his men could recover balance, they were caught in a withering cross-fire in the narrow Sault au Matelot. They fought as best they could, but assailed from all sides and unable to break through the second barrier they finally surrendered. The American losses in the assault numbered 461, to say nothing of those poor unidentified souls who fled from history as they fled for safety over the uncertain ice of the Saint Lawrence. The defenders lost five killed and thirteen wounded.

A man of vigorous temperament, a man like Maclean for instance, might well have finished the American army as a fighting force, by a prompt sally against the American camp. But Carleton stayed where he was, allowing the wounded Arnold to muster the remnants of the assault force, most of whom would have been happy to hurry back to Montreal. And so, for the next four months, Arnold's army remained outside the walls of Quebec, while several hundred Americans remained inside, as Carleton's prisoners of war. At least they were warmer than their comrades. Meanwhile Washington arranged to send reinforcements to rebuild Arnold's army, the good ladies of Philadelphia collected blankets in a door-to-door canvass to ease the distress of their troops in the far-off frozen north, and Congress resolved to appoint commissioners to find out why the invasion had failed.

From January to May, the Americans pretended to carry on the

siege of Quebec. Then on the 6th of that month, British vessels
appeared below the city, carrying reinforcements. Carleton
opened the gates and his men poured out upon the Plains of
Abraham. The besiegers offered no resistance. They fled from
their batteries without firing a shot, leaving their matches burning. Every man took his own course, many of them throwing
down their arms in order to hasten their flight. One observer
wrote, 'As we pursued them we found the road strewed with
arms, cartridges, cloathes, bread, pork.'[24] Schuyler's version to
Washington said, 'Our forces were so dispersed that not more
than two hundred could be collected at headquarters.'[25] But once
again Carleton would not let his men have their heads. It was
enough simply to frighten the enemy and let some of Allan
Maclean's Highlanders enjoy the dinner prepared by the
American officers for themselves, but of which they had no opportunity to partake.

IV

The news of the defeat at Quebec came as a stunning blow to
Washington. The invasion of Canada had been his first adventure
in strategy on the grand scale and it had failed. The whole
strategic situation would have to be re-assessed. During 1775 the
Americans had held the initiative and had almost succeeded in
adding Canada to the United Colonies. The British had been on
the defensive from the day Ethan Allen aroused the astonished
Captain Delaplace from his bed in Ticonderoga on 10 May.
With his offensive now shattered by the walls of Quebec,
Washington began to see the Canadian operation in a different
context. He knew that even though the American troops were
still on the Saint Lawrence, the British garrison at Quebec would
probably sit out the siege until the arrival of massive reinforcements in the spring. Then they would be in a position to
move from the defensive to the offensive. More and more
Washington began to think about New York and the Hudson
Valley, and the waterway that linked New York and Montreal.
Once the British did take the offensive in Canada, was it not
likely that they would turn south towards Lake Champlain and
the Hudson? And what about that British army, now in Halifax,
commanded by Sir William Howe? Was it not likely that it
would be used to seize New York – after all, New York was a
better base than Boston, with a good harbour and a river leading

directly, by way of Lake Champlain and the Richelieu, to the Saint Lawrence. What if London should conceive the idea of sending troops south from Canada to link up with British troops moving north from New York along the waterway which linked the two countries? Because he thought in these terms, Washington could see the campaign which had started as a contest for the control of the Saint Lawrence developing into one for the control of the Hudson. That is why he did not, despite the urgent need of the army in Canada for reinforcements, expend all his resources in that direction; and why he sent his second-in-command, General Charles Lee, to supervise the defences of New York. He did, of course, send help to Canada; but not in great numbers. He could not stop worrying about New York; and in an appreciation prepared for Congress in April 1776 Washington stressed the necessity of strengthening the army in New York as well as the army in Canada. [26]

With the coming of warm weather in the north the situation grew more and more critical for the Americans. With the roads no better than quagmires, the American transport system broke down, thus cutting off the foodstuffs, ammunition and medical supplies so badly needed by the troops. Waggons and boats, formerly obtainable from the Canadians for money were certainly not available for love, particularly after the Americans substituted useless paper for hard coin. The habitants, remembering the evils of inflation and uncontrolled issues of paper money during the closing years of the Seven Years' War, would not touch the Continental paper bills, and to get what they wanted the Americans had recourse to force. This kind of action hardly reflected what the habitants thought freedom and liberty should mean, and they began to pay more and more attention to the remarks of people like *Civis Canadensis* who had written in the *Quebec Gazette*,

> These people [i.e. the Americans] to whom you have done no harm come into your province to take your property with arms in their hands under the pretext of being well-wishers, can you think that these people who are without food and ammunition will allow you to enjoy peacefully the fruits of your labours, no: they will take your grain and your cattle and everything you have...and they will pay you with notes; ...what will you do with such money? Nothing. [27]

They listened too, to Simon Sanguinet when he denounced the
'tyranny' the Americans had brought to Canada and urged them
to chase 'the brigands' out of the country. [28] As the Canadians
grew more hostile, the Americans grew more repressive and by
the spring of 1776, American rule in Canada was based upon
naked force. Both Wooster and Arnold saw the Canadians as
only waiting for an opportunity 'to join our enemies'. When the
Commissioners appointed by Congress reached Montreal they
were appalled at the degree of animosity which the American occupation had aroused and urged the immediate recall of Wooster
before he could do any more damage to the American cause in
Canada. [29]

The Americans were not only losing the war for the minds of
the Canadians, they were also losing the war for Canadian
territory. British influence had continued to remain strong
among the western Indians and in the spring of 1776 both Indians
and fur traders began to think in terms of renewing trading contacts. Despite the American prohibition forbidding any fur
traders from leaving Montreal, several managed to slip out of the
city to join a band of Indians gathering at Fort Oswegatchie on
the Saint Lawrence. Here the post commandant, Captain George
Forster, had assembled a force of regulars, volunteers and Indians
numbering about 250 and set off for the Cedars, a point on the
river between Lake Francis and Lake St Louis, where a detachment of Americans was posted. There is no need to go into
details about Forster's moves. It is sufficient to point out that he
not only overcame the American detachment at the Cedars but
also a relief force which Arnold had rushed forward from Montreal. At this point Arnold, aware of the arrival of British reinforcements at Quebec and anxious to avoid getting caught
between the British regulars on the one flank and the Indians on
the other, expressed his willingness to make a deal with Forster.
Embarrassed by the fact that he had nearly 490 prisoners under
guard, and hopelessly outnumbered by Arnold's men, Forster,
too, preferred to negotiate rather than to fight. By promising to
spare the lives of his prisoners from the tomahawks of the Indians,
he persuaded Arnold to enter into an agreement for the mutual
exchange of prisoners. Arnold agreed. Congress, however, was
incensed at what Arnold had done, and although the American
prisoners returned home safely, their British counterparts were
not allowed to leave their prison camps in the United Colonies. [30]

Forster's action at the Cedars was, in the larger picture of the war, little more than a minor engagement. It did not achieve a greater success because it had not been co-ordinated with the threat from Quebec. But it was a signpost pointing the direction in which the war was moving. In little over a week later, at Trois Rivières, on 8 June, Carleton smashed the last American attempt to establish a defence line between Quebec and Sorel. The astonishing thing is that the British commander again failed to take full advantage of his success. Instead of allowing his regulars to push rapidly ahead in pursuit of the enemy, he held them on the leash to such an extent that two French Canadian observers wondered if it were not really Carleton's intention that all the Americans should escape.[31]

After their defeat at Trois Rivières the Americans were at no time in any condition to rally and resist Carleton's advance. Sick, divided, ragged and undisciplined, they could scarcely hope to stand up to an army of 8,000 British regulars. Sick and well alike, they were no better than a mob of exhausted, panic-stricken men, subsisting largely on plunder. For the Americans it was a matter of steal or starve. Even the reinforcements sent by Washington became infected with the virus of defeat and joined the rout. 'Lousey as the Devil, for want of soap',[32] famished and plague-stricken, they struggled up the Saint Lawrence to Sorel. and up the Richelieu to Saint Jean. From May to July 1776, the Americans suffered no fewer than 5,000 casualties from gunshot, disease, wounds and desertion. The Southerners in particular were hard hit, Morgan's riflemen being almost wiped out. Even the new general, John Thomas, sent by Congress to retrieve the situation, died of smallpox, the enemy which his successor in command, Brigadier-General John Sullivan, described as 'ten times more terrible than Britons, Canadians and Indians together'. Under these conditions the order emanating from Congress to contest 'every foot of ground' was a patent absurdity.[33]

Carleton, now in complete control, continued to move ponderously and with deliberation. He split his pursuing force at Sorel, leading one wing himself to Montreal and sending the other under Burgoyne to follow the enemy up the Richelieu. But not to engage them in battle. Carleton's instruction to Burgoyne said just that; he was to follow closely 'but without hazarding anything' until Carleton himself should be able 'to co-operate' with him.[34] In consequence Burgoyne hazarded nothing, and his advance guard reached Saint Jean just in time to see Arnold push off in the last boat leaving the burning fortress. It marked the end of an American occupation which had lasted from 3 November until 18 June. From Saint Jean the Americans hurried on to Ticonderoga. They even by-passed Crown Point in their flight to safety. As far as the British regulars were concerned the pursuit after the engagement at Trois Rivières was no more than a field exercise. Everywhere they went they were greeted as liberators. 'All is joy,' wrote Burgoyne. So eager were the Canadians to assist the British troops in driving out the invaders that the British General had scarcely enough ammunition to satisfy their demands. But Burgoyne was under no illusions. The Canadians, he said, were always ready to throw in their lot with the man with the biggest battalions. 'They would be the same', he wrote, 'to the Emperor of Morocco' should they believe that he commanded the largest legions.[35]

The stage was now set for the very strategy that Washington feared most, the recovery of Ticonderoga, followed by a British offensive south along the Hudson River towards New York. Ticonderoga was in a weak state, and although Washington appointed a new general, Horatio Gates, whose powers were such that he was named 'dictator in Canada for six months',[36] it would obviously take time to restore both the numbers and the morale of the defeated army. Even Washington himself had lost some of his confidence. 'An unaccountable kind of fatality seems to have attended all our movements in Canada since the death of poor Montgomery', is what he wrote on 20 July.[37] Certainly from the British standpoint, now was the time to strike a telling blow against the Revolution. Howe in Halifax had his eyes on New York and on 26 August he landed his troops on Long Island. Even though they did not make the most of their initial attack, the British soon found themselves firmly established at the mouth of the Hudson River. It is interesting to speculate what might have happened had Carleton launched a similar attack on receiving news of Howe's success. Is it beyond the realm of possibility that such an imaginative action might have gone far towards opening the line of the Hudson to the British, thus sealing off the main area of revolutionary activity? But because Arnold was building a fleet on Lake Champlain, Carleton believed he had to build one; except that Carleton was not Arnold and worked much more slowly. That is why it was 7 October before Simon Fraser's brigade was ordered to move south and 9 October before Pringle's fleet set sail on Lake Champlain.

At Valcour Island Carleton's vessels virtually drove Arnold's ships out of the water in a running battle between 11 and 13 October. Six days later Fraser occupied Crown Point without meeting any resistance. But by this time the situation had stabilised itself as far as the Americans were concerned. Where Carleton was cautious, Howe was indolent. After occupying New York, he dallied and dawdled in the city and did not rouse himself to military action until the end of October and not until early November did he move to occupy Forts Lee and Washington on the lower reaches of the Hudson River. But these actions, which might have spurred Carleton and Burgoyne in Canada at an earlier date, came too late to make any contribution to the British campaign in 1776. On 27 October Fraser made a demonstration in front of the walls of Ticonderoga and that was all. When Gates refused to accept the challenge to battle, Carleton withdrew his troops into winter quarters in Canada along the Richelieu and the Saint Lawrence. One of those who took part in these events wrote,

> this little army...after having done as much as the situation of the country and the climate wo'd admit of, by driving the enemy from Canada, destroying their fleet and then following close to their Dens, was obliged to return to Canada to its great regret, which it did on 2 November in a very regular manner, without being in the least molested by the Enemy, and the whole got into their winter Cantonment ab't the 12th of the same month. [38]

During the winter of 1776-7, Burgoyne returned to England and drew up a plan for a British offensive in 1777. It envisaged the occupation of Lake Champlain and the occupation of the Hudson by armies operating from Canada and from New York. The plan was basically a repeat of what Washington had feared might be attempted in 1776, but with rather less chance of success in 1777 than in the previous year. By 1777 the Americans were prepared; and in October Burgoyne found himself too far south to get any help from Canada, and too far north to derive any benefit from Clinton's belated drive from New York. Unable to advance, or to retire, Burgoyne surrendered his sword at Saratoga on 16 October 1777. His defeat removed any fears that Washington might still have harboured about the fate of the Hudson River.

In 1778 Congress began to think again in terms of another expedition to Canada, this time under the command of the Marquis de Lafayette. But Washington looked upon the proposal with a cold eye. So too did Schuyler and Arnold. Gates and Lafayette liked it, but the very name of Canada had become a word of ill-omen in the ears of those American soldiers who still remembered the disastrous events of 1775-6 too vividly to support what many of them considered to be a half-baked scheme concocted by Gates for his own self-glorification and by Lafayette for the possible recovery of Canada for France. Nothing, not even larger bounties, would induce them to enlist for service in an inhospitable land of winter chills and summer ague. The result was that the Canada proposal never got beyond the talking stage, and in January 1779, Congress voted to defer indefinitely any invasion of the British colony to the north.

V

What had gone wrong with the American invasion scheme? When that question was put to Sam Adams he cried in anger and frustration, 'The subject is disgusting to me – I will dismiss it.' [39] But there were others who were not prepared to dismiss it. Some members of Congress, searching for scapegoats, talked of cowardice and drunkenness among senior officers of the American army in Canada. That cowardice and drunkenness were to be found in the ranks is undeniable, and instances, too, among the officer corps; but neither cowardice nor drunkenness played a major role in the defeat of the American forces before Quebec, or at Trois Rivières. [40] George Washington found the explanation in the manpower policy, the reliance on volunteering and short-term enlistments. He had from the outset questioned the advisability of both, but it had been impolitic for him to say so. Now he set out to persuade Congress to grant a special bounty to men already in the Continental Line in order to encourage them to extend their service 'for the continuance of the war'. [41] It was not a popular proposal, but on 26 June 1776, Congress went as far as to offer a bounty of ten dollars to each man who would enlist for three years; and on the reorganisation of the army in

September this sum was raised to twenty dollars. To any man who agreed to serve for the duration of the war – and there were few who were willing to do so – an additional gift of one hundred acres of land was offered. [42]

Perhaps Congress itself was to blame for the defeat of its forces in Canada. John Adams thought so when he accused Congress of 'embarrassing and starving the war in Canada'. [43] Most of the officers agreed with him. They never had enough men, enough medication, enough transport or enough money to achieve what they were expected to achieve. There was always too little and it always came too late.

But there was another factor in the Canadian defeat. That was the fact that American intelligence painted too optimistic a picture of the extent and nature of the assistance to be expected from the local population. The whole invasion had been predicated upon the assumption that both the English and French civilian populations were wholeheartedly in favour of the Revolution and that they would provide the means of waging war in Canada in the revolutionary interest. As it was, the Canadians adopted a policy of watching and waiting; and even the Anglo-American merchants in Quebec and Montreal, with a few notable exceptions like Price and Walker, while offering their 'condolences and good-will' to the people of Massachusetts, hesitated to elect delegates to go to Philadelphia to take part in the sittings of the Continental Congress. And because they could not get the assistance they expected and required, the Americans found themselves faced with a task more formidable than they had anticipated. Without strong local support it took the Americans two months to reduce Fort Saint Jean, thus setting back the invasion time-table and forcing a winter campaign upon an army ill-equipped to conduct it. Perhaps we can lay the blame on John Brown, whose spying journey to Montreal in February 1775 was the first act of hostility against Canada in the war of the American Revolution.

The events on the banks of the Richelieu and the Saint Lawrence in 1775 and 1776 may appear to be of small moment in the general history of military operations. And yet, they should be remembered, if only because they constituted a preview of the changes in warfare and strategy barely yet discernible on the historical horizon. The Canadian invasion was the first military operation in which an old-style eighteenth-century military force was pitted against a new-style nineteenth-century military force: for Carleton's men were paid professionals, men with no ideological stake in the war in which they were fighting; those led by Montgomery and Arnold were amateurs convinced of the virtue of their cause. Because theirs was a revolutionary army, the Americans were ready to discard the rigidity of the old--fashioned professional army and to adopt the elasticity of the amateur. It was largely as a result of the American Revolution and the French Revolution that the new citizen armies became the popular form of military organisation. Because troops and officers alike were revolutionaries, aggressive, mobile, combative strategy replaced the slow strategy of siegecraft, 'limited' war was superseded by 'unlimited' war, and the dynastic state gave way to the national state. Nineteenth-century and twentieth-century wars, therefore, became wars between peoples, rather than wars between ruling governments. Total war, that twentieth-century contribution to the history of warfare, came slowly. But its origins may be traced to the invasion of Canada which the Continental Congress authorised in June 1775.

Notes

1. Liddell Hart, *Thoughts on War* (London, 1943), pp. 229, 236.
2. Michael Howard (ed), *The Theory and Practice of War* (London, 1965), p.7.
3. Chevalier de Johnstone, *Dialogue in Hades*, Quebec Literary and Historical Society, n.d., p.28.
4. J. F. C. Fuller, *Armament and History* (London, 1946), pp. 101-2.
5. J. C. Miller, *Triumph of Freedom* (Boston, 1948), p. 88.
6. See G. H. T. Kimble, *Canadian Military Geography* (Ottawa, 1948); also G. F. G. Stanley, *Canada's Soldiers, the Military History of an Unmilitary People* (Toronto, 1974), pp. 1-3.
7. Hart, *Thoughts*, p. 80.
8. D. S. Freeman, *George Washington, a Biography* (New York, 1951), Vol. III, pp. 533-4.
9. Miller, *Triumph*, p. 90.
10. Freeman, *Washington*, III, pp. 436-8.
11. G. F. G. Stanley *Canada Invaded* (Toronto, 1973), pp. 21-3.
12. Freeman, *Washington*, III, p. 532.
13. *Ibid.* pp. 536-7.
14. Miller, *Triumph*, p. 91.
15. Freeman, *Washington*, III, pp. 537-8.
16. J. R. Elting, *The Battle of Bunker's Hill* (Monmouth Beach, 1975)
17. Gustave Lanctot, *Les Canadiens Français et leurs Voisins du Sud* (Montreal, 1941), p. 107.
18. Miller, *Triumph*, p. 95.
19. *Ibid.*, p. 91.

20. Kimble, *Geography*, p. 48.
21. Stanley, *Canada Invaded*, p. 69.
22. Miller, *Triumph*, p. 96.
23. An account of the assault will be found in Stanley, *Canada Invaded*, pp. 87-104. Additional details will be found in Appendix I of the French translation of this book, *L'Invasion du Canada 1775-1776* (Québec, 1975), pp. 183-8.
24. S.S. Cohen (ed.), *Canada Preserved, the Journal of Captain Thomas Ainslie* (New York, 1968), pp. 88-9.
25. Freeman, *Washington*, IV, p. 96.
26. *Ibid.*, IV, p. 84.
27. *Quebec Gazette*, 5 October 1775.
28. Abbé Verreau, *Invasion du Canada, Collection de Mémoires Receuillis et Annotés* (Montréal, 1873), pp. 103-5.
29. *The Journal of Charles Carroll of Carroltown during his visit to Canada in 1776 as one of the Commissioners from Congress* (Baltimore, 1876), pp. 38-41.
30. For an account of the fighting and negotiations at the Cedars see *An Authentic Narrative of Facts Relating to the Exchange of Prisoners taken at the Cedars: supported by the Testimony and depositions of his majesty's Officers with several original letters and Papers, together with Remarks upon the Report and resolves of the American Congress on that subject* (London, 1772).
31. Verreau, *Invasion*, pp. 134, 240.
32. Miller, *Triumph*, p. 100.
33. Freeman, *Washington*, IV, p. 122.
34. Stanley, *Canada Invaded*, p. 132.
35. Miller, *Triumph*, p. 101.
36. C. H. Jones, *History of the Campaign for the Conquest of Canada*, (Philadelphia, 1882), p. 99.
37. Freeman, *Washington*, IV, p. 143.
38. G. F. G. Stanley (ed.), *For Want of a Horse, being a Journal of the Campaigns against the Americans in 1776 and 1777 conducted from Canada* (Sackville, 1961), p. 90.
39. J. H. Smith, *Our Struggle for the Fourteenth Colony* (New York, 1907), Vol. II, p. 450.
40. Miller, *Triumph*, p. 101.
41. Freeman, *Washington*, IV, p. 104.
42. C. J. Bernardo and E. H. Bacon, *American Military Policy , its development since 1775* (Harrisburg, 1961), pp. 13-14.
43. Miller, *Triumph*, p. 101.

The Blessings of the Land: Naval Officers in Upper Canada, 1815-1841

W. A. B. DOUGLAS

'My Lord , there exist in the Colony I have lately left, a considerable number of naval officers of character and experience who having been cast ashore by the last peace settled themselves in the backwoods of Upper Canada.' Sir Francis Bond Head to Lord Glenelg, 3 August 1838. (CO/42/445/570.)

Veterans of the Napoleonic Wars were thrust upon society, often with nothing but naval and military service to prepare them for life in a competitive world where security was the exception rather than the rule. It is little wonder that so many took up the free land grants to which they were entitled in British North America, Southern Africa and Australasia. In Upper Canada, where such grants or equivalent benefits were given out between 1815 and 1843, discharged soldiers and seamen, reduced officers of the Royal Navy, Royal Marines and the army, arrived in their thousands. Some were placed in military settlements, others allowed to settle as ordinary immigrants. Military settlements were less than successful; individual settlers on the other hand fared just about as well as other British immigrants of their class. That is to say, they did not compare favourably with their North American counterparts as pioneer farmers or even, it has been argued, in general cultural attainments. [1] At the same time, special consideration was shown to retired and half pay officers; this tended to make up for some of their shortcomings in a formative society. The large amount of land granted to each officer; the small but nevertheless steady financial subsidy that many received in the form of half pay or private income; the status of rank – these were useful assets to count against the liabilities of inexperience and improvidence. Indeed, the significant proportion of magistrates selected from the ranks of reduced officers in these years suggests that even if they did not adapt very well they still played an important part in the community. [2]

We have formed our knowledge of half pay officers in Upper

Canada from a series of rather disparate sources. Travellers' accounts and diaries often refer to their activities; studies of settlement and of land policies have made reference to the regulations concerning their grants; and events brought a measure of fame or notoriety to some – particularly, during the rebellion of 1837, the naval officers among them. Although naval officers represented a small proportion of all military settlers, they formed a group that lends itself to identification and analysis. The numbers are manageable – there are less than 200 involved – and the group is remarkably homogeneous. Unlike army officers, who tended to give their loyalty to a regiment or a corps, naval officers were all the servants of one master – the Admiralty. And in spite of vast differences in social and geographic origin they developed common interests as a result of naval service. This characteristic opens the way to several fruitful lines of investigation. Data concerning their wealth and property, their family connections, their attitudes, their role in the community and the roles of their descendants, merit the attention of historians.[3] Within the compass of a short article one can hardly do more than point the direction to such exhaustive analysis by examining patterns of immigration and settlement, but in doing so it is possible to analyse the policies which attracted naval officers to Upper Canada, to assess the results, and perhaps to lay the basis for comparative studies with other parts of the Empire.

I

The naval officers of Upper Canada belonged, of course, to that most impressive among elites, the Royal Navy. Unchallenged mistress of the seas in 1815, the navy opened the way to honour and fortune more surely than any other branch of the fighting services.[4] Providing a young man had the right connections or made the necessary impression, providing he was prepared to put up with frightful inequalities and brutal conditions of service, he could expect as a naval officer, even if he had the most slender prospects, to secure a firm place in an exclusive club, and an accepted position in polite society. The three principal inducements to recruiting were prize money, freight and land grants. When ships were captured in war or condemned by Admiralty Courts for illicit trading, the financial proceeds were often enough to make the fortunes of individual officers, or at

least to provide them with independent means. Similar expectations could be held out for freight money – the fee paid to
commanders of ships transporting specie. Whether or not such
windfalls came the way of a sea officer there was always a further
choice – to take advantage of the regulations that from the
mid-eighteenth century had permitted half pay officers to accept
land grants in the colonies. [5] In the time-honoured language of the
naval prayer, seamen looked forward to enjoying 'the blessings
of the land with the fruits of their labours'.

So long as active employment was assured, the prospects of
enhancing a naval officer's financial situation never completely
faded from his sight. Much depended upon advancement in the
service, which could be obtained by patronage in the first instance and thereafter by a combination of patronage and merit.
Venality often obscured the higher military virtues in such cases,
and the sentiments of the naval prayer could assume a more
worldly guise:

> Hardy is picking up a good deal of freight money in the
> South Seas, and will no doubt return £20,000 the better for
> his command, which in time of peace is no bad thing. Lord
> Colville has also done well at Cork, having already put into
> his pockets about £5,000; when you get your flag you must
> get a slice of the good loaf . . . .[6]

The recipient of this letter, written by the Comptroller of the
Navy Board in 1822, was Captain Robert Barrie, Commissioner
of the dockyard at Kingston. Even in this remote outpost of the
Royal Navy he was enjoying considerable material advantages;
he raised pineapples in his hothouse, kept the best cellar in
Canada and obtained for himself land that on his departure some
years later would net him a profit of at least £975. His pious
avowal that '...mine is a profession *I would not recommend* to
anyone who has the sense to earn his bread by the plough', if not
sheer hypocrisy, must rank as fashionable romanticism. [7] More
realistic was Lieutenant Charles Rubidge, whose slice of the loaf
was typical of the unemployed half pay officer in time of peace:
'I had come to the determination to go to Canada', he explained,
'for I found that with a limited income of £100 a year it was impossible to maintain, with proper respectability, that situation in
life which my profession called for.'[8]

Before jumping to the conclusion that Charles Rubidge represented the norm and Robert Barrie the exception it is necessary to apply more rigorous tests. What attracted these people to the province was land, and through the Upper Canada Land Papers and related documents it is possible to discover exactly what land or land rights were granted. [9] It is a reasonable assumption that seems to be borne out by other evidence that every naval officer settling in the province took advantage of the grant to which he was entitled; therefore the lists of land grants or equivalent benefits provide a solid foundation for analysing the group. Using the earliest date at which each officer's name appears in the records as receiving a location ticket or remission of money to purchase property, it is possible to estimate when he arrived as a settler in the province and what quality he possessed. Because dates and locations are not clear in every case the breakdown is limited to 153 names. This included thirty officers of the rank of commander and higher, fifty-four lieutenants, thirteen midshipmen, thirteen pursers, ten masters, seven surgeons and twenty-six other officers, including twelve officers of the Royal Marines. By far the greatest influx took place between 1832 and 1835, when seventy officers arrived. Twenty-four had come in the first years following the War of 1812. In the eleven years between 1820 and 1831 the flow was down considerably, for a total of only forty-four, and after the period of maximum emigration already indicated the flow subsided to a trickle, only thirteen more officers taking up their entitlements after 1836 until the privilege came to an end seven years later in 1843.

These are suggestive figures. It is especially interesting that the peak years were after the final abolition of land grants to ordinary immigrants in 1832. [10] They also coincided with the beginnings of an improving situation in the Royal Navy for the active employment of officers. [11] Thus although the arrivals of 1818 and 1819 could perhaps be related to the drastic naval retrenchment of those years, the general pattern of immigration between 1815 and 1843 cannot be said to reflect the patterns of active service by naval officers. Rather, when considered in conjunction with other evidence, immigration figures show a definite correlation with the land policies of the Colonial Office and the political objectives of Lieutenant Governors.

The Proclamation of 1763 contained the first scale of grants of Crown Lands in the colonies, as a reward for military service. [12]

The amount of land granted varied from time to time – between 1815 and 1832 it was as follows:

Post captain and above	1,200 acres
Commander	1,000 acres
Lieutenant, Master, Purser and Surgeon	800 acres
Midshipman	500 acres [13]

Most other eligible settlers were entitled to no more than 200 acres, so that half pay officers, like a few other privileged grantees, enjoyed an enormous advantage; but at first naval officers found it difficult to obtain the grants to which they believed they had a claim, because local authorities only had instructions to accommodate officers of the army. [14] Captain Robert Hall, who was Commissioner of the dockyard at Kingston, made representations to the Admiralty that were followed early in 1816 by instructions from Lord Bathurst, Secretary of State for War and Colonies, to General Sir Gordon Drummond, administrator of Upper Canada, to allow grants to naval officers who had three years service on the Lakes. [15] In July 1817, Bathurst instructed Lieutenant-Governor Francis Gore to extend this privilege to all naval officers who had served in the Lakes. In fact, naval officers who applied received grants, even without such service, providing each officer formally obtained leave from the Admiralty every twenty-four months to remain as a settler in the province. [16] Such encouragement to emigrate was in accord with the policy of countering the alarming growth of American settlers – a policy in which military settlers and military settlement played a large part – but the Admiralty seems also to have perceived the tactical advantage of persuading naval officers to settle near the Great Lakes frontier region. Hall petitioned the Lieutenant-Governor in November, 1816, to set aside land adjacent to naval posts as naval settlements, and proposed purchasing and settling the land on either side of the Governor's Road between Blandford and the Grand River 'as it is the best, and most rapid communication we can have with Lake Erie and actually indispensable in the Event of a future War'. [17] Consequently in subsequent years a number of naval officers and discharged seamen settled in enclaves. The Comptroller of the Navy Board showed some interest when he advised Hall's replacement, Robert Barrie, that 'The half pay officers of every rank (Naval) who are residing will be subject to your call in the event of an armament, and I suspect there are many of them...' [18]

Sir Byam Martin's vagueness on this point was matched by Barrie's lack of interest. His efforts were directed towards preserving the struggling naval posts at Penetang, Grand River, Isle aux Noix and Kingston, in the face of ever-increasing economy. In 1819 Lieutenant-Governor Sir Peregrine Maitland received instructions from the Colonial Office to purchase twelve square miles of land from the Six Nations Indians in the Bay of Quinte area as a naval settlement: Barrie made it clear that he regarded the allocation of land grants as a thankless task, that he would not go to the trouble for seamen but would restrict grants to officers, and that 'in the distribution I certainly will take care of No. one'.[19] Whether or not Barrie himself followed through on this precise method of speculation, the practice was sufficiently widespread to prompt special orders by Sir Peregrine Maitland in 1821 forbidding the granting of lands to officers who were serving on full pay in Upper Canadian stations.[20] At the same time, under Maitland's regime the settlement duties before possession of a land grant was confirmed frequently took several years to complete. William Henvey, a lieutenant stationed at Kingston, and one of those who acquired land but did not take it up, gave an honest account of his feelings on the matter as early as 1817:

> ...[In my opinion there can be no comparison between] the ideal charms of fashionable life [and] the more substantial comforts of the cottage;...the truest happiness is surely to be found when Pomp, Pride and Arrogance reign *not*. My inclinations would lead me to follow your example, but my profession and reason dictate otherwise. I should have been highly amused to have seen Jack steering a plough; exclaiming 'steady, very well thus' as he turned the soil of Navy Hall, for such I declare you must term it. It is well he sticks to the turf so manfully, few sailors could boast of such perseverance.[21]

Settlement policies not having been particularly successful in Upper Canada between 1815 and 1826, Lord Bathurst instituted the New South Wales system, named after the practice being followed in the colony of that name in Australia. A value was placed on Crown Lands and settlers had to purchase property at the going rate. This was to ensure that prospective immigrants were not paupers but men with capital and education who would make a real contribution to the province. [22] Regulations issued in 1826 brought military officers into the scheme. They would still be allowed to take up their grants, but only after selling their commissions. [23] Even though these officers, like loyalists and certain poor settlers, were therefore exempt from adhering to the sales system they were committing themselves irrevocably to a new life. The principle could not apply to naval officers because there was no purchase of commissions in the Royal Navy, and no system of retirement. This is an important distinction; it provided a permanent and very strong tie between the settler and his paymaster in England. In August 1827, the Admiralty issued regulations permitting a naval officer to take up his grant on producing a certificate of service from the Admiralty, but few took advantage of the concession. [24] In the next five years it seems that only seven officers — two lieutenants, two midshipmen, a lieutenant of the Royal Marines, a surgeon and an assistant surgeon — took up their land.

It was the impact of Edward Gibbon Wakefield's ideas which seems to have transformed the pattern — that and the upsurge of interest accompanying the formation of the Canada Land Company. [25] 'Emigration', wrote Seeley some years later in *The Expansion of England*, 'is in itself only a private affair; it does not, as such, concern Governments . . .' [26] Wakefield advocated colonisation, which gave imperial purpose to emigration. The Public Land Act of 1832 abolished all grants of land in Upper Canada, thereby formalising a situation that had developed by 1831. [27] Lord Goderich then ordered the discontinuation of free grants of land except to military settlers, [28] but plans were already afoot to substitute the remission of purchase money with which half pay officers could buy land at public auction. Lord Goderich, E. G. Stanley and T. Spring-Rice, the Colonial Secretaries between 1831 and 1835, demonstrated an increasingly unsympathetic approach to military settlers of all classes. In 1834 Spring-Rice argued: 'Gentlemen who have ceased to belong to the Service should not...be allowed the advantages to which they were entitled while in the army/navy — Being no longer officers, there is no reason why they should enjoy the privileges of officers . . .' [29] In spite of such pressures, as well as the upheavals of the Mackenzie Rebellion of 1837 and the influence of the

Durham Report of 1839 which reflected so much of the Colonial
Reformers who had influenced policy in the early 1830s, special
advantages for half pay officers of the army did not come to an
end until stopped by a Horse Guards General Order of 12
January 1841. The Admiralty, which had lagged behind the
Horse Guards in issuing such regulations, did not produce a
similar order until 21 December 1842. [30]

The sharp rise in the number of naval officers settling each year
under this policy – 18 in 1832, 15 in 1833, 25 in 1834, 12 in 1835 –
followed the overall pattern of increased emigration to the
province,[31] but by 1837 naval officers were evidently being attracted elsewhere, probably to other parts of the Empire where
the advantages of free land were to continue for many more
years.[32] That Upper Canada ceased to attract half pay officers is
beyond doubt – had it been otherwise they would not have
refused the advantages still open to them by the regulations until
1842,[33] at a time when emigration to the province was enjoying
another sharp upturn. The amount of land they could purchase
varied with location and quality, and probably did not equal the
amount authorised by the scale in existence until 1832,[34] but they
could pick and choose to a greater extent, and Sir John Colborne
saw to it that half pay officers could buy at the upset price – the
cheapest going rate – without having to compete in an auction.
He also was prepared to arrange advantages like the right to
build grist mills.[35] Such privileges enabled naval officers to
preserve their station in life in the remoteness of the 'backwoods
of Upper Canada'; circumstances after 1837 deprived them of
such advantages sufficiently to discourage further addition to
their numbers.

II

Common interests were enhanced by geographic proximity.
Naval officers tended to settle near each other even though they
were located in townships from one end of the province to
another.[36] Following the general pattern of land alienation, most
of those who settled before 1830 obtained their grants in the
vicinity of the Ottawa Valley, but in addition to the 32 locations
in this region there were another 14 near Rice Lake and 19
scattered along the shores of Lake Ontario from Kingston to
Niagara and north-westward from the Bay of Quinte to Not-

tawasaga Bay. After 1830 only six more locations were made near the Ottawa River – the rest were divided between the western and central regions of the province. Most of them – 67 – were to be found in the central region stretching in an easterly direction from St Vincent township on the shore of Nottawasaga Bay, around the north shore of Lake Simcoe, then in the area of the Kawartha Lakes and Rice Lake. Another 47 locations after 1830 were in the south-western part of the province. There were distinct differences in the types of land taken up and some locations included lots in more than one township, particularly in the 1820s when speculation was more prevalent than in later years. One cannot therefore claim that there was a constant pattern of intercommunication by virtue of their location, but naval officers did congregate at some focal areas, which both reflected a settlement policy and brought about some group solidarity.

Interestingly enough, this did not become pronounced until after 1832. Attitudes like that of Robert Barrie towards the proposed naval settlement on the Bay of Quinte did not help. Some early settlers, it is true, received their grants in the settlement which was eventually set up, not on the Bay of Quinte after all but near Rice Lake. For instance Charles Rubidge after some difficulty acquired his lot in Otonabee township in the area set aside for naval settlers. [37] Christopher Bell on the other hand, a man of evident capacity who first obtained a location in Pakenham township, in the Ottawa Valley, in 1825, shrewdly went about acquisition of strategic lots on the timber frontier in subsequent years. [38] John Harris, who was at first told he would have to accept his grant within the naval settlement, petitioned the Governor for special consideration and received lands near those of his wife's family, the Ryerses of Long Point, in the London District. [39] In their way, these three men were all successful in adapting to pioneer life, and they illustrate the relative isolation of early naval settlers. Christopher Bell had commanded a gunboat in the Battle of Plattsburgh, had there lost a leg, and been taken prisoner, later emerging from a court martial with honour for the part he had played in the battle. He was allowed, four years after settling in Pakenham, to locate further up the Ottawa Valley in Horton township in 1829 on condition of building a sawmill on his lot, on the River Bonnechere, 'at great expense and with but little prospect of immediate gain.' In 1829 he received a licence to cut red pine, to be renewed each year, along the river and a tributary as far as Golden Lake. In 1832 he received authority to construct a dam and paper-mill across the river at the second falls, and in 1836 was authorised to collect tolls on slides erected on his property. [40]

Charles Rubidge, who is better known to historians than Bell, borrowed £200 to bring his wife and four children to Upper Canada in May 1819 and on arrival at Cobourg found support from 'an old and esteemed friend', Commander Walter Boswell, RN, who was also taking up land in the country. Rubidge suffered like so many others from the tedious process of selecting and obtaining a ticket for a lot. Restricted to the naval settlement, he could only procure his land by the generosity of Captain Francis Spilsbury, RN, who stepped aside to allow Rubidge to take precedence in view of his large family. Rubidge then discovered that a location ticket for the same land had been issued to David Jones, who was not even a naval officer. Early in 1820 this difficulty was settled, and Rubidge persevered with the cultivation of his property. He had a log house built by two local men for $100, hired two Americans to chop four and a half acres of land at $6 an acre, and employed a man who had followed him out from England as a hired hand. He knew nothing about farming, even in England, 'but if a man will give his mind to any common thing of the kind', he later wrote, ' and not think it a hardship, it is surprising what he may do, as in this case in a few days I found no difficulty'. [41] By 1825, thanks to his half pay, he had repaid his debts and completed the necessary improvements to secure a patent for his 800 acres. [42] In 1834 he was unsuccessful in his attempt to procure the position of agent for emigrants in the London district, but he played a large part in the schemes of assisted emigration initiated by Peter Robinson in the 1820s, bringing out emigrants from England in 1831 and Ireland in 1839. [43]

Charles Rubidge took full advantage of his naval ties, and later probably helped attract other naval officers to settle in the lands between Cobourg and Peterborough. John Harris, who deliberately detached himself somewhat from naval surroundings in order to take up his land, also placed importance in naval connections. Impressed into the navy and promoted in 1810 at the age of 28 to the rank of Master, [44] Harris was ordered in 1812 to the Lakes in Canada. In 1815 he joined three of the most dis-

tinguished hydrographers of the nineteenth century – Captain
W. F. W. Owen, Lieutenants (later Vice-Admirals) A. T. E.
Vidal and H. W. Bayfield – in surveying Lake Ontario and Lake
Erie. While engaged in this work on the north shore of Lake
Erie, he met and married Amelia Ryerse, the daughter of Samuel
Ryerse and niece of Egerton Ryerson. Two years later Harris
settled in Woodhouse township, near Lake Erie, although he had
to wait two more years to obtain the location he was entitled to,
in nearby Dorchester township. [45] In 1821 Harris succeeded to the
vacant office of Treasurer for the London District, [46] and in 1826
moved with the District offices to the site of the new town of
London. [47] He might have emulated the example of Rubidge and
improved his land, but the soil in Norfolk County was notorious
for its poor qualities [48] and it was probably fortunate that
circumstances and family connections opened up the opportunity
of an official post. His naval friendships remained strong partly
through his own and partly through his remarkable wife's
efforts. [49]

Although a number of naval settlers followed Rubidge into
Otonabee, Asphodel and several other neighbouring townships
near Rice Lake in the 1820s, it was not until Sir John Colborne
made concerted efforts to encourage 'respectable' emigrants in
the 'thirties that a sense of community among naval officers
seemed to develop in other parts of the province. It would be
misleading to suggest that there was a fellowship unique to naval
officers, or restricted to settlers with naval and military
backgrounds – in fact the relationships were those of family and
class extending to all settlers of a region. There was all the same a
special bond between sailors, expressed partly in the choice of
locations. There were many examples of this bond [50] – one of the
most enlightening was the experience of Commander Henry
LeVisconte. [51] In 1834 he set out for Upper Canada to explore the
possibilities of settling. One of his first encounters with a naval
officer in the province was with Captain Alexander Dobbs, en
route from Kingston to Toronto. Dobbs, who had married
Richard Cartwright's daughter (the ward of John Strachan) [52] and
remained in Upper Canada after the War of 1812, was off to settle in the Newcastle district, which he strongly recommended.
This was enough for LeVisconte who after the usual round of
calls at the capital – Sir John Colborne, Peter Robinson (Commissioner of Crown Lands), Colonel Rowen (the Civil

Secretary), and such residents of Toronto as Commander George
Truscott, to whom he had a letter of introduction – set off for
Cobourg. He went directly from there to Seymour township,
where he received a welcome dinner from Thomas Allan and
William Kay, pursers on half pay from the navy. LeVisconte was
accompanied by a Captain Masson of the Royal Artillery, and
they 'went next morning in a skiff to see some lands near Grosse
Ile where Captain Masson chose lots No. 7 in the 1st. Concession
of Seymour and No. 8 in the second Concession and I chose No.
8 in the first concession and No. 9 and 11 in the Second being the
most eligible we could find . . .' Having selected his lots,
LeVisconte went by stage-coach from Cobourg to Rice Lake, 'by
steamer to Otonabee near Mr. Rubidge's. . .walked to Peterboro'
5 or 6 miles called at Mr. Taylor's, Col. Brown's, Major Sharp
[Royal Marines] and dined with Lieut. Smart [Royal Navy].
Called at Dr Conins [Surgeon, Royal Navy] and Mr. Rubidge's
and ret'd by Steamer and coach to Cobourg.'[53] Sixteen weeks to
the day after leaving England he had returned to his home in
Devon, and the following year he sold out to bring his family to
their new home, secure in the knowledge that he would be
among friends, a large proportion of whom were in fact sailors
like himself.[54]

Blandford and Oxford townships near London, on the junc-
tion of the Thames River and Governor's Road, attracted a
number of naval and military officers. Vice-Admiral Henry Vansittart arrived with his family in 1834 to take up lands procured
for him in advance by Commander Andrew Drew, who acted as
the Admiral's agent and partner. Drew, Commander Philip
Graham and Lieutenant Edward Buller had taken up their land in
the township in 1832 and 1833. All of them had lots fronting on
the River Thames except for Vansittart, who chose to set up his
estate some way back from the river. Vansittart and Drew invested a large amount of private capital in land both in Blandford
township and elsewhere in the province.[55] We have a revealing
picture of life among these worthies from the Canadian Journal
of Alfred Domett,[56] and Anna Jameson's *Winter Studies and
Summer Rambles.*[57] Enormous pleasure was found in the novelty
and stimulus of pioneer life. Philip Graham's neighbour,
Lieutenant-Colonel Alexander W. Light was 'a fine clever
animated man, with a great deal of odd learning about the Bible
(the Septuagint), Bellamy and the prophesies. . .the youngest old

man I ever saw...'. Alfred Domett was a frequent visitor to
Light's House in 1833, where he 'dined, drank whisky toddy
with maple sugar out of pewter mugs, slept on the floor, heard
such excellent songs from Captain Graham and passed many a
day in a room which the Colonel delighted in as reminding him
of a barrack room . . .' [58]

Further west, in Moore and Sarnia townships, there was a
similar community of naval officers. The agent for those
townships was Henry Jones, a purser on half pay. For many years
he had tried to establish an Owenite community on the shores of
Lake Huron [59] – not too surprisingly, this Socialist experiment had
resulted in failure. As agent for Moore and Sarnia, however, he
not only procured choice waterfront lots on the St Clair River
for himself but reserved others for Commander R. E. Vidal, his
brother Captain A. T. E. Vidal, Captain William Elliot Wright
and Captain Thomas Ledlie Crooke. [60] When A. T. E. Vidal
returned to active employment in order to survey on the West
Coast of Africa special measures were authorised by the Executive Council of the province to exempt him from the normal
requirement of residing on his property in order to qualify for a
patent. [61] Another Vidal brother who had served in the navy as a
purser, Emeric Essex, remained in England but kept in touch
with his family in Upper Canada. [62] Like Vansittart and Drew in
Blandford, the Vidals invested large sums besides their remission
of purchase money in property and property improvement. From
Henry Jones' diary it is also clear that there was frequent visiting
between the naval officers who settled in Moore and Sarnia, and
of course A. T. E. Vidal's old friend of Kingston days, John
Harris, kept in touch. [63] Moreover both the Vidal and Harris
families corresponded regularly with W. F. W. Owen, who
settled in his old family home on Campobello Island, and eventually moved to Woodstock, New Brunswick. [64]

The documentary evidence of little enclaves of naval officers
growing up in certain townships is supported by oral tradition in
Blandford – where the descendants of earlier American settlers
refer to the English landowners as 'Codfish Gentry'. [65] Just north
of London, Ontario in Adelaide township, which later was
divided into Adelaide and Metcalfe, an oral tradition has survived that suggests a similar enclave borne out by the letters of
Thomas Radcliffe. [66] The earliest naval settler here was Lieutenant
Christopher Beer, one of the few to take up land according to the

regulations of 1827. Other naval officers who arrived between 1832 and 1836 were George William Harris, a lieutenant in the Royal Marines, Joseph Kerr, an assistant surgeon, Lieutenant Shepherd McCormick and Lieutenant John Radcliff. Radcliff was accompanied by his soldier brother who settled close by and was described by Sir George Arthur in 1838 as the leader of an extensive settlement.[67] Another settler of interest was Mrs Patrick Donnelly, the widow of a naval surgeon who having been resident many years in Lower Canada had died of cholera while tending patients in the London District during the epidemic of 1832 before he could take up the land which he could have acquired in the upper province.[68] The Lieutenant-Governor took an interest in Mrs Donnelly's case, and she was settled with her young family in Adelaide township, where her sons attempted to clear and till the land.[69] Tradition has it that the naval and military settlers assumed the leadership in developing a sense of community here. They visited frequently, organised festive occasions and attempted to establish themselves as a form of aristocracy – perhaps better described as a squirearchy. A picture has come down to us of Beer, said to be a giant of a man six foot six inches in height, dancing at sugaring-off festivals with one foot in a carpet slipper – the result of a wound sustained in the Napoleonic wars.[70]

Generally it is true to say that naval and military officers were encouraged to settle in groups, partly for military and partly for socio-political reasons. Except for the Rice Lake settlement, naval officers did not seem to choose land in accordance with this policy until the 1830s, but then they did so almost invariably, drawing comfort from having neighbours of a like class and background. Where they succeeded as settlers, it was probably because they could afford to hire hands to do some of the most demanding work in clearing land, and to build their homes.[71] Certainly some proved unequal to the task, and others enjoyed a position in society that made settlement duties unnecessary.[72] It is clear that the naval background of these settlers acted as a unifying force among them in the new society. Furthermore, they provided the necessary source of officials – especially magistrates – in newly settled townships; and they were near convenient routes to the border regions most likely to be threatened by an attack from the United States. The Rice Lake settlement was in good communication with Cobourg and Kingston; the townships near Lake Simcoe were within easy reach of the naval and military establishment at Penetanguishene (hence to Lake Huron) and to the provincial capital of York (or Toronto, as it became in 1834) on Lake Ontario. Similarly, settlers in the south-western part of the province were near the best road connecting Lakes Ontario and Erie. It is interesting to note how close many naval officers were to the best water routes: the St Clair River in Sarnia and Moore townships, the Thames River where it joined Dundas Street in Blandford and Oxford townships; Bear Creek in Adelaide township.

III

Ties of nationality, class and profession took formal shape in 1832 with the establishment of the United Services Club in York. Alfred Domett is the most informative witness to this event:

> Monday Oct. 7. I went to the British Coffee House to leave some letters and to my surprise learned that Captain Graham R.N. was at that moment in the house. I had heard that he commanded a steamer in the Lake. I found that he had just given it up. I went upstairs where were a number of military and naval officers organizing a United Services Club for Upper Canada. Their objects were to provide comfortable apartments for themselves and families whilst visiting York and do away with the necessity of dining at the public tables which they are at present under. The establishment of such a club would, they imagined, give a loyal tone to the politics of the Upper Province, make the British Government an authority more respected, and induce many half-pay officers now in England to emigrate, by holding out prospects of society to them pleasant and showing that they constituted a body numerous, united and influential. They said there were about 400 officers in the Province who would decidedly support the Club. The governor (of course) gave his sanction to it. Dr. Dunlop ['Tiger' Dunlop, who was an assistant surgeon in the army before his career with the Canada Land Company] and Colonel Light [of Blandford] presided at the meeting. They are both in some sense literary men. [73]

The club itself does not appear to have functioned as successfully as its founders hoped, but the fact of its existence and the aims professed by its original members reveal a common need among some settlers with military and naval backgrounds. An analysis of membership provides a useful indication of the unifying strands among naval officers in the province. [74]

There were only ninety-eight members in all. Of the twenty-nine naval officers only John Harris of London, Charles Rubidge of Otonabee and Walter Boswell of Cobourg had settled in the early 'twenties. Two well-established residents of York, Augustus Baldwin and John Elmsley, also belonged. Their co-operation was to be expected – both were well-known Tories in the Executive Council, but on the other hand neither was typical of the naval officers settling in the province. Baldwin had emigrated in 1817 to join the rest of that famous family, including his brother William Warren Baldwin, at the opposite end of the political spectrum. [75] John Elmsley was the son of the first Chief Justice of Upper Canada and had returned to the province after his service as a naval officer from 1815 to 1824. [76] Also from Toronto was Arthur Gifford, a purser who had emigrated in 1823 and secured his position in the civil establishment in 1828 as second clerk to the Lieutenant-Governor. [77]

Almost all the other naval officers in the club had taken up their land in 1832 or later. Oxford and Blandford townships had the largest single representation, nine members showing that address, including five naval officers, no doubt influenced by Colonel Light. Most members were from the central and western parts of the province and although a few listed Kingston, Cobourg and Colborne as their address, there appeared to be little interest among settlers in the eastern part of the province. It will be recalled that forty-seven locations of land by naval officers after 1830 were to be found in the south western region; the United Services Club attracted the interest of fifteen members from Oxford, Blandford, Adelaide, Sarnia and Moore townships, as well as from London, St Thomas, Niagara and Goderich. In the same period there were sixty-seven locations in the central region of the province, but there were only nine naval officers from that region who joined the club, from Collingwood, Medonte, Otonabee, Oro and Seymour townships, and from Penetanguishene and Cobourg. This suggests that there was more contact between Toronto and the western communities of the province during the short life of the club. What is clear above all, however, is that it was recent emigrants who fostered and supported this visible expression of a professional elite, while among the older settlers it was only those who had some active link with government who seemed to think the project worth while.

Those who appeared on club rolls however continued to keep in touch after 1836.[78] This was most evident during the rebellion of 1837, when circumstances brought a number of naval officers together against insurgents on the Niagara frontier in December of that year. The point made by W. H. Draper, in his report on the uprising in the London and Gore districts, was an important one: '...at Woodstock, London, Adelaide and other places the people gathered for the purpose of putting down the insurrection, and were making active efforts for that purpose before it was even known at the seat of government that there had been a rising in the London District'[79] Andrew Drew left Blandford township on 12 December and travelled all night to meet Allan MacNab's force of three or four hundred men at Ancaster.[80] John Harris left London when the militia were called out on 14 December to march to St Thomas.[81] After Dr Duncombe's uprising at Oakland had been quelled, Drew stayed with MacNab's force and marched to Oxford township to disperse rebels there. With the news that Mackenzie's forces had appeared at Buffalo and encamped on Navy Island, Drew went post haste to Chippewa, probably accompanied by two other Blandford naval settlers, Philip Graham and Edward Buller. By 20 December everything was in train for organising a force of armed vessels and boats capable of transporting 1,000 men from the Canadian shore to Navy Island.[82] Messages had gone out to certain half pay officers of the navy who were already responding. Shepherd McCormick arrived at Chippewa on 22 December and immediately started to prepare a scow for mounting a 24 pounder gun — his own suggestion.[83] It seems probable that Christopher Beer had accompanied McCormick from Adelaide. Drew also sent for Lieutenants William Milne of London, James Battersby of Ancaster and John Elmsley of Toronto.[84] On 26 December John Harris set off on his own initiative to offer his services, accompanied by a young protégé and son of a naval officer in England, H. C. R. Becher.[85] There were then seven half pay naval officers on hand to help organise naval forces when the steam vessel *Caroline* made her fateful appearance on 29 December.

The *Caroline* had been chartered by the Patriots. She was broken out of the ice to come down to Buffalo and act as a ferry for men and equipment between the American shore and Navy Island.[86] By the time this happened the patriot forces on Navy Island had such internal problems that they no longer posed a real threat to MacNab's force and Head had forbidden the planned attack on the island.[87] But Drew and MacNab believed, or chose to believe, that the steam vessel would enable the rebels to increase their strength too much for safety; and the reason for the Lieutenant-Governor's reluctance to attack had been the fear that the rebels would be strong enough to inflict a defeat. Thus they decided to cut the vessel out, and the deed was done with gusto that night.[88] No doubt this was an ill-advised decision; certainly, in view of the diplomatic consequences of the next four years, when conditions verged on open hostilities between Great Britain and the United States as a result of this adventure, Sir Francis Bond Head's triumphant and persistent proclamation of 'the first naval victory in Queen Victoria's reign' had a faintly disreputable ring about it.[89] But the merits of the case do not concern us here. Quite apart from the effect it was to have on Drew's naval career, to the participants and loyal inhabitants of Upper Canada the exploit was a vital tactical and moral success. At the very least it hastened the demise of the patriots in that region.[90] Speaking of the settlers in the province 'who had acquired experience in the Army and Navy of Britain' and 'whose glory it is to devote their lives to the service of their Sovereign', the Select Committee of 1838 expressed the popular view:

> With hands and hearts like these a militia is soon rendered efficient and formidable; and it may be doubted whether any country of equal population has better materials for self defence, than the Province of Upper Canada.[91]

The reputation of half pay officers, especially naval officers, had never been higher and never would be higher again in Upper Canada. Only eight months later Sir George Arthur would send home Robert Baldwin Sullivan's defensive report on the state of the province lamenting the American intellectual influence through which half pay officers were 'stigmatized as the bribed pensioners of a corrupt Government, while they were merely enjoying in a British Colony the reward of long services and exercising their rights as freemen . . .' [92]

In the immediate aftermath of the rebellion, when the forces of conservative loyalism seemed triumphant, euphoria prevailed among many of the naval officers in the province. War seemed likely and their special expertise would then be in demand. 'My only hope now', wrote Commander Vidal to his niece in England, 'is that John Bull...will make Jonathan pay...or else declare war...to give Jonathan such a dose as will teach him to behave himself for 50 years to come at least. . ... If I was sure my house would be in ruins tomorrow by it, I would still hold up both hands for war.' [93] Robert Graham Dunlop had earlier gained the Admiralty's permission to accept the honour of becoming Colonel Commandant of the 3rd Regiment of Huron Militia. Now that he saw war with the States looming, he quickly began importuning the Admiralty for active naval employment. [94] It was in this year of crisis and excitement that Captain Frederick Marryat travelled through the United States and Canada, adding his prestige as a naval celebrity to those of his profession who resided in the province. [95] There were of course other arrivals of note, and they each had a bearing on the naval officers of Upper Canada – George Arthur, Sir Francis Bond Head's successor as Lieutenant-Governor; Lord Durham, appointed Governor-General of Canada; and Captain Williams Sandom appointed to command naval forces in Canada. Arthur proved sympathetic to the views and aspirations of naval settlers; Durham provided them with cold comfort; Sandom represented their swan song.

This officer was sent in February 1838 'to prepare a flotilla, if it should be necessary, in the waters of the St. Lawrence or the Canadian Lakes'. [96] He was to be under the orders of Vice-Admiral Sir Charles Paget, Commander-in-Chief of the North American and West Indies Stations, and was to co-operate both with Sir John Colborne and Sir George Arthur. The naval establishment in the Lakes had been dismantled in 1835, but when he arrived in the Canadas there was already a naval organisation on the Great Lakes. Brought into being as the Naval Brigade by Sir Francis Bond Head's order of 20 December 1837, [97] a provincial marine continued to exist on paper under Drew, with John Elmsley as his second-in-command, even after the vessels requisitioned to watch Navy Island had been laid up for the rest of the winter.[98] In April Sandom started to build up the necessary force to watch for patriot activity. He had a few officers at his disposal and the authority to appoint half pay officers to his establishment if necessary. The Admiralty had provided him with a commission for John Elmsley, but Sandom did 'not consider it essential at present [21 April 1838] to give Lieutenant Elmsley any notice of his appointment'.[99] He did acquire the services of William Kay,[100] one of the pursers on half pay who had welcomed Henry LeVisconte to Seymour township in 1834. In June, having gathered a small flotilla together,[101] and disregarding the existence of a provincial marine, he tried to supersede Drew with an officer of his own choice. In view of Drew's rank and proven capacity Sandom reluctantly had to appoint him to command in Lake Erie and Lieutenant Duffill (his own candidate) at Toronto.[102] By 19 November 1838 five half pay naval officers resident in Upper Canada were on Sandom's establishment. They were David Taylor, a master on half pay, the purser William Kay, Commanders Andrew Drew and Philip Graham and Lieutenant James Harper, who like Graham had experience of commanding steam vessels in the Lakes.[103] Sandom's view of these officers was patronising. Their most recent experience, not having been in ships of the Royal Navy, was considered of no account.[104] Nevertheless, when more help was needed in the winter two more officers were acquired – Christopher Beer and James Battersby, both of *Caroline* fame.[105]

Sandom's relationships with local authorities and with his Upper Canadian personnel were uneasy at best. He was continually quarrelling with Arthur and with army officers who 'forgot their place' by issuing instructions as to the disposal of vessels. He engaged in a long dispute with the Lieutenant-Governor over the official use of naval vessels by Sir George Arthur on passage to various parts of the province.[106] In the winter of 1838-9 he accused Andrew Drew of absenting himself without leave from his command in Lake Erie. This resulted in no immediate charges, but Drew insisted on a court martial to defend his name and to protect the unparalleled opportunity resulting from the *Caroline* affair to return to active naval employment.[107] And although Sandom very soon revised his opinion of Harper, the best pilot on the Lakes and exceptionally knowledgeable in steam engines,[108] it was necessary in the spring of 1839 to submit an adverse report on John Elmsley. [109] The circumstances of that report reveal the extraordinary relationship that subsisted both between authorities and individuals charged with the naval defence of Upper Canada.

By the end of October 1838, the activities of the 'Patriot Hunters' in the United States and on the Upper Canadian border had convinced Arthur that there was a very real threat to the province, especially in view of the absence of fortified posts. [110] The naval implications were that with Captain Sandom's aid the force in Lake Erie needed to be expanded from one to three steam vessels, and in Lake Ontario three steam vessels should be chartered. Burlington Bay was to be protected by booms and a gun boat. [111] To get the men for this rapid expansion Arthur expanded the provincial marine. [112] When a group of patriots landed near Prescott and brought about the Battle of the Windmill in November 1838, matters took on an even more urgent aspect. Andrew Drew, now known variously as 'Commodore, Provincial Marine' and naval officer commanding on Lake Erie, could not raise the men necessary for the new steam vessel he was fitting out at the Niagara frontier. Consequently he wrote to John Elmsley, who on 28 November was placed in command of the Toronto Divison of the Naval Brigade as a Captain of the Militia.

My dear Elmsley

I am distressed beyond measure for seamen. For God's sake send me all you can and I will satisfy them about wages. You had better send me one company of the Provincial Marines with competent officers to join me at Fort Erie, and of course to act under my directions: to serve either afloat or on shore as occasion may require, and any seamen you send off forthwith may form part of that company.

You will perfectly understand that the companies you are now raising will be permanently attached to your Division at Toronto, and will return there as soon as others can be raised for service here. I have not yet heard from you. It is necessary you should make a Report to me of your operations, and what directions you have received from His Excellency that I may know what orders to give. If all is quiet I shall be in Toronto in about Ten Days.

Do pray send me forthwith all the seamen you can. Here

is where they are wanted – you will not require them at Toronto or if you do want men, landsmen will serve you just as well.

I understood you and was also told by Mr. Reed that you had sent me 50 men; whilst only 6 have arrived under Mr. Boyce – I am so straightened that I am thankful even for these.

Pray, do all you can to help me – and send them via Niagara to Point Abino, where a Steamer will be.

Ever yours [113]

Drew, as his letter shows, was circumspect with Elmsley, who was not only a member of the Executive Council but also the largest single landowner in Blandford township. [114] Drew had judged his man well. Elmsley planned to lead a party of men to Niagara in his quality as a Lieutenant-Colonel of Militia. He had assumed this rank when made second-in-command of the provincial marine, and an hour or two before leaving he approached his father-in-law, Mr Justice Livius Sherwood, armed with the Militia Act and arguing that if he was entitled to parity with ranks in the Royal Navy, he might have superior authority to that of a Commander in the Royal Navy. [115] When the argument failed to convince Sherwood, Elmsley promptly resigned, rather than hold a rank that he claimed to be beneath his dignity. As he suggested next day to Christopher Hagerman, then Attorney-General of Upper Canada, he simply felt entitled to command over Drew. [116] If he could not be in overall command Elmsley chose to offer his services as a private volunteer. [117]

If this had been the full extent of Elmsley's protest no harm would have been done, but that impetuous and passionate man could not let well enough alone. As soon as it was clear that the rank he wanted was not forthcoming, he made his way back to the vessel where his men were waiting and with a few well chosen words undermined the whole expedition. He told the officers they were now to rank only as corporals, then boarded the steam vessel *Traveller,* telling the officers in charge of a marine detachment there that the oath administered to them was illegal, that they were not bound to serve and that the men were free to go as they pleased once they had accounted for the clothing they had drawn under Elmsley's authority. [118] At five-thirty in the evening Sir George Arthur sent Colonel F.A.

Mackenzie-Fraser, Assistant Quartermaster General, to the steam vessel *Chief Justice Robinson* (still under construction in Toronto harbour, and acting as a receiving ship under Elmsley's command) to collect the sailors needed by Drew. Mackenzie-Fraser found the officers and men tipsy and impertinent, and only two volunteers came forward out of twenty-five men. The officers on board then interfered to say they had engaged to serve not under Commodore Drew but Captain Elmsley and him alone. The unfortunate emissary from the Lieutenant-Governor reported this affair, and received a polite note from Elmsley saying that since he had given up the command of the vessel he had nothing more to do with her. [119] Elmsley then wrote to Lieutenant-Colonel Halkett, military secretary to Arthur, brazenly requesting a few days leave of absence as Executive Councillor to help complete a crew for the force in Lake Erie in his capacity as a private volunteer. [120] Halkett's reply permitted Elmsley no further course of action until he 'shall have had the opportunity of offering explanation upon a course of conduct which appears so very unaccountable'. [121]

The result of Elmsley's intrigue was his suspension from the Executive Council and the forfeiture of confidence in him at the Admiralty. He had acted in a manner 'discreditable to the public spirit and even to his duty as an officer and his loyalty as a subject'. [122] Captain Sandom simply returned the Admiralty commission which Elmsley had declined to accept when called upon to do so.

In spite of these complications, the necessary naval defence forces were successfully brought into being. Relations between Sandom and Drew were still bad, but after forcing his court martial and being vindicated, Drew went on to find employment and promotion in 1842 as a post captain, appointed to HMS *Wasp* on the West Indies station. [123] For other naval officers the events of subsequent years were anti-climactic. There was no war, and no need for their special skills. For those serving under Sandom the chief desire by the spring of 1839 was to return to their farms and homes. [124] Shepherd McCormick, who lost the use of his right arm in the *Caroline* affair, left Adelaide township not only because he could no longer work his land but also according to his own account because, like Andrew Drew in Blandford, he was being hounded by Mackenzie's sympathisers. [125] He was given the lucrative position of collector of Customs at Cobourg, and in addition seems to have received a small pension from the Admiralty. [126]

The triumph of the Reform cause after 1841 did not spell the end of the influence of naval officers in the life of what was now Canada West. It was not until 1842 that the naval establishment of the Lakes was again reduced, [127] but there were still more lasting examples of influence than that. Elmes Steele, for instance, became a reform member of Parliament. [128] John Harris, who never gave up hope of returning to active naval employment, continued amid some controversy as Treasurer of the London District until 1846. [129] Such men kept close ties with the mother country – they would probably without exception have considered themselves 'true Britons', and it is questionable whether many came to regard themselves as part of that exclusive group which had given the ruling class of Upper Canada its special flavour before 1841. But as a separate group of naval officers, in spite of strong professional and social ties, their time was running out. New arrivals were no longer swelling their numbers.

The last of these men to receive the benefits of the land granting system was Commander Robert Otway, who with his remission of purchase money in 1843 bought land in Ashfield township, Huron County but settled eventually in Toronto. [130]He may well have been influenced in his decision to emigrate by Captain Marryat, who was an old family friend. [131]Otway, whose naval career had lasted from 1805 to 1837, published in 1834 the first work ever written on the application of steam to naval vessels, a book that has been adjudged one of the best of its kind. [132] Canada for Otway was a pleasant place to retire to and remain comfortably within his means. For Andrew Drew it was indeed a difficult place to leave in some respects – 'We find', he wrote to John Harris in 1842, 'we have left a great many of our comforts behind us in Canada particularly the horses which we miss very much.' [133]

In the generation since the Napoleonic Wars the naval officers of Upper Canada had given their own dimension to the affairs of the province. Some by their own strength of character and, perhaps, business acumen, turned their position to advantage. Some could not make ends meet or adapt to life in the backwoods. All, by policies of the Colonial Office and special encouragement under the regime of Sir John Colborne, Sir Francis Bond Head and Sir George Arthur, found their position

enhanced through their quality as half pay officers. Already ac-
customed to authority, their locations in the province and their
interrelationships ensured that the group remained not only
recognisable but powerful. This became clear when rebellion
first broke out, and when war threatened. But although rebellion
gave naval officers in the province unexpected professional opportunities, it also revealed the detrimental effect a few of them
could have on Anglo-American relations when they were not
subjected to rational political guidelines. Moreover, they had
developed, in their new homes, local interests that were bound to
conflict with their professional obligations so long as they were
not confirmed in positions of the naval establishment of Upper
Canada. In its most extreme form this contradiction led to the
ridiculous behaviour of John Elmsley, and the intrigues of Captain Williams Sandom against Andrew Drew. Level-headed men
like Christopher Beer simply wanted to get back to their farms in
1839. In years to come, in places like Woodstock and Sarnia,
where naval officers had played a major part in founding the
towns, there continued 'all the marks of English fashionable
life',[134] but this 'passed away in a dream, surviving only in some
still honoured names and in a memory that lingers round the
place with a pleasant old time fragrance'. It was a satisfactory
enough legacy. Some of the names were indeed preserved in
following generations by more than a memory. They included
E.W. Harris, a founding director of the London Life Assurance
Company; Major-General J.H. Elmsley who served in the South
African War, commanded a brigade on the Western Front in the
First World War and was General Officer Commanding the
Canadian Expeditionary Force to Siberia in 1918; Sir Sam Steele
of the North West Mounted Police, commander of the
Strathconas in the South African War and one of Sir Sam
Hughes' protégés in the Canadian Expeditionary Force of
1914-18; Colonel Henry Beaufort Vidal, Adjutant-General of the
Canadian militia from 1904-1908; Senator Alexander Vidal,
pillar of the Liberal Party and champion of prohibition in the
late-nineteenth century. And perhaps most colourful of all was
Walter Moberley, the famous explorer and surveyor for the
CPR, son of Captain John Moberley of Penetanguishene.
Whatever tradition they fell into, whether remembered as
codfish gentry or as aristocracy, the naval officers of Upper
Canada played a distinctive and in the end an unforgettable part
in shaping Canadian society.

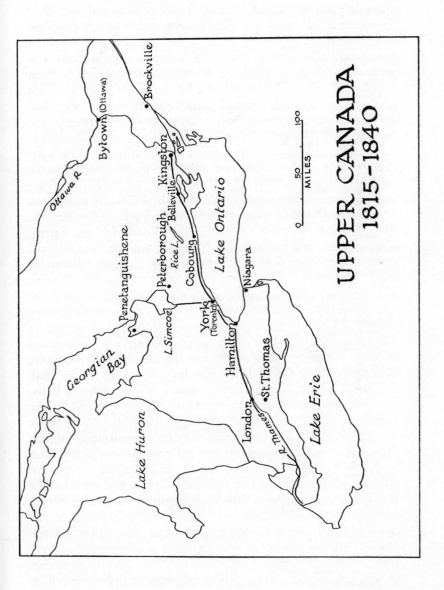

UPPER CANADA
1815-1840

Notes

1. A.R.M. Lower, *Canadians in the Making: A Social History of Canada* (Toronto, 1958), pp. 197,200, 205-6, 208; Lillian F. Gates, *Land Policies of Upper Canada* (Toronto, 1968), p. 303; Helen Cowan, *British Emigration to British North America* (Toronto, 1928), *passim*; Norman Macdonald, *Canada, 1763-1841, Immigration and Settlement* (London, 1939), pp. 39-40, 50, 61: Gilbert Patterson, *Land Settlement in Upper Canada 1783-1840* (Ontario Department of Public Records and Archives, Sixteenth Report, 1920); S.D. Clark, *The Social Development of Canada* (Toronto, 1942), p. 114.
2. G.M. Craig, *Upper Canada: The Formative Years, 1784-1841* (Toronto, 1963), p.130.
3. See, for example, John Porter, *The Vertical Mosaic* (Toronto, 1965), pp.25-8, 215; S.F. Wise, 'God's Peculiar People', in W. L. Morton (ed). *The Shield of Achilles: Aspects of Canada in the Victorian Age* (Toronto, 1968). pp. S. F. Wise, 'Upper Canada and the Conservative Tradition', in *Profiles of A Province, Studies in the History of Ontario*, a collection of essays commissioned by the Ontario Historical Society to commemorate the centennial of Ontario, Ontario Historical Society (Toronto, 1967), pp.20-33; J. Howard Richards, 'Lands and Policies: Attitudes and Controls in the Alienation of Lands in Ontario during the First Century of Settlement'. *Ontario History*, vol. 50 (1958), pp.193-209; Elva M, Richards, 'The Joneses of Brockvillle and the Family Compact'. *Ontario History* vol.60 (1968), pp. 169-84.
4. Michael Lewis, *The Navy in Transition, 1814-1864*(London, 1965); see also *idem, England's Sea Officers* (London, 1939) pp.60-77. 122-42.
5. Order in Council, 30 April 1751, PAC, MG 12A, Admiralty 1 series, In Letters (henceforth Ad. 1), vol. 5163.
6. Sir Byam Martin to Commissioner Robert Barrie, 5 April 1822, Barrie Papers (Letters from Kingston), Royal Military College of Canada (henceforth Barrie Papers, RMC).
7. Barrie to Mrs Clayton, 13 November 1818, Barrie to his sister Fanny, April 1824, A.N. McDonnell to Barrie, Ancaster, 31 May 1834, *ibid.*
8. Charles Rubidge to Captain Basil Hall, cited in Edward Guillet, *The Valley of the Trent* (Toronto, Champlain Society 1957), p.353.
9. The following papers have been consulted Public Archives of Canada (PAC) RG1, Series I. Records relating to Land Matters 1764-1867; RG5, A1, Upper Canada Sundries; Correspondence of the Civil Secretary, 1766-1841; RG8, C series, British Military Records 1767-1883; Public Archives of Ontario (PAO) , Canada Land Papers, vols. 1125-42, esp. Registers for Military Warrants and Fiats and the Journal of Military and Naval Officers' Land Rights, 1832-44. Statistics derived from these sources have been compiled by simple card-sorting techniques.
10. Patterson, *Land Settlement*, pp.159-60; Gates, *Land Policies*, p.173.
11. Lewis, *The Navy in Transition*.
12. Adam Shortt and Arthur C. Doughty, *Documents Relating to the Constitutional History of Canada 1759-1791* (Ottawa, 1907), 119-22; Patterson, *Land Grants*, pp.18, 122.
13. Maitland to Major-General Darling. ? April 1828, PAC. C631, f.7; see also C633, f.179.
14. Commissioner Robert Hall to G.W. Croker, 3 August 1817, transcript in PAC, MG 12A, Ad.1, vol. 510.
15. Bathurst to Drummond, 6 January 1816, U.C. Land Books K, f.175.
16. Bathurst to Gore, 31 July 1817, cited in Patterson, *Land Settlement*, p.119; evidence of the continuing requirement to obtain leave is in the Captain's Letters, which contain numerous examples of letters requesting leave or renewal of leave to re-

main as settlers. Microfilm, PAC, MG 12A, Ad. 1, vols. 1435-2738.

17. Hall to Gore, 12 November 1816, in Upper Canada Executive Council Minutes 22 January 1817, PAC, U. C. Land Book K. ff.55-6.

18. Martin to Barrie, 7 March 1822, Barrie Papers, RMC.

19. Barrie to his mother, Mrs Clayton, 12 October 1819, *ibid.*

20. Patterson, *Land Settlement,* p. 136; Gates, *Land Policies,* p.131.

21. William Henvey to Amelia Harris, 19 December 1817, Harris Papers, Victoria University Library, Toronto (henceforth, Harris Papers, Toronto, as distinguished from a second set of Harris Papers at the University of Western Ontario).

22. Craig, *Upper Canada,* 139.

23. Patterson, *Land Settlement,* p.149; Gates, *Land Policies,* pp.172-3.

24. Regulations for grants of land to officers of the navy, PAC, C631, f.286.

25. Donald Winch, *Classical Political Economy and Colonies* (London, 1965), pp.78-81, 87-9, 109-12.

26. John Seeley, *The Expansion of England* (London, 1883), p.102.

27. R.W. Hay to Lord Fitzroy Somerset, 4 July 1831, cited in Cowan, *British Emigration,* p.175.

28. Circular letter of 7 March 1831, PAC, C631, f.190; see also R.W. Hay to Ensign Evans, 20 July 1831, *ibid.,ff.208-9.*

29. Hay to Somerset, 12 August 1834, C632, f.186.

30. U. C. Executive Council Minutes, 19 July 1843, PAC, Canada Land Book B, f.225; Land petitions P/24, 0/8, *ibid.,* ff.292,373.

31. Cowan, *British Emigration,* pp.184-90.

32. C-in-C. Memorandum for Officers of the Army, 5 September 1843, PAC, C633, f.179; See also memoranda of 29 June 1848, August 1848, and 28 November 1849, *ibid.,* pp.223-6, 227-8, 349.

33. Evidently provincial legislation in 1837 made it impossible to alter the regulations earlier; see Sir George Arthur to Lord Durham, 31 July 1838, CO 42/449, pp. 345-55.

34. The scale was as follows:

Commander and above	Over 25 years	£300
Field Officers, Royal Marines	Over 20 years	£250
	Under 15 years	£200
Lieutenants, Warrant Officers	Over 20 years	£200
ranking as such, Captains of	Under 15 years	£150
Royal Marines		
Subalterns of Royal Marines	Over 20 years	£150
Assistant Surgeons of the Royal Navy	Under 7 years	£100

PAC, Upper Canada Land Books P. 242, 23 July 1832; Q. 449, 3 July 1834; R. 411, 23 May 1836; Land Petitions D, Bundle 72, 1832. Andrew Drew, who received a remission of £300 sterling, purchased about 700 acres, John Ireland, 'Andrew Drew and the Founding of Woodstock', *Ontario History,* LX (1968), pp. 229-45.

35. Colborne to Goderich, private and confidential, 21 September 1832. CO 42/411, 473; Colborne to ? 6 May 1834, CO 42/413, f.74.

36. Data concerning settlement has been compiled from information in Warrants and Fiats and the Journal of Land Rights, PAO.

37. Guillet, *Valley of the Trent,* pp.354-6.

38. PAO, Historic Sites and Archaeological Board of Ontario, working file, Christopher Bell.

39. John Harris to Amelia Harris, 20 June 1816, Harris Papers, Toronto; Harris to Lord Bathurst, 15 August 1817, Goulbourn to L.-Gen. Sir J.C. Sherbrooke, 13 January 1818, PAC C624, ff. 10-11; George Gowler to Harris, 31 March 1818, Harris to Lt.-Col. Cockburn, 20 June 1818, Cockburn to Harris 21 June 1818,

Petition of John Harris, 22 February 1819. PAC, Upper Canada Land Petitions, Bundle H 12, No.11, 1819; Minute of Thomas Ridout, 23 February 1819, Upper Canada Land Book K., f.8

40. File on Christopher Bell, *loc. cit.*

41. Charles Rubidge to Sir Peregrine Maitland, 22 January 1820, cited in Guillet, *Valley of the Trent,* pp.61-2.

42. *Ibid.,* pp. 354-6.

43. *Ibid.,* Rubidge to Colborne, 25 January 1834, PAC, Upper Canada Sundries, 137, f.75082; Rubidge to S. B. Harrison, 26 July 1839, Sir George Arthur to Lord Normanby, 11 September 1839, CO 42/462, ff.267-8.

44. Harris Papers, UWO.

45. PAO, Warrants and Fiats.

46. PAC, RG 5, B1. I am indebted to Professor F.H. Armstrong, University of Western Ontario, for this reference.

47. F.H. Armstrong, *Handbook of Upper Canadian Chronology and Territorial Legislation* (London, Ont. 1967), pp. 171, 173.

48. A.R.M. Lower, *Settlement and the Forest Frontier in Eastern Canada,* (Toronto, 1936).

49. Harris Papers, Toronto and UWO, *passim.*

50. See for example the John Thompson diary, 20 July 1834, PAO; A.S. Millar (ed.), *The Journals of Mary O'Brien 1832-1838* (Toronto, 1968).

51. Henry Le Visconte diary, 1834-5, PAO.

52. G.W. Spragge (ed.), *The John Strachan Letter Book 1812-1834* (Toronto, 1946), pp. 116, 135, 158, 168, 174, 245.

53. LeVisconte Diary, 31 March – 21 July 1834.

54. *Ibid.*

55. Ireland, 'Andrew Drew and the Founding of Woodstock', discusses the partnership in detail with a great deal of perception.

56. E.A. Horsman and Lillian Rea Benson (ed.), *The Canadian Journal of Alfred Domett: Being an extract from a Journal of a Tour in Canada, the United States and Jamaica, 1833-1835* (London, Canada, 1955).

57. London, 1838, New York, 1839.

58. Domett, *Canadian Journal,* p.59

59. John Morrison, "The Toon o' Maxwell" – An Owen Settlement in Lambton County, Ont.', Ontario Historical Society, *Papers and Records,* vol. XIII (1914), pp. 5-12.

60. Province of Ontario, Department of Mines and Surveys, Moore and Sarnia townships, Office Plan (incorporating information from the land grants of 1832-3).

61. 'He has been ordered upon active Service on the Western Coast of Africa . . . has resided upon his location in the township of Moore upwards of a year and expended more than twelve hundred pounds in improvement. And praying that his patent may now issue. Recommended in consequence of the peculiar circumstances of the case.' PAC, Upper Canada Land Books Q.666, 28 March 1835; Land Petition, V, Bundle 43, 1835.

62. Emeric Essex, a purser on the Lakes of Canada during the War of 1812, painted the water-colours of Kingston and Sackett's Harbour now in the Massey Library of the Royal Military College. Correspondence between his family in England and those of his brothers in Upper Canada may be found in the Vidal Papers, University of Western Ontario.

63. Diary of Henry Jones (the son of Henry Jones Sr. who was the naval officer). Sarnia Public Library. Excerpts were printed in *Willison's Monthly,* April 1929-September 1929.

64. Owen to John Harris, 18 June 1840, Harris Papers, Toronto.

65. Information from Miss Louise Hill, Woodstock, Ont.

66. 'What renders this settlement peculiarly agreeable is the circumstance of its being

mostly peopled by British; many of them, families of respectability, living within a few minutes walk of me…Last July [1832] this township was a wilderness without habitation; there are now upwards of two thousand inhabitants, and houses within every half mile along the road.' Lt. Thomas Radcliffe to his agent, cited in Rev. T. Radcliffe (ed.), *Authentic Letters from Upper Canada: with an Account of Field Sports, by T.W. Magrath, Esq.* (Dublin, 1833), p. 302.

67. Revised List of Twenty-seven Gentlemen recommended as Members of the Legislative Council of Upper Canada, 1838, CO 42/488, f.372; J.B.Robinson to Sir George Arthur, 11 December 1838, C. R. Sanderson (ed). *The Arthur Papers,* 3 vols, (Toronto, 1943-49), vol II, p.439.

68. PAC, MG 12A, Supplementary, No. 9, Patrick Donnelly (extracts from Admiralty papers showing his services).

69. Maria Donnelly to Colborne, 5 July 1833; Peter Robinson to Colborne, 18 July 1833; Maria Donnelly to Colborne, 22 July 1833, Upper Canada Sundries, vol.131, ff.72358-69; Petition of Maria Donnelly, 20 August 1834, *ibid.,* vol.144, ff.78816-19.

70. Information from Mrs Enna Field, Strathroy, Ontario.

71. See for instance the diaries of John Thomson and Mary O'Brien, and Domett's *Canadian Journal.*

72. For an example of relaxing settlement duties, which were 'injurious as forcing the Settlements of the Officers into the bleak parts of the Province where they did not succeed as Settlers', see PAC, Upper Canada Land Book, A. 355.

73. *Canadian Journal,* p.23.

74. The club proceedings are to be found in PAC, C1476.

75. F.H. Armstrong, 'Augustus Baldwin', forthcoming article in *Dictionary of Canadian Biography,* vol. 11.

76. William R. O'Byrne, *A Naval Biographical Dictionary, comprising the life and services of every living officer in Her Majesty's Navy* (London, 1849); Armstrong, *Upper Canadian Chronology,* pp. 12, 13.

77. One other member who should be noted here is Commander Robert Graham Dunlop, 'Tiger' Dunlop's brother. He was the only member to reach the Legislative Assembly, representing Huron County in the Assembly from 1835 to 1841. Two other naval officers served in such capacities – James Edward Small and Ambrose Blacklock. Small was the son of a former Clerk of the Executive Council; he represented Toronto from 1834 to 1836, and York (3rd Riding) from 1839 to 1845 as a reform candidate. His naval career had however been limited to a few months' service as a midshipman in the Lakes during the War of 1812, and he was not a member of the United Services Club. Blacklock was a surgeon who represented Stormont from 1828 to 1830. He did not appear in the United Services Club membership either. Armstrong, *Upper Canadian Chronology,* pp.9, 15, 42, 53, 76; *Idem* . . . 'James Edward Small', forthcoming biographical article, *D.C.B.,* vol. XI.

78. Club proceedings after 1836 have not apparently been preserved.

79. CO 42/477, f.144.

80. Drew to Sir Charles Wood, 20 December 1837, Ad. 1/1751; and see reference 82 (below).

81. Amelia Harris to H.C.R. Becher, 15 December 1837, Harris Papers, UWO, file marked 'Harris – re. Caroline'.

82. Drew to Wood, 20 December 1837, Ad. 1/1751; Arthur to Glenelg, 17 December 1838, enclosure L. deposition of Andrew Drew. CO 42/452, pp.234-40.

83. Arthur to Glenelg, 17 December 1838, Enclosure I, deposition by Shepherd McCormick, CO 42/452, pp. 225-9.

84. Drew to Wood, 20 December 1837, Ad. 1/1751.

85. Becher, it should be noted, had been at the December assizes in Toronto when the Montgomery Tavern incident occurred. Harris was trying, through Arthur Gif-

ford, to have Becher made Surrogate Registrar for the London District – an attempt that resulted successfully in Becher's appointment at the age of 22 in 1839. H.C.R. Becher, diary, typescript, pp. 8-9, Becher Papers, UWO; Armstrong, *Upper Canadian Chronology.*

86. Testimony of Gilman Appleby, captain of the *Caroline,* at Lockport N.Y., October, 1841, CO 42/475, f.48, 249.
87. John Ireland, 'Andrew Drew: The Man who Burned the *Caroline',* Ontario History, vol. LIX (1967), pp. 137-56; J.C. Dent, *The Story of the Upper Canadian Rebellion,* 2 vols. (Toronto, 1885), vol. II, pp. 175-93, 223.
88. Dent, *op. cit.*
89. A.B. Corey, *The Crisis of 1830-42 in Canadian American Relations* (Toronto, 1941), p.179; Sir Francis Bond Head, *A Narrative,* S.F. Wise (ed.), (Toronto, 1969).
90. R.E. Vidal to Anna Jane Vidal, 29 March 1838, Vidal Papers, U.W.O.
91. C.O. 42/445, ff.98-9.
92. Arthur to Lord Glenelg, 10 August 1838, enclosure, Co 42/449, f.246.
93. Vidal to Anna Jane Vidal, *loc. cit.*
94. Dunlop to Sir Charles Wood, 14 December 1838, Ad. 1/1753.
95. Becher diary, May 1838, Becher Papers, UWO.
96. Sandom to Arthur, 9 May 1838, CO 42/446, f.432.
97. Lt.-Col,. Strachan to Allan McNab, 20 December 1837, enclosure to Head to Glenelg, 9 February 1838, CO 42/444, f.226; Sandom to Wood, 4 May 1838, Ad. 1/2563.
98. The Militia Act of 1838 made specific provision for such a contingency, I Victoria Cap. 8, articles 44 and 46; cf. CO 42/457, f.492; see also Ireland, 'Drew: The Man Who Burned the *Caroline'.*
99. Sandom to Wood, 1 April 1838, Ad. 1/2563.
100. *Ibid.*
101. *Ibid.*
102. Sandom to Wood, 31 October 1838, Ad. 1/2564; Ireland, 'Drew: The Man Who Burned the *Caroline'.*
103. Harper commanded the steam vessel *Queen Victoria* when Henry LeVisconte visited Upper Canada in 1834, LeVisconte Diary, PAO.
104. Sandom to Wood, 19 November 1838, Ad. 1/2564.
105. Sandom to Wood, 12 January 1839, *ibid..*
106. Sandom to Wood, 21 August 1838, Ad. 1/2563; see also Sandom to Wood 12 January 1839, 29 April 1839, 2 June 1839, Ad. 1/2564-2565; Arthur to Lord John Russell, 9 November 1840. CO 42/472, ff.58-9.
107. Ireland, 'Drew: The Man Who Burned the *Caroline'.*
108. Sandom to Wood 1 June 1839, Ad. 1/2565; Sandom to Wood, 19 August 1839, Ad. 1/2566.
109. Sandom to Wood, 24 February 1839, Ad. 1/2564; Sandom [?] to Sir John Barrow, 25 February 1839, CO 42/465, ff.32-5.
110. Arthur to Glenelg, 30 October 1838, CO 42/451, ff.129-30; findings of board on defensive measures, *ibid.,* ff.183-6.
111. *Ibid..*
112. Arthur to Glenelg, 31 October 1838 and enclosure, *ibid.,*ff. 214, 221.
113. Arthur to Glenelg, 22 February 1839, enclosure No.6 CO. 42/457, ff.381-492.
114. Ontario, Department of Mines and Surveys, Blandford and Oxford townships, Office Plan (incorporating information from the survey of 1826 and subsequent grants).
115. Arthur to Glenelg, 22 February 1839, CO 42/456, f.458.
116. Hagerman to Macaulay, 7 February 1839, CO 42/457, f.490.
117. Elmsley to Halkett, 1 December 1838, *ibid.,* f. 390.
118. Report by Colonel F.A. Mackenzie-Fraser, 30 November 1838, *ibid.,* f. 389; Halkett to Elmsley, 1 December 1838, *ibid.,* ff.390-1.

119. Mackenzie-Fraser's report, *loc. cit.*
120. Elmsley to Halkett, 1 December 1838, *ibid.,* f.390.
121. Halkett to Elmsley, 1 December 1838, *ibid.,* f.391.
122. Minute by James Stephen on Sir John Barrow to Stephen, 15 February 1839, CO 42/465f. 29. Sandon to Wood, 24 February 1839, Ad. 1/2564.
123. Ireland, 'Drew: The Man Who Burned the *Caroline*'; Drew to John Harris, 2 November 1842, Harris Papers, Toronto.
124. Sandom to Wood, 1 March 1839, Ad. 1/2564.
125. Memorial of Lt. Shepherd McCormick, 13 April 1839, CO 42/467, ff.297-8.
126. Armstrong, *Upper Canadian Chronology*, p. 215.
127. Corey, *The Crisis of 1830-1842*, p. 179.
128. Elmes Henderson, 'The Public Services, etc., of Commander Elmes Steele, R.N.', Ontario Historical Society, *Papers and Records,* vol. **XXIV** (1927), pp. 373-80.
129. Armstrong, *Upper Canadian Chronology*, p.173.
130. Royal Military College of Canada, Otway papers, microfilm of the original belonging to Mr Otway Hayden of London, Ontario.
131. *Ibid.*
132. F.L. Robertson, *The Evolution of Naval Armament* (London, 1921).
133. Drew to Harris, 2 November 1842, *loc. cit.*
134. Rt. Rev. Arthur Sweatman, Bishop of Toronto and one-time rector of Woodstock, writing about the year 1900, cited in W.E. Elliot, 'The Parish of Woodstock', O.H.S., *Papers and Records,* vol.**XXX** (1934), pp. 83-95.

The Militia Lobby In Parliament
The Military Politicians and the Canadian Militia, 1868 – 1897

DESMOND MORTON

'The survival of any militia organization during the dreary decades of the 1870s and 1880s owes something to the influence of the militia lobby. Its other legacy…was the miasma of political intrigue which debilitated and divided the commanders of the Canadian Expeditionary Force…

'…(I)n a House like this', complained Peter Mitchell, 'with Colonels on his right, Colonels on his left, Colonels all around him and in front of him, with every fourth man a Lieut. Colonel', it was not easy for an enemy of military extravagance to carry the day.[1]

The highly independent New Brunswick MP was exaggerating only slightly. About one member in five in the Canadian House of Commons in 1877 can be identified as a senior officer in the active or reserve militia. In the first seven parliaments elected after Confederation, between a quarter and a sixth of the MPs indicated in their biographies that they held some kind of militia commission.[2] As a militia lobby in Parliament, they represented the interests of several thousand militia officers and at least a paper strength of approximately forty thousand volunteers scattered across the Dominion. Included in the ranks of the military politicians were such redoubtable figures as Lieutenant-General Sir Sam Hughes, Lieutenant-Colonel James Domville, Lieutenant-Colonel Armand Lavergne and three prime ministers, Lieutenant-Colonel Sir John Abbott, Lieutenant-Colonel Sir Mackenzie Bowell and Major Alexander Mackenzie.

In the years after Confederation, Canadian politics became a battleground for a bewildering array of sectional, religious and economic interest groups; to these competing forces the militia lobby may fairly be added. In an era of restricted franchise and small electorates, the impact of any organised group could be significant and there was hardly a constituency in Canada which could not boast a company or two of volunteer militia. Contemporary politicians recognised the phenomenon. The annual parliamentary debate on the Militia Department estimates was nicknamed 'Colonel's Day' and most non-military members stayed away. An astute practical politician like Adolphe Caron, Minister of Militia from 1880 to 1892, recognised that one of the major responsibilities of his portfolio was retaining the allegiance of the militia vote. 'I believe the volunteers will give us a big lift...' he reported to Sir John A. Macdonald in 1881 on the eve of an expected federal election. 'That is what I am trying to work.'[3] Since Cabinet colleagues were usually reluctant to support increased militia expenditure, his task was not easy. Whatever historians may think or claim, the *Canadian Military Gazette* insisted that disgruntled militia voters were responsible for the Liberal collapse in 1878 and the Conservative defeat in 1896.[4]

Far more important than the influence of military considerations on Canadian politics was the impact of politics on the militia. To outsiders, the force was a 'Military Tammany' and an 'Augean Stable' of corruption and patronage. Appointments, promotions, contracts, discipline, even the replacement of worn-out uniforms were guided by partisan considerations, only slightly masked by lip service to the current British principle that politics and military administration were to be rigidly separated.[5]

The presence of so many colonels in the House of Commons was testimony to the fact that both politics and soldiering were amateur avocations for most Canadians. During the 1860s, as a result of the Trent Affair, Civil War alarms and the Fenian raids, militia organisation had expanded rapidly in British North America. The civic eminence which made a man the natural choice to command the county militia battalion could also make him the logical person to represent the county in Parliament. High rank in the militia offered a politician public prominence, social prestige and a chance to distribute promotions and other favours in his battalion. Political influence could help a colonel to enlarge his corps, lobby for a drill shed or new uniforms and even frustrate the military ambitions of a political rival.

Such influences could only be truly powerful if the essential military functions of the militia had become marginal. There were repeated calls on the services of Canada's post-Confederation military system. Expeditions to the Red River in 1870 and

1871, the North-West campaign of 1885, the Yukon Force of 1898-9, two Russian war scares in 1878 and 1885 and a long list of calls to the aid of the civil power against strikers, Orangemen and other disturbers of the peace showed that the militia could be useful.[6] They did not resolve the continuing dilemma of Canadian defence: left to its unaided efforts, the country was indefensible. The treaty of Washington in 1871 and the hurried withdrawal of British garrisons from central Canada served notice that no sane British government would again contemplate war with the United States and, whatever an occasional eccentric soldier might imagine, no sane Canadian politican would expect it to. Between diplomatic reality and defence plans based on a possible replay of the War of 1812, there was a serious contradiction.

It could only partially be resolved by a little-known feature of the pre-Confederation settlement. In 1865, the Colonial Secretary, Edward Cardwell, had assured the Canadian negotiators that provided Canada 'would devote all her resources both in men and money to the maintenance of her connection with the Mother Country...the Imperial Government fully acknowledged the reciprocal obligation of defending every portion of the Empire with all the resources at its command'.[7] Even when the British forces were withdrawn, Cardwell's commitment was maintained and it was reiterated at intervals in the ensuing years. For Canada, it was a second line of security, an insurance policy with an admittedly shaky company; the premium was set at the level of Canada's unprecedented 1865 militia budget, a million dollars a year.

In the absence of any more objective basis for determining the defence budget of an indefensible country, the million dollar figure became a measure for Canadian military effort in much the same spirit as an annual two billion dollar expenditure became the standard a century later. Occasionally, governments fell below the million dollar level: in the year in which Mitchell complained of extravagance, Canadian military spending fell to an all-time low of $625,000.[8] In a belated and obviously embarrassed reply in 1888 to a long series of unanswered Colonial Defence Committee inquiries, Caron insisted that, since Canada had spent more than twenty-six million dollars on the militia, works and fortifications since Confederation, she had more than fulfilled her responsibilities under the Cardwell commitment.[9]

Budgeting the money was one thing; spending it rationally was another. As A.B. Keith reminded readers of Sir John French's sharp critique of the Canadian militia in 1909: 'It must always be remembered that the overwhelming strength of the United States on the one hand and the improbability of a rupture on the other render military training in Canada of somewhat doubtful value and reality.'[10] Alfred Gilpin Jones, a Liberal Minister of Militia in 1878, expressed a more authentically Canadian viewpoint: '...[he] has always felt that the amount we paid annually for military purposes was more to show the Horse Guards our willingness as far as possible to take upon ourselves a fair share of our own defences than for any other purposes'.[11]

The creation of valuable but undoubtedly premature institutions like the Royal Military College at Kingston was one way of impressing the British with Canadian sincerity; appointing a senior British officer to command the militia was another.[12] The Government might have spent the balance on attempting to fill some of the gaps left by the departed British garrison, for the Canadian militia soon showed the lack of trained instructors, new equipment and modern arms, to say nothing of trained staff officers and the administrative, transport and medical services which enable an army to take the field. With unconscious rationality, it did not do so, since the Canadian militia was not going to campaign as an army. When it did so, in 1885, hospitals and transport were successfully improvised and the Hudson's Bay Company played an unsung but indispensable role as quartermaster for the expedition.[13] Even more important, few of the militia's own officers saw any necessity for such reforms. Instead, through the militia lobby, they defended their own interests and their own limited concept of the militia institution.

Even before the young Dominion had formally adopted its new militia system, the 'Colonels' had demonstrated their power. When Sir George Etienne Cartier, as Minister of Militia, introduced the first Militia Bill during the 1868 session, a number of sections brought criticism from officers, with Alexander Mackenzie leading the attack for the Liberals. The provisions for compulsory service seemed defective and it was hard to see how discipline could be enforced if a volunteer could obtain his discharge simply by giving six months' notice. However, the section which drew the greatest fury from militia MPs was one granting all militiamen, regardless of rank, a mere fifty cents a day in drill pay. Parliamentary procedure prevented the officers from proposing a higher rate for themselves and eventually the Conservative officers, led by Major Mackenzie Bowell, joined the Liberals in a furious assault on the salaries proposed for militia staff officers. In vain, Cartier and Macdonald tried to rally enough votes to defeat the Colonels' amendments. After three successive divisions, in which the majority against the Government rose from one to four, the Ministers had to capitulate. [14]

The militia officers' grievance was soon remedied by granting them a dollar a day and, later, by adopting a pay scale graduated by rank, but they soon had other grievances. Militia officers were responsible for recruiting their own companies but, as peace and tranquillity dried up the reservoir of military enthusiasm, young Canadians found other outlets for their leisure. The Act of 1868 included extensive compulsory features if sufficient volunteers failed to appear and hard-pressed officers soon clamoured to have them invoked. Cartier adamantly refused. In his view, military institutions in Canada would only survive in peace-time if they were sustained by voluntary enthusiasm: peace-time conscription would condemn them to an early death. [15] The Minister was almost certainly right but that did not dissuade many militia officers from opposing the Government in the 1872 election: Lieutenant-Colonel George Denison even boasted that he had helped to defeat Cartier in his Montreal-East constituency. [16]

Within a few years, the problem of recruiting had been solved, though not with universal satisfaction. The commercial depression which began in the early 1870s at first produced droves of unemployed men, eager for even a few days of paid militia service. By 1875, the drastic fall in government revenue forced the Mackenzie Government to make sharp cuts in militia expenditure. After a series of expedients, a pattern of training and organisation emerged from the shrunken estimates which endured for the ensuing twenty years. Within the force, the establishment of rank and file was cut by a third, leaving the number of militia units (and officers' vacancies) virtually unaltered. Recognising their potential value in the event of domestic disorders, the militia units in the cities were allowed to train throughout the year. The rural battalions, on the other hand, were only authorised to muster for two-week summer camps in alternate years. As continuing, corporate entities, they virtually ceased to exist. [17]

The decision to maintain an impressive list of battalions, batteries and troops of militia scattered across the country owed very little to military needs and a great deal to the political influence of the militia lobby. As Colonel Henry Fletcher, Lord Dufferin's military secretary, had observed in a memorandum to the Government, the military problem of Canada, given a fixed amount of money, was to choose between numbers and efficiency. [18] There was no doubt which the officers preferred. Successive British commanders of the militia urged a reduction of its strength to the number the country could afford to train annually, with some money left over to replace worn-out and obsolete arms and equipment. Both Macdonald and Mackenzie agreed that Canada also needed a small regular army to cope with urban riots and the growing possibility of an Indian revolt in the North-West. Yet when Sir Alexander Campbell, as Minister of Militia, produced a plan in 1880 which would have allowed both annual training and a small regular force within the million dollar budgetary limit, his scheme was hurriedly shelved. Reducing the force by half would have meant stripping two thousand influential local citizens of their militia rank, status and allowances. It would have required rare political courage. To do so in order to finance a standing army would only have demonstrated political insanity. [19]

Instead of allowing the force to shrink, most militia officers deployed their political influence to encourage expansion and their own prospects of promotion. 'I am in daily, almost hourly receipt of letters from Colonels and Captains and corporals and Mayors and Wardens and constables about this Essex Battalion', moaned one MP to the Minister of Militia, 'and either you have to give them a sixth company or I have to retire from public life and I don't care a d – which alternative finds favour in your eyes.'[20] Responding to the assurance of its commanding officers that 'you can always rely on the Grenadiers being a good Conservative Regiment', [21] Sir Adolphe Caron overruled his British general and gave the Toronto battalion two extra companies on the eve of the 1891 election. After Toronto had proved its loyalty to the Macdonald government, prominent local citizens had their wish for a kilted battalion satisfied by the creation of the 48th Highlanders. [22]

Expanding the force could pay political as well as career

benefits. From a purely military standpoint, there was little real benefit from the biennial musters of the rural militia since few of the men served for more than one camp and it was notorious, particularly in Quebec, that the ranks were padded with men who would never be fit for real service.[23] Nevertheless, a persistent theme of the militia lobby during debate on the militia estimates was the need to increase the share devoted to annual drill, usually at the expense of the staff, the permanent corps or even the Royal Military College. As Colonel Denison never tired of reminding politicians, drill pay was virtually the only form of public money which penetrated down every dusty concession road in the country.[24] In nineteenth-century Canada, public spending was expected to inspire political gratitude.

The different treatment of city and rural militia naturally produced serious differences within the militia lobby. With the advantage of regular training and a dependable though modest income from government grants and allowances, the city battalions had a chance to thrive, sometimes evolving into active sporting, social and even political clubs. The military year was enlivened with mess dinners, dances, church parades, excursions and occasional explosive quarrels.[25] In a Canada acutely conscious of social status, a commission in a city regiment could be a badge of respectability. As the Montreal *Herald* explained to its readers: 'In Canada, an officer is useful to his regiment because he has the means to spend and the will to spend it; the regiment is useful to him because the paths toward social distinction are smoothed for the militia officer.'[26] Lord Minto, while Governor-General, confessed that officers whose social standing might not otherwise entitle them to be received at Rideau Hall were acceptable if they came in uniform.[27]

Being an officer in a rural battalion could also be expensive. 'After paying mess and band accounts, contributions to this and that call, paying for a substitute or, what is the same, losing their pay while at camp, from their employer at home, not only men, but officers of rural corps frequently go much more deeply into their pocket than there should be a necessity for in rural or city corps', insisted Sam Hughes.[28] There was also less social prestige in a rural battalion. Most of the men were collected only for each camp. The younger officers were more likely to be farmers' sons than rising young lawyers and businessmen. The cost of an officer's uniform was an additional deterrent but it was indispensable for attendance at the military schools, established for the artillery in 1871 and for the cavalry and infantry in 1883. The schools also placed a heavy emphasis on 'gentlemanly' conduct and on elaborate mess etiquette, guaranteeing a humiliating ordeal for many an unsophisticated rural youngster. [29]

Bitterness between the two elements in the militia reflected tensions in Canadian society as a whole. In 1880, when a young officer of the highly successful Queen's Own Rifles of Toronto, who also happened to be a Conservative MP, suggested in Parliament that there should be a reduction of the force to allow annual training, the rural members of the militia turned on him in fury. Lieutenant-Colonel Arthur Williams of the 46th Battalion, a fellow Conservative, indignantly acknowledged that '...rural corps, as a rule, did not understand the art of dressing themselves with that neatness that so marked the city corps, but he felt satisfied that when endurance and pluck were required that those from the country would be found to be quite equal in efficiency to those corps that the hon. gentleman seemed to praise so highly.'[30]

Friction between the rural and urban militia could only be resolved by a return to annual training, a promise which became a hardy perennial among politicians with a substantial contingent of rural militiamen in their constituencies. In the 1896 election, both Liberal and Conservative politicians pledged themselves to annual camps but the new Liberal administration discovered that its Conservative predecessor had made no provision for them in its hurriedly abandoned estimates. When Laurier's Minister of Militia, Dr Frederick Borden, a veteran militia surgeon, set out to honour the campaign promise, he had to overcome the opposition of most of his Cabinet colleagues. [31] Borden, urged by his experience, also pushed forward the creation of a Militia Medical service and other ancillary corps.

Prior to 1896, the militia lobby seems to have made little effort to expand total militia spending; its chief concern was to reduce other areas of military spending. There were only a few targets. It would have been hard to complain that too much was spent on new arms and equipment since, until 1894, almost nothing was done to replace material bequeathed by the British in the 1860s. It was easier to resume the assault on the militia staff, whose salaries in 1874-5 consumed $61,105 of the annual militia expenditure, compared to $315,557 for annual drill. Even the British officers at the head of the force agreed that the country's collection of deputy adjutants-general, brigade majors, storekeepers, accountants and inspectors was too large and that some of the incumbents regarded their positions as sinecures. [32] Unfortunately most of the incumbents had also obtained their positions through political influence and it was easier to denounce an over-sized staff in general than to risk the wrath of a powerful patron by removing a protégé. When the Mackenzie government boasted of achieving significant reductions, it was accused of moving only Conservatives. [33] British Columbia, Manitoba and even Prince Edward Island insisted on becoming separate military districts as part of the price of entering Confederation and additional staff vacancies had to be created.

Militia staff vacancies, despite their meagre pay and dispiriting prospects, possessed great attraction for gentlemen in financial distress, a group which was certainly in evidence on the fringes of Canadian government during the Macdonald era and before. Few other appointments in the Government's patronage conferred both a steady income and a measure of social status. Accordingly, even when they condemned the staff, military politicians were rarely slow to push their own nominees when vacancies occurred. [34] Political patronage extended, of course, to academic appointments at the Royal Military College. An important qualification of the Rev. A. Kearley Jones as professor of English in the opinion of Lieutenant-Colonel G.A. Kirkpatrick, was the fact that 'All his family have been staunch old Conservatives and he is a son in law of Dr. Strange who was dismissed from the surgeoncy of A Battery...because he insisted on his right to vote for Sir John.' [35]

Hostility to the staff was soon transferred to the permanent corps, particularly after 1883 when they became major rivals for scarce militia funds. By 1884, expenditure on the schools, with their small, permanently embodied units, began to exceed the annual vote for drill and, by 1891, the regulars were costing twice as much as the rest of the force and giving the militia lobby no commensurate satisfaction. While they might grudgingly accept permanent schools as a means of training junior officers and non-commissioned officers, the volunteer militia was suspicious of any tendency to supplant its own position as the first line of the Dominion's defence. That suspicion was made manifest with the advent of Major-General Ivor Herbert at the end of 1890 and the beginning of a process of reforming and altering the role of the militia which would eventually make it almost unrecognisable.

Herbert's reforms coincided with the beginning of the decline of the militia lobby, at least in Parliament. Only five years earlier, in the North-West campaign of 1885, the 'Colonels' had been at their height. Four of them, all Conservatives, were sent off at the head of their battalions; a fifth grudgingly went along as a second-in-command. A Conservative colonel from Cornwall who happened to be a doctor was placed in charge of the medical arrangements, another served as chief surgeon for Major-General Fred Middleton's column while a Conservative senator was sent west as Purveyor-General. Many of the military politicians made sure that their opinions on the management and strategy of the campaign were conveyed directly to the Minister of Militia. [36] Colonel Arthur Williams, whose Midland Battalion precipitated the final charge at Batoche on 12 May 1885, became a hero to the Canadian officers through his outspoken criticism of General Middleton and other British officers. His death from typhoid fever at the end of the campaign transformed him into a martyr. [37]

Unlike his predecessor, Major-General R.G.A. Luard, Middleton's embarrassed departure from Canada was due to the Bremner fur scandal, not the remorseless hostility of the militia lobby,[38] but militia antagonism was at least a factor in the refusal of the Macdonald government to back a loyal and once-valuable servant. Unlike earlier commanders of the militia, Middleton's successor, General Herbert, arrived with a concept of imperial defence as well as such varied gifts as wealth, energy and a command of French. Unlike his predecessors, he perceived that the rough and ready rural militia would be the backbone of any Canadian military effort, not the city battalions which, in his view, had degenerated into mere political clubs. [39] The key to reforming the Canadian militia was the reorganisation of the scattered permanent corps into a small, highly trained regular army, capable of being a model for the militia in Canada and a reinforcement to Britain's badly strained army overseas. With Herbert, the concept of Canada's twentieth-century military role as the source of expeditionary forces to fulfil imperial and international commitments was finally born. It was not enough to reorganise the permanent corps: having won the right for his new regiments to wear the imperial cypher, 'VRI', Herbert persuaded the officers to form a 'VRI Club' as a conscious declaration of their difference from the rest of the force, and as their own pressure group. In 1894, when militia drill was cancelled to save money to buy new rifles, the permanent force infantry was assembled at Lévis to the fury of militiamen. [40]

Herbert's progress had been possible only because he served a series of weak and inattentive Ministers of Militia, the by-products of a senescent Macdonald Conservative party. The militia voice in Parliament was also in decline and largely found on the Conservative benches. In 1874, eighteen Conservative officers and twenty-five Liberals — roughly the balance in the full House of Commons — sat as MPs. In 1878, Conservatives out-numbered Liberals by thirty-four to six and by 1891, numbers had dwindled to thirteen Conservative colonels to a single Liberal. The militia's voice was more clearly heard outside Parliament, perhaps through the *Canadian Military Gazette,* which began publication in 1885. Despite its dependence on govern-ment advertising revenue, the Herbert reforms helped precipitate it into increasingly open attacks on the Conservative administra-tion. By 1885, it was warning its readers: 'If militiamen really wish to see the force maintained on a proper footing they must see to it that their votes and influence are used to some purpose.' [41]

The counter-attack succeeded at least temporarily. A new Conservative Minister of Militia cancelled the order for rifles, promised drill for the entire force in 1896, and cut the strength of the permanent force by 20 per cent. Herbert, who had gone to England on leave early in 1895, did not return. When the VRI Club met without its patron, only eleven chastened permanent force officers appeared. Membership was thrown open to other militiamen and the president meekly proclaimed that instruc-tional duties were the only real task for the permanent corps. [42]

For the militia lobby it was only a partial and temporary vic-tory. A year later, in 1896, the entire direction of Canadian military development was transformed. The Venezuela crisis, with its transient possibility of war with the United States, launched a rearmament programme which did not end until the First World War. The new weapons and equipment were too complicated and expensive to be subjected to the slipshod ad-ministration of the post-Confederation militia. No longer could training camps be shifted at a politician's whim: permanent camps with extensive ranges were essential if the militia were ever to practise with their new rifles and artillery.

The brief risk of war brought the British Government to a fresh realisation of its dangerous commitment to Canadian defence. While a fresh generation of staff officers wrestled in Whitehall with the problems of war with the United States, a succession of able officers arrived from England to command the Canadian militia and lead it to reform. Willingly, they did battle with what Major-General E.T.H. Hutton continually referred to as 'the Upas tree' of political influence.[43] Though both Hutton and Lord Dundonald seemingly failed in their attempts to uproot political influence and to place the militia 'above' politics, their struggles popularised the notion of separation of military and political affairs. Paradoxically, since their struggles were with Frederick Borden, Laurier's Minister of Militia, they were aided by another event of 1896, the overthrow of the Conservative government. With predominantly Conservative militia officers facing a Liberal administration, it was a time for negotiation, not revenge. Like Caron, Borden wanted to attract militia votes and he could not do so by massively alienating Conservative officers.

The militia lobby was by no means dead after 1896, though its strength in Parliament had dwindled by the 1900 election to a mere five Conservatives and three Liberals. Until his defeat in 1904, Lieutenant-Colonel Andrew Thompson was an articulate and progressive critic of his own party's militia policy while Lieutenant-Colonel James Domville's struggle to retain command of the 8th New Brunswick Hussars illustrated the militia lobby's perennial willingness to deploy political influence against sensible regulations and simple justice.

Unquestionably the most redoubtable of the military politicians was Sam Hughes, the editor, railway promoter and outspoken Orangeman who entered Parliament in 1892. His defence of the rural militia and strident assaults on British generals and the permanent corps reflected most of the militia lobby's antipathies and, characteristically, carried them to extremes. Frederick Borden's management of Hughes was a demonstration of his skill in disarming Conservative opponents. A complicated shuffle of appointments enabled Sam's brother to transfer to the command of another battalion, allowing the Conservative MP to become a commanding officer in his own right.[44] Two and a half years later, Borden and his colleagues cleared a way for Hughes to go to South Africa, over the bitter resistance of General Hutton and, in later years, Borden manufactured further appointments and staff vacancies for his turbulent critic. Hughes more than repaid the favours by becoming the passionate defender of the Ross rifle – to the degree that Liberal responsibility for acquiring that badly flawed weapon has almost faded from history. [45] When Hughes became Minister of Militia in the Borden government, some of the atmosphere of the militia lobby returned to Ottawa. A council of senior officers was summoned as a counterweight and a snub to the professional staff officers. Hughes resumed the old quarrels with British officers and forced out his chief of the general staff, Major-General Colin Mackenzie, in circumstances reminiscent of the battles with Herbert, Luard and Hutton. The myriad of honourary and substantive colonels created in the early years of the First World War was a symptom of the past with bitter consequences for recruiting and administration in Canada and overseas.

The survival of any militia organisation during the dreary decades of the 1879s and 1880s probably owes a good deal to the influence of the militia lobby. Its other legacy, conveyed by Sam Hughes, was the miasma of political intrigue which debilitated and divided the commanders of the Canadian Expeditionary Force and which offered such a shameful contrast to the sacrifice of its members.

Notes

1. Canada, House of Commons, *Debates,* 19 April 1877, p. 1617.
2. For an estimate of the militia members in the House of Commons, see Desmond Morton, *Ministers and Generals: Politics and the Canadian Militia, 1868-1904* (Toronto, 1970), p.201, Table II, based on biographies in the *Parliamentary Guide* and *Parliamentary Companion.*
3. Caron to Macdonald, 14 August 1881, Public Archives of Canada (henceforth PAC) Macdonald Papers, vol.200, p. 84377.
4. *Canadian Military Gazette,* 12 July 1904.
5. For a discussion of the issues see Morton, *Ministers and Generals, passim;* Norman Penlington, *Canada and Imperialism, 1869-1899* (Toronto, 1965): and R.A. Preston, *Canada and 'Imperial Defence'* (Toronto, 1967).
6. On militia roles, see C.P. Stacey, 'The Military Aspect of Canada's Winning of the West'. *Canadian Historical Review,* vol.XXI, no.1 (March, 1940); and Desmond Morton, 'Aid to the Civil Power: The Canadian Militia in Support of Social Order'. Canadian Historical Review, vol.LI, no.4 (December, 1970); and in Michiel Horn and Ronald Sabourin, *Studies in Canadian Social History* (Toronto, 1974), pp.417-34.
7. Cardwell to Monck, 17 June 1865, Public Record Office, London, CO 42/693, pp.350-1. On the commitment, see C.P. Stacey, *Canada and the British Army* (Toronto, 1963), pp. 179-88; and Kenneth Bourne, *Britain and the Balance of*

Power in North America (London, 1967), pp. 287-90.

8. 'Abstract of Expenditures of the Department of Militia and Defence' (memorandum in the library of the Department of National Defence).

9. 'Report of the Minister of Militia and Defence', 23 January 1888, CO 42/795, pp. 299-300.

10. Minute (n.d.) CO 42/939, p. 492.

11. House of Commons, *Debates*, 16 April 1878, p. 2052.

12. See R.A. Preston, *Canada's RMC*(Toronto, 1969) and Morton, *Ministers and Generals*, pp.27-30.

13. See Desmond Morton, 'Administrative Aspects of the Canadian Campaign in the Northwest in 1885', *Canadian Defence Quarterly*, vol. III, no.1 (Summer, 1973).

14. *Journals of the House of Commons*, 1868-9, pp. 391-4. See also Eugene Forsey, *Freedom and Order: Collected Essays* (Toronto, 1974), pp. 123-4.

15. See, for example, 'Memorial to Cartier: The Volunteer Militia', in P.R.O., Carnarvon Papers, vol. 170, pp. 3-4, and R.H. Davis. *The Canadian Militia: Its Organization and Present Condition* (Caledonia, 1873). For Cartier's views, see Sir Joseph Tassé, *Discours de Sir George Cartier Barronet* (Montreal, 1893), pp. 707-9.

16. George T. Denison, *Soldiering in Canada* (Toronto, 1900), p. 186.

17. See reports of the Department of Militia and Defence, 1877-1896, *passim;* Desmond Morton, *The Canadian General: Sir William Otter* (Toronto, 1974), pp. 61-2.

18. Lt.-Col. Henry Fletcher, *Memorandum on the Militia System of Canada* (Ottawa, 1873), p. 3.

19. For Campbell's proposal, see draft Order-in-Council, 30 October 1880, PAC, RG 9, II A 1, vol. 604, pp. 192-201.

20. J.C. Patterson to Caron, February 22, 1889, PAC, Caron Papers, file 10729.

21. Lt.-Col. G.D. Dawson to Macdonald, 22 January 1890, *ibid.,* file 14014.

22. On the new battalion, see *ibid.,* file 15006; House of Commons *Debates*, 25 September 1891, p. 6182.

23. Desmond Morton, 'French Canadians and the Canadian Militia, 1868-1914', *Histoire Sociale/Social History*, no. 3 (June, 1969). The limitations of the camps were a recurrent theme in the departmental reports and in the *Canadian Military Gazette*. For an extensive indictment of the state of the militia, see Lord Stanley to Mackenzie Bowell, 18 February 1892, PAC, Bowell Papers, vol. 10, pp. 4783-97.

24. See, for example, Denison to Macdonald, n.d. and memorandum, PAC, Macdonald Papers, vol. 332, pp. 150174-6, and Two Militiamen, 'A Plea for the Militia', *Canadian Monthly*, February 1879. (The two appear to have been Denison and Lt.-Col. T.C. Scoble of the Toronto Engineer Company.)

25. For example, see Morton, *Ministers and Generals*, p. 116 and *idem, The Canadian General*, pp. 77-8, 152-4.

26. Montreal *Herald*, 4 September 1902.

27. Minto to St. John Brodrick, 3 May 1899, National Library of Scotland, Minto Papers, box 10.

28. Hughes to Lt.-Col. C.E. Montizambert, 29 November 1898, PAC, Hutton Papers, p. 1108.

29. The criticisms are reflected in House of Commons, *Debates*, 22 March 1889, pp. 796-7, and 6 June 1895, pp. 2197-2223. See also Hughes' memorandum 're Militia', n.d. (1892 or 1893), PAC, Sir John Thompson Papers, p. 21455.

30. House of Commons, *Debates*, 31 April 1880, p. 1362.

31. Fielding to Borden, 21 August 1896, Public Archives of Nova Scotia, F.W. Borden Papers, p. 177.

32. *Report of the Department of Militia and Defence*, 1874, pp. xvii-xx, for example.

33. House of Commons, *Debates*, 10 April 1877, pp. 1347-5?.

34. For examples of pressure, see Caron Papers, *passim*, for instance file 12326-7 on filling a vacancy for a surgeon at a military school.

35. Kirkpatrick to Caron, 4 September 1883, *ibid.,* file 3114.

36. See for example, letters from Colonel Guillaume Amyot in *ibid.,* vol. 199, published by Desmond Morton and R.H. Roy, *Telegrams of the North-West Campaign, 1885* (Champlain Society, Toronto, 1972). *passim,* and Desmond Morton. 'Des Canadiens Errants: French Canadian Troops in the North-West Campaign of 1885', *Journal of Canadian Studies,* vol.V. no.3 (August, 1970). For the later history of the Amyot correspondence, see *inter alia,* n.a., *'Sir Adolphe Caron C.C.M.G. ministre de la milice et ses détracteurs ou luit années d'administration militaire'* (Montreal, 1889).

37. See Denison, *Soldiering,* pp. 300-1; G.H. Needler, *Louis Riel* (Toronto, 1957), p.4; and Desmond Morton, *The Last War Drum: The North West Campaign of 1885* (Toronto, 1972), pp. 90, 142.

38. On Luard, see Morton, *Ministers and Generals,* pp. 59-68.

39. Herbert to the Duke of Cambridge, 19 April 1891, Royal Archives, Windsor Castle, Cambridge Papers.

40. Morton, *The Canadian General,* pp. 147-9.

41. *Canadian Military Gazette,* 15 May 1895.

42. *VRI Magazine,* March 1896; Morton, *The Canadian General,* p. 157.

43. On Hutton's policy, see *Canadian Military Gazette,* 1 November 1898. See Norman Penlington, 'General Hutton and the Problem of Military Imperialism in Canada, 1898-1900', *Canadian Historical Review,* vol. XXIV, no. 2 (June 1943). For another view, see Morton, *Ministers and Generals,* ch. VII.

44. Cotton to Adjutant-General, 14 May 1897, F.W. Borden Papers, p. 2020.

45. See Morton, *The Canadian General,* pp. 248-51, 290-2.

Wolseley, The Khartoum Relief Expedition and The Defence of India, 1885 – 1900

ADRIAN PRESTON

When Wolseley left Charing Cross Station on 31 August 1884 to extricate Gordon from the Soudan, his was an embattled reputation. Barely two years before, the Egyptian campaign had convinced him of what his closest admirers had always suspected, that he was the greatest commander his country had produced since Wellington. Yet despite that climactic campaign it was clear to any student of military politics that Wolseley's career, hitherto unchecked, had now run into heavy weather. He had failed to turn the Eastern Question to any grand strategical advantage while obscurer officials were secretly manipulating the springs of policy. The chief commands in the Balkans, Zululand, Afghanistan and the Transvaal – even the Adjutant-Generalship – had been either denied him or conceded under such grudging conditions as to minimise the potential he saw in them. His administration of Cyprus and his settlement of Zululand had been exposed by events as unworkably flashy and doctrinaire – mere stepping-stones to the Indian Command which continued to elude him. His stable of ghost-writers, his calculated use of after-dinner speeches, his truckling to the press, his cliquish practices and indulgent nepotism were now open secrets. The intemperance and theatricality of his attacks upon the Horse Guards and the Indian Army had vitiated a quite genuine case for a thoroughly professional short-service army and had driven otherwise unsympathetic critics to defend those very institutions he had assaulted. In this, the sequel to the Egyptian campaign, he was embarking although he did not know it upon his last command.[1]

Hicks's inexplicably muddle-headed defeat had worried Wolseley – as indeed it had convinced anxious generals in India – that the Mahdi might be more than a mere saintly Moslem prophet, and as early as 4 January he had urged the Government to instruct the commander of the garrison at Khartoum to retreat as fast as possible by any route that he could find before he was

surrounded by a sea of insurrection which had every prospect of
becoming a direct invasion of Egypt proper. A retreat, he warned the Government, was always one of the most difficult military
operations to carry out and its dangers were immensely increased
and intensified when conducted by inefficient native troops exposed to the full blast of the Mahdi's propaganda. It would be
necessary to combine the British and Egyptian forces under the
consolidated unitary command which Hicks's expedition had
fatally lacked, and he himself was ready at a moment's notice to
lead any diversionary raid which would help Gordon to
withdraw the beleaguered garrison unmolested.[2] The
Government declined the offer, feeling that Gordon alone,
equipped only with his personality and his reputation, could
somehow or other pacify an immense and mutinous province.

The repulse of Baker's distractive raid at Suakin – which he
himself had offered to conduct – now galvanised Wolseley into
fresh fits of tough talk. It had seriously imperilled not merely
Gordon's negotiating position – which was weak to start with –
but the whole of British military prestige in the Near East.
Wolseley explained to Hartington,

> Unless 'something' is now done, and done at once, to
> manifest your power and strength in the most un-
> mistakeable manner, it is tolerably certain that Gordon will
> soon find himself shut up in Khartoum, unable to do more
> than hold his own there as long as his provisions last, even
> assuming he is able, with his genius for command, to infuse
> sufficient courage into the miserable troops that now con-
> stitute the garrison of that place.

A brigade of Wood's Army should take up a threatening position
at Wady Halfa; fresh blows with strong forces should be struck
in the East Soudan; and an Indian Contingent should land at
Suakin. If these elementary precautions were not taken, Wolseley
warned, he could not see what Gordon could possibly achieve at
Khartoum. 'He will be besieged...and it is folly to imagine he
would be able to cut his way out. The result I foresee is, an
irresistible demand on the part of our people to have him relieved, and to relieve Khartoum under such conditions would mean a
costly war of considerable proportions.' No army could march
from Suakin to Berber if it were opposed, since the last hundred

miles were for operational purposes entirely without water. If Khartoum were besieged in force, therefore, any army sent to its relief would have to advance from Assuan into Egypt proper along the Nile Valley, 'a very long and tedious operation'. It was precisely because he wished to avoid such a war that contained so many of the ingredients of disaster that he now proposed the show of force with which to cover Gordon's retreat. He concluded,

My dread, is that unless action is at once taken we shall be forced into war before many months elapse. It is bold measures and a decided policy at moments like the present that stave off wars with all their horrors and attendant cost: it is half-measures and no policy beyond waiting upon events that cause us insensibly to drift into war. Something desperately should be done. [3]

But for reasons of its own, infamous and otherwise, the Government prevaricated; and while it did so Wolseley began to intrigue to supplant Stephenson – the local British commander of the Forces in Egypt who was at the same time pressing identical proposals on the Government – as the likely commander of the relief force, [4] by thrusting upon the Cabinet in a way that Stephenson could not, specific plans of operations which so guaranteed a rapid and clear success that it could not fail to select him to implement them. [5] To this, despite the protests of the Admiralty, the Royal Engineers, the Indian Army and the Intelligence Department and of both Baring and Stephenson on the spot, the Government eventually succumbed, [6] but it refused to place in Wolseley's hands a dormant Commission as Governor of the Soudan on the grounds that he had made a mess of his former governorships in Natal and the Transvaal [7] and that if Gordon disobeyed and refused to be relieved Wolseley might combine with him in a spectacular military promenade into the interior of Africa. [8] Wolseley's basic plan was one of approach rather than of operations. It was worked out in detail with all the technical expertise which his former Canadian colleagues could command, and it therefore visualised repeating on a vastly increased scale his earliest but largely forgotten triumph – the Red River Expedition. Like that earlier bloodless operation, this would be a gigantic ferrying service, a contest against time and nature rather than against men, and therefore a test of Wolseley's logistical skill. For this reason, no serious thought was given to the probability of the Mahdi's resistance or to the question of what the force should do were Gordon to refuse, or be unable to accept, its help. [9]

Yet the historian cannot fail to notice that for all his initial talk of desperate urgency, for all his scoffing that other plans were too clumsy, top-heavy or defeatist, for all his insistence upon professional merit, unity of command and swiftness of execution, Wolseley's handling of the Soudan campaign was a patchwork of muddle and confusion. It seems that Wolseley was as bewildered as Gladstone by Gordon's infrequent and outrageous messages and sheltered behind them to excuse the grandiose preparations which as Adjutant-General and President of the Mobilisation Committee he was putting in hand to make this a truly homeric spectacle, 'the biggest operation the English Army has *ever* undertaken'. [10] He padded his staff with comforting relatives, influential courtiers and titled *flaneurs* who could only compound the frictions, inertia and mistakes which inevitably beset all campaigns in which lean and crisp operations are most required. To Wolseley's remarks at the Engineers' dinner that the 'Crimean days of patronage and nepotism had gone forever', Ponsonby was prompted to observe that 'no doubt Lord Raglan appointed his own nephews on the staff and many of the Staff appointments were given for private reasons. But in Egypt the War Minister had 2 sons ADCs, the Duke one son (he would have had 2 but the other was ill), Adye had one son. All Childers' Private Secretaries were on the Staff. Patronage and nepotism were just as much there as in the Crimea.' [11] The same held true for the Soudan; with the result that when news came of the fall of Khartoum a general desertion of disappointed medal-hunters took place. In spite of Wolseley's understandable and unceasing complaints that Gladstone should have let him off the leash sooner, his own recently published diary of the campaign provides striking proof that once launched he was determined to take his own time. For two months he languished in Cairo, building up a force that seemed grossly inconsistent with the specific and non-punitory objectives it was his mission to fulfill. The confidential diaries of Wolseley's own battalion commanders reflected these apprehensions. One of them wrote,

Wolseley seems as unpopular here on active service as at home. No one has a good word for him, and really much that he has done lately shows him to be a snob and a self-interested man. It is the general opinion that he is responsible for the supercession of Stephenson which no doubt was very hard lines. It requires explanation why Stephenson was refused the 3000 troops he asked for while Wolseley has about 7000 given to him. People say he is trying to bolster up the expedition into a big business so as to reap extra credit himself and get an Earldom, and that his employment of every man in the service almost who has a handle to his name is only part and parcel of the same selfish game and innate snobbishness. I have always thought him a much-abused man but I cannot help, in the face of all he does, coming round to the belief that he does not care a jot for the taxpayers' money and sinks patriotism with a view to raising his reputation by a big display. I don't believe so many troops are necessary for this job. . . . [12]

When news of Gordon's predicament finally compelled Wolseley to detach the Desert from the River Column, he found himself doing what he had never done before – directing rather than commanding the decisive operations of his armies and co-ordinating in detail the movements of two widely separated columns, groping forward in largely unknown country, and dangerously exposed to imminent defeat. Indian and Engineer officers such as Napier, Roberts and Kitchener, or strategists such as Hamley and Clarke who had their own reasons for favouring the desert route, could now only watch with arid satisfaction as the Mahdi tempted Wolseley's broken and wasted force into a series of inconclusive battles and brought it to a complete standstill two days' march from Khartoum.

To the official historian of the Royal Engineers and to Kitchener who compiled an unusually moving lament to the fall of Khartoum and who some fifteen years later, despite Wolseley's vigorous protests, was to command the Anglo-Egyptian force which avenged it, Wolseley's eccentric choice of the Nile route, his ignorance of Dervish tactics and his inexcusable failure to provide for his armies combined to insure Gordon's certain death. [13] To Roberts, Wolseley's obsession with the Nile strategy, and indeed with the whole amphibious basis of British war policy of which it seemed a part, remained a tragic and indefensible enigma.[14]

Exactly ten years before, he had embarked upon a career as a professional strategist in the first of a series of commissioned memoranda in which he argued with convincing economy and with one ear instinctively tuned to the rumblings of mutiny that Russian intrigue and aggression in Central Asia, like the Mahdi's in North Africa, could only be decisively broken in battles in Western Afghanistan conducted from a base and along lines of communication and supply which were as short and as impenetrable as man and nature could make them. Such an orthodox Indocentric strategy effectively ruled out those ancillary seaborne operations in the Baltic, the Persian Gulf, the Black Sea and the Mediterranean upon which British soldiers and governments, lacking the manpower to field large armies, had been traditionally nurtured and which, providing they attracted a powerful Continental ally, they stubbornly preferred. Since the war scare of 1870, Britain's strategic counter-measures to Russian designs upon Turkey and Central Asia and ultimately upon the Mediterranean corridor and India itself were implicit proofs in themselves that as the spreading web of interior railroads conferred upon land-powers capacities for defensive concentration and manoeuvre greater than those traditionally enjoyed by sea-powers, then Roberts' arguments for the continental Indianisation of British strategic policy seemed not only logical but unanswerable. The Admiralty's refusal in 1878 to guarantee the forcing or seizure of the Dardanelles by ships alone and the subsequent annexations of Cyprus and Egypt to establish direct naval control of the Mediterranean corridor reflected the general indecisiveness of sea-power and diplomacy in themselves to prevent a Russian occupation of Merv or Constantinople or to deter Russian advances towards India. Yet, with the Swiss and Italian civil wars and the Prussian defeats of Austria and France which had deprived Britain of reliable sources of foreign mercenary contingents and of the effective military allies she had always needed to supplement her manpower, it seemed that only India could provide the resources and the base of operations – the centre of strategic gravity – which could turn British sea-power to decisive advantage in a war against Russia or which in less critical circumstances could cover, support or salvage British expeditions compromised abroad. [15]

With the deaths of Cavagnari, Colley and MacGregor, Roberts had emerged as the best-known surviving spokesman of Lytton's controversial strategic policies and the abortive Simla Commission reforms which the fall of Merv had vindicated while Wolseley's armies were embroiled in Egypt. Exploiting Wolseley's fall from grace at the time of Majuba and his own ascendancy as the Indian champion of long-service reform, Roberts had jobbed and intrigued as feverishly as Wolseley had ever done to secure his claim to the Indian command. He did so by cultivating the Conservative Opposition and its supporting strategists (such as Hamley, Clarke, Wilkinson, Dilke and Chapman) with an articulated strategy of Indian defence which it was logical that he as Commander-in-Chief should implement. [16] As Wolseley squandered the remnants of his reputation and resources in the sands of the Soudan, as the Russian assault upon Penjdeh drove home the logic of Roberts' strategic appreciation that India was the pivot of Imperial power, and as Gladstone's Government tottered to the brink of dissolution, Roberts' hour now seemed at hand and he became more outspoken in his criticisms of Wolseley's handling of the Soudan campaign.

Like most Indian generals at the time of the Hicks' disaster he had asked himself whether the Mahdi would confine his jehad to the Soudan and lower Egypt or whether he would encourage it to spread towards India, and if the latter he hoped to be selected for the command of any Anglo-Indian force which might be sent to contain it. [17] After struggling all the way to Dongola, Roberts wrote to Grant Duff, [18] Wolseley's battered armies were no nearer to Khartoum than the alternative base at Suakin which was protected by the fleet and which could provide a rapid conduit for Indian reinforcements. Instead they were thinly scattered across a desert of hostile and mounting insurrection. Whether by accident or design, the Mahdi had played a clever game. He had captured Khartoum just as Wolseley had committed himself by dividing his force into widely separated columns which he could not possibly control or co-ordinate. It was a potentially disastrous situation which could only be retrieved by the strongest forces and the ablest commanders that Britain and India could provide. It was clearly a case, as it had been in the Crimea and in South Africa, of asking the Indian Army to save British generals from the consequences of their own incompetence.

Major Ian Hamilton, one of Roberts' young disciples, agreed.

Wolseley's fatal mistake, he wrote years later, lay in the creation
of the Desert Column as the principal strike force, to which the
smaller but tougher River Column was to be sacrificed. For the
Desert Column was to be "the go" as they called it then; into *that*
the cream of the British Army had been poured with no niggard-
ly hand. Far from the nursemaids of Hyde Park, mounted now
on magnificent, groaning camels, the Household Cavalry and the
Guards performed the most wonderful evolutions:

> The Desert Column was a brain freak of his. No one but
> Wolseley, in the days of railways, as leading soldier of the
> greatest industrial nation of the nineteenth century, could
> by his creating fancy have persuaded bovine Hartingtons
> and serious Gladstones to re-embark upon the methods of
> the ninth century. Had he stuck to his boats those river
> men, the other poor common soldiers, the outsiders, would
> have saved him; they would have enabled him to rescue
> Charles Gordon (which he was by no means mad keen
> about) and to wipe the floor with Roberts's march to Kan-
> dahar (on which he was absolutely set). But the pressure of
> the Ring; the urge to do something for his pals; the pic-
> turesqueness of the idea of putting London society on
> camels and marching them over a desert; these were too
> much for ... . The scheme was semi-social, semi-political .
> Charles Gordon was doomed when Wolseley hatched out
> the Desert Column.

When Earle was killed at Kirkeban, the command of the
Column devolved upon Brackenbury, an intellectual administrator but a paper soldier who in hastening to retire
forfeited forever the chance to fight

> an earlier Omdurman; to save millions of lives; to save
> Gladstone's soul; to save Wolseley's prestige from the
> knock from which it never recovered...Wolseley had only
> himself to blame; for his arrangement of the force to suit
> those whose influence, respect and admiration he courted;
> for his failure to press on through one channel when the
> other, favourite channel, failed. Wolseley was not built to
> catch the eye of the crowd and clearly he cared nothing for
> their regard. In bidding for the eye of the few, he failed

himself and his command...There was no personal touch
and so the legend of Wolseley was dead. [19]

There was a time when Lord Napier might secretly have
agreed, but he was generally more charitable than either Roberts
or Roberts' protégés in his assessment of Wolseley's predicament.
He had always managed to keep one courtly step ahead of
Wolseley in his wars and chief commands, something which
Wolseley found insufferable and which inflamed a malicious
streak in his character. Napier had captured the Balkan command
without too much trouble in 1878, his chief rival being, not
Wolseley whose stringent ambitions were implicit in every
memorandum he wrote, but Simmons who could not be spared
from Whitehall. [20]Where Wolseley had later seized the chance,
Napier had chivalrously declined to supersede the harassed but
ultimately successful Chelmsford in South Africa. [21] As an
Engineer, a former Military Member and acting Viceroy of India
who was not afraid of changing his mind as fresh conditions of
strategy arose, Napier displayed a profound and occasionally explosive revulsion to the cheap bourgeois habits and sinister
Caesarism which Wolseley had dragged into British military
politics, pitting the British against the Indian Army and striking
mischievous comparisons between them.

For Wolseley's failure throughout the developing crises with
Russia and Afghanistan to foist himself into the Indian Command
and in the course of a war to set himself up as a virtually
autonomous counterweight to the Duke of Cambridge had
rankled bitterly. The very considerable efforts of Eyre, Colley
and Lytton to prepare the way for him had been frustrated by an
implacable and impenetrable alliance of the Horse Guards and Indian bureaucrats who saw in Wolseley's firebrand buccaneering
all the makings of a recond Mutiny. [22]As Russian generals in
Central Asia forced strategists to the conclusion that India rather
than Britain or its self-governing colonies was the true centre of
Imperial strategic gravity, Wolseley retaliated in both the Egyptian and the Soudan campaigns by relegating Indian commanders
and contingents to operational roles which, however brilliantly
carried out, could not detract from the control or credit of the
War Office of the British Armies which he personally
commanded. [23] Even in his preparations for the Boer War,
Wolseley as Commander-in-Chief was 'very anxious to do the

job without calling upon India'. 'I don't want it to be thought', he wrote to Bigge, 'that we must always get help from India when we go to war in our Colonies.' [24] Whenever there had been a minor reverse overseas or a breakdown in army reform, there had always been 'a cry to get someone from India to put us right. God help the Army if we have to take our lessons from India. In 1855-6 such was the cry and in 1857 all India and its Army was in revolt against us.' [25] 'Wolseley has never concealed his contempt for Native troops', wrote one of Roberts' informants from the War Office, and it had been aroused when he was Governor of Cyprus because some Gurkhas had not been able to keep in step with the Grenadier Guards. [26] On several occasions over the next twenty years Wolseley was called to book by Queen Victoria for tactless and disparaging remarks upon the efficiency and reliability of the Native Army. [27] By 1885, his 'arrogance and temper, and his ill-conceived dislike i.e. jealousy of Indian officers and the Indian Army at large' had prejudiced all reasonable claim to the chief command. It was obvious that he had lost the confidence of both Liberals and Conservatives who considered he would have made 'a very unpopular and unsafe Commander-in-Chief.' [28] In a letter to Ponsonby on 25 July 1885 Salisbury explained why.

'We are not yet free from the peril of war. It may come this autumn: or next year: or later: but the probability on the whole is that we shall not escape it. It will be a critical struggle: and we ought not to throw away a single chance. Now Roberts, beyond comparison, is the man who knows most, and has done most in Afghan warfare: and we ought not to forego the advantage of placing the conduct of operations under his care if we can help it. It is vital in this matter to have a man whose merit has been tried, and who thoroughly knows his work... . I think that Roberts has been quite the equal of Wolseley in the brilliancy of his successes, as well as in the importance of the field upon which they have been won. There is a general inpression in the Army that Wolseley has had much more than his share of opportunities of distinction... . [29]

Such exclusion on the grounds that Wolseley was 'wanted at home for our European wars', [30] merely intensified his prejudices, with inevitable repercussions upon the forumlation of strategy. The great debate in the 1880s between the Eurocentric and Indocentric advocates of Imperial defence became as embittered and as sterile as it did because it was heavily charged with the conflicting interests and professional ambitions of those rival commanders, namely Roberts and Wolseley, who stood most to gain or lose. [32] Every senior appointment both in India and Britain became the occasion and the focus for this internecine and sometimes malicious struggle. Although Wolseley distrusted Wood and Buller, he was more than ready to recommend them for Aldershot or the Adjutant-Generalship if by so doing he could forestall Roberts; while Roberts on the other hand was prepared to violate the traditions of an outraged Army by promoting his protégé. White, to the Chief Command over the heads of Greaves, Wood or Buller who although more senior and experienced were despicable Wolseley men. Wolseley himself admitted to Bigge – what he had never told anyone before – that the 'one great reason' he had accepted the Commander-in-Chiefship in 1895 'was to keep Roberts out of it'. 'I knew he would Indianise our Army,' he explained, 'and bring in customs that we try to avoid here.' [32] For somewhat similar reasons he had protested Kitchener's selection to command the Second Nile Expedition, preferring Talbot instead. [33] In South Africa, he blamed all of Buller's misfortunes upon Sir George White who had 'proved himself to be absolutely incapable and ignorant of War's first principles'. Roberts had committed even greater blunders, but had concealed them by criticising Buller. All in all, he wrote, 'our Indian generals have not done well: White, Symonds and Gatacre, all failed, and poor Kitchener is no better'. [34]

It was talk of this kind which particularly infuriated Napier. He wrote to the Military Secretary at the Horse Guards,

> Think of Ali Musjid, Peiwar Kotal, action near Kandahar, near Giriskh, Ghazni, Charaniah. On every occasion we had succeeded in India. Compare it with Africa. The latter was a series of misfortunes and disgraces, lightened by the defensive battle of Ulundi and the hunting down of the ruined Cetewayo. What the defeat of Secocoeni was we do not know. Roberts and Stewart have had real battles... . What has Wolseley done? Ashanti was in-

complete. Sartorius with a few Africans went on to the end after Wolseley had turned back: he had difficulties to overcome no doubt. The Red River Expedition may be learnt from Butler's *Lone Land*. I would not detract for a moment what Wolseley did in Africa. But really his name is built up from his own and his followers' talk. If he should have a great field to display these qualities he may justify the confidence in him, but he has it to do.[35]

As for the Nile Expedition,

Stewart's dash was a desperate effort to make up for lost time and was a brilliant affair for the troops. Had it succeeded it would have rivalled anything in History. But had they even reached Khartoum they were too weak and exhausted to clear the Arabs away. The basis of the whole expedition was thoroughly faulty. For that the Ministry may be entirely to blame. The weakness of the boat carriage was that the main column was chained to the Nile and might have been harassed daily without the power of pursuit. Any serious attack on their communications would have been fatal.[36]

After the Penjdeh crisis had broken out, Napier had urged the Horse Guards in the event of a Russian war to prosecute the Soudanese and Central Asian campaigns at the same time and with equal vigour. To wind up the Soudan or subordinate it to a Central Asian campaign would only release Wolseley for the chief command in India which public clamour would make it difficult for the Government to refuse. Napier would normally have been expected to endorse a Central Asian campaign over peripheral operations in the Soudan. But the Duke of Cambridge agreed and felt that to keep Wolseley out of both England and India he should be offered the High Commissionership in Egypt or the Viceroyalty in Ireland.[37]

For these and other reasons – the petty squabbling among his rear and base commanders, Buller's fatal logistical oversights, the inexperience of the boat-crews and the deaths of Stewart, Eyre and Burnaby – Wolseley failed to reach Khartoum in time. Those whom Wolseley had deliberately shelved from glory –

the despised Wood, the Indians and the Engineers – now found themselves blameless of defeat; and Wolseley turned all the savage force of his despair against an ascetic non-Ringer, Sir Charles Wilson, whose stubborn and skilful defence of Metemmeh during those last anxious days may well have saved the entire expedition from utter rout.[38] But even if Wolseley had had unlimited time and troops at his disposal, it is hard to imagine that the result would have been much different. As Napier and Hamley had remarked, Wolseley's whole operation was monstrously and fundamentally flawed by the very river to which it was tied, and by the claims which disease and desert warfare would make upon the fighting component of his force and its freedom of manoeuvre. Encircled and exhausted at the end of a fixed and vulnerable life-line by a mutinous population which denied him both information and supplies while the Mahdi's massed and fanatical hosts poised themselves around the emaciated garrison, Wolseley's boasts about sweeping the Mahdi into the sea sounded ludicrously hollow and if carried out would have brought upon himself a defeat as disastrous and decisive as Hicks' had been. As it was a combination of circumstances – the Penjdeh crisis, the fall of Gladstone's government and the Mahdi's death – thrust upon him the bitter humiliation of a long and unharassed retreat. The Christmas cards specially struck from engravings commemorating the relief of Khartoum,[39] the vacant Order of St Patrick and the dormant commission as Governor-General of the Soudan he had vainly requested of Gladstone – all now seemed singularly irrelevant and repugnant.

For Wolseley knew that he had suffered on the Nile no less than a dramatic military defeat which the legion of his critics would allow him no chance to redress. One example need suffice. Wolseley was anxious that Hamley be prohibited from reviewing Brackenbury's semi-official account of the operations of the River Column.[40] Since Tel-el-Kebir, when Wolseley had suppressed Hamley's despatches claiming that the Highland Division which he commanded had been decisive of Wolseley's ultimate victory, Hamley had relentlessly censured Wolseley's generalship. Their feud had become a professional *cause célèbre*. Wolseley had written down Hamley as a mere paper theorist – the so-called English Jomini – whose monumental *Operations of War* was a greater burden to the British Army than the Duke of Cambridge, who understood nothing of the accidents and

realities of modern warfare and who out of sheer perversity and
spite had identified himself with the Roberts school of Imperial
strategic policy. But other critics, such as G.S. Clarke, abler than
Hamley and sympathetic to him, seized upon the official history
and Wolseley's revision of the *Soldier's Pocketbook* and ruthlessly
exposed them both:[41]

> The new matter consists [wrote Clarke] chiefly of com-
> placent vindication of his own infallibility and aggressive
> vituperation of all who have presumed to question that at-
> tribute. The 'ladies and gentlemen' who dared to uphold at
> least the practicability of the Suakim-Berber line of advance
> into the Soudan are objurgated as wild visionaries and
> theorists destitute of practical knowledge of war. He taunts
> them with the jibe that 'Jomini never had an independent
> command in war'. True; but it is not less true that Jomini
> had a responsible share in the direction of military
> operations contrasted with which the expedition which
> Lord Wolseley has personally conducted have been petty
> raids.... . The ascribed revision has not eliminated from its
> pages blunders in military chronology, history and
> topography, such as would disgrace a Sandhurst cadet; and
> in regard to contemporary matters lapses are rife which can
> scarcely fail to engender the suspicion that the author does
> not keep himself abreast of the march of progress in the art
> of war.... . Common decency, it might have been expected,
> would have prompted an officer who has held 'independent
> command' to delete from his pages words of impertinence
> and futile obloquy, written while as yet he was a junior
> officer, hungry for notoriety at any cost.

Although Wolseley might draw Ponsonby confidentially
aside, abuse Wilson as a useless commander who lost his head,
castigate Clarke as the evil genius of the piece[42] and confess failure
to the Queen in a broken voice,[43] the effect of Khartoum upon his
career was at once more significant and more decisive. It was
significant because the capitulation of the garrison and the
massacre of Gordon demonstrated to an anguished world that
Wolseley's failure had been complete and irrevocable. That it
was his first and only setback in the field was neither accurate in

fact nor sufficient as mitigation. Indeed those closest to affairs knew that in Ashanti Wolseley had not only disobeyed orders in sacking Kumasi but had retreated, leaving others dangerously in the lurch, before negotiating the treaty it was his express mission to conclude.[44] In Natal, Zululand and the Transvaal his legalistic and arbitrary approach to complex and volatile problems had erupted into war and resistance. He had been excluded from the Indian Command as a dangerous and self-seeking radical who might stoop to Caesarism to overthrow the military prerogatives of the Crown.[45] Khartoum was therefore decisive in the sense that Wolseley believed that only if a great European war broke out within the next five years could he hope to salvage and redeem his reputation.[46] Beyond that point he would be too old. It was this belief which accounts for Wolseley's frequent loose talk about pre-emptive or preventative war and his fierce struggle to see British strategic policy defined in such a way that any war against Russia would be fought primarily in Europe and not in Asia. It also meant that Wolseley had forfeited, finally and irrevocably, all claim to the Indian Command and that his chances of toppling and succeeding the Duke of Cambridge were narrowly confined to the inevitability of a European war.

But Khartoum had also led others, most notably Salisbury, who had long regarded Wolseley's vulgar pyrotechnics with something approaching revulsion and who in fact had been chiefly responsible for denying Wolseley the Indian Command successively in 1880 and 1885, to question – or indeed altogether ignore – more confidently then they had done before Wolseley's judgement on the broader political aspects of national security: aspects for which his own restricted experience and questionable success in colonial warfare and administration and his capricious system of command by clique had not fitted him to deal. On such issues therefore as the invasion scare, Indian versus Imperial defence and Irish Home Rule (when it was rumoured that Wolseley would resign his commission and lead an Ulster Army against it), Salisbury was inclined to put his trust, if he put it at all, in safer, official experts such as Roberts, Wood, Buller, Brackenbury or Clarke, or in harmless amateur strategists such as Wilkinson or Dilke who had a less compromised and Caesarist conception of the role of military adviser and who indeed had recommended that the Commander-in-Chiefship to which Wolseley aspired should be abolished.

In 1895, as the Hartington Commission, the resignation of the
Duke of Cambridge and the question of his successor set in motion the last laboured convulsions of the military politics of the
Victorian Age Wolseley could write to his wife with the settled
if still prickly candour of humbled ambition.

> For the last ten years I have had nothing to do, and serving
> in peace under the   ignorant obstructionism of an old
> bumble-bee like the Duke of Cambridge, one is denied
> even the satisfaction of making the Army efficient as a
> fighting machine.... My calculations of the future have been
> absolutely wrong.... For the last twelve years nothing has
> gone as I had wished.

His legendary good luck had deserted him at Khartoum. For
years he 'had depended on a great war that would have shaken
all Europe in either 1887 or 1889'. It was bound to come; no
special powers were required to predict that. But his own time
was running out; and even if he did become Commander-
-in-Chief it would be a hollow and much diminished position,
without power of initiative and a handy scapegoat in the event of
disaster.[47]

In Salisbury, Lansdowne, Roberts, Brackenbury, Chapman,
Clarke and Kitchener he smelled an organised plot to take over
the War Office, the Commander-in-Chiefship and the direction
of operations in the Soudan and South Africa and place them in
the hands of Indian officers whom he believed in Afghanistan,
Burma and Chitral had been guilty of carefully concealed
blunders and whose training was not conducive to the
Europeanised warfare expected in South Africa.[48] It was a plot
which ironically the Duke of Cambridge had suspected earlier
(1878-80) of Wolseley and his Ring with respect to the Indian
Army,[49] and it was one which Wolseley now found himself
struggling hard to smash. After all, he had a unique personal interest in avenging the deaths of Colley and Gordon, and by insisting upon his choice of commanders and general control of
operations he might go some way towards retrieving his
shattered reputation. In the circumstances, his resistance was
bound to fail, and Wolseley, powerless and forgotten, could only
commiserate with his wife and the Queen (who had always disliked the political infiltration of Indian military influences as sub-

versive of the prerogatives of the Crown) that the disastrous extension of the Boer War into an indecisive guerilla action was ascribable to the overly Continentalised concepts and commanders from India which had been crudely thrust upon them. [50]

Throughout history, few commanders once as popular as Wolseley was can have left office as he did in 1900 under such clouds of disgrace, reproach and disloyalty. Yet when Wolseley came to compose his memoirs in the solitude of the Sussex Downs it was not out of bitterness but in the pathetic awareness that something, somewhere, had gone tragically wrong. He wrote:

> These memoirs are to me the ghosts of proud joys long dead, the memories of moments when as a young man I won some reputation, and was well regarded by the soldiers who followed me. I dream now of the past only... .
> Among the many dreams of my boyhood and early manhood was the hope that I might as a successful Commander do England such service in the field that I should in dying for her leave behind me a reputation not only as a successful leader but as the patriot soldier of the Crown who had lived for England and to whom the Almighty had accorded the privilege of dying for her... . How poor has been my life's work when compared with the lofty aspirations of my youth! I had no father...to teach me how to curb and direct those ambitions and to instruct me in worldly wisdom... to direct my studies, to point my mistakes and advise me how to avoid them. [51]

There can be little doubt that during the formative stages of his career, especially in Canada and at the War Office in the 1860s and 1870s, Wolseley looked to both MacDougall and Airey as father substitutes. [52] But their advice – indeed their whole cast of mind – had been moulded by pre-Crimean traditions of Peninsular and maritime warfare. It is also true that War Ministers such as Cardwell and Childers (and to a lesser extent Hardy, Stanley, Hartington and Smith) exploited Wolseley's celebrity and radicalism, and his willingness to indulge in intrigue, quite as much as he extracted from them all the political leverage of which they disposed, to steamroller through reforms which had the effect of diminishing costs at the expense of the military prerogatives of the Crown without significantly improving the tactical efficiency of the Army. Moreover, by 1885, Wolseley's own intellectual resilience had been very much weakened by the deaths of Home and Colley, by the gnawing controversies surrounding his various colonial settlements, by the emergence of Roberts and MacGregor as powerful strategists in their own right and by the potential defection of Brackenbury, Wood and Buller.

Two things therefore had gone wrong. By 1885 Wolseley's prejudices and mannerisms had alienated every significant element of British political and military society: the Indian Army, the Engineers, the Admiralty, the politicians, the strategists and the war correspondents, all of whom in one way or another were indispensable to the formulation of strategic policy. Secondly, the essential conditions and requirements of that policy had been revolutionised by Russian advances in Central Asia. While Wolseley had clung stubbornly to the primacy of home defence and colonial warfare by which Cardwell's reforms — and indeed Wolseley's own career — could be best explained and justified, India and the Continental resources of which it disposed had become the real fulcrum of Imperial defence and war policy. When these two factors were juxtaposed, or indeed combined, as they were in mid-1885, Wolseley's downfall, or at least the unlikelihood that he would attain quite so smoothly the position of unbridled pre-eminence he sought, was assured.

The planning, composition and conduct of the Khartoum Relief Expedition had exposed to even the most charitable critic all the abuses, corruption, intrigues, deceptions and distortions to which the Cardwellian or indeed any system was susceptible if left in the hands of ungovernable men like Wolseley. At the same time, the Russian assault on the Afghan village of Penjdeh, climaxing what Indian strategists had conditioned themselves to imagine was the final stage in the systematic pacification of Central Asia preparatory to the conquest of India, had thrust that problem squarely and inescapably into the lap of British politicians. Each crisis in its own way had demonstrated the hollowness of any general system of Imperial defence which failed intelligently to adjust resources to interests. The Russian withdrawal from Afghanistan, like the British withdrawal from the Soudan, was the result of such miscalculation. The conflict of interests, which even Gladstone was forced to respect, between military vengeance in the Soudan or strategic deterrence in India exposed Cardwell's basic failure to provide not simply against the contingency of a rash of small wars which might have an overall global character, as the Airey Commission suggested, but perhaps more fundamentally against the shifting balance of international military power towards America, Germany and Russia, and within the Empire from Britain and the self-governing colonies towards India.[53]

The very conditions which had discredited Gladstone, Wolseley and the Cardwellian system were also those which thrust Salisbury, Roberts and the role of India in Imperial strategy to the centre of domestic and military politics. The political and official machinery depicted by Continental theorists such as Goltz, Upton and Leer for organising and directing the 'nation-in-arms' in accordance with the classical principles and objectives of strategy now seemed, after years during which Indian strategists had been pleading for the same things,[54] suddenly and especially appropriate to the conditions and needs of Indian defence. Two of these strategists, Chesney and MacGregor, unshelved that monumental classic of Indian Army reform – the Eden Commission Report – which had been urged upon Gladstone's Government and the Home Council by three successive Viceroys in a series of elaborate despatches;[55] and with the backing of Dufferin, Lansdowne and Churchill they began implementing it in bits and pieces so far as that was possible against the hardening opposition of Roberts and Collen who as Commander-in-Chief and Military Secretary respectively stood most to lose by the abolition of the Commander-in-Chiefship and the interposition of a General Staff. The influence of the Eden upon the Hartington Commission Report was extensive and direct, and its main provisions were elsewhere reflected in the writings of Brackenbury, Wilkinson and Clarke, who by adapting them to the idiosyncracies of British civil-military relations sought to make the peace-time formulation of strategic policy at once more continuous, expert and accountable.[56]

To Wolseley – as to Roberts – all this gadgetry seemed neither necessary, congenial nor workable. Indeed in the hands of clever men like Brackenbury it would become positively dangerous and subversive. It would usurp and neutralise the unique and predominant authority which he exercised in the shaping of military policy as his Government's principal official adviser: an

authority which he – like Roberts – intended to extend and for-
tify when once he had slid into the seat vacated by the Duke of
Cambridge. Thus on his return to the War Office in October
1885, Wolseley found himself increasingly circumvented or ignored by War Ministers (such as Stanhope, Brodrick and
Lansdowne) or Ministers who had made themselves experts in Indian defence (such as Dilke, Churchill and Chamberlain) who
courted the advice of those who would strengthen the Indian
rather than the British Army as the main instrument of Imperial
policy, and select Asia rather than Europe as the principal theatre
of its operations in the belief that this was the least controversial
method not only of increasing Imperial military power and
British political control over it, but of doing so at Indian rather
than British expense. It is only fair to remind ourselves, however,
that Wolseley did not seek a settled definition of national
strategic policy except as a means of so electrifying the country
about the possibilities of invasion that he could impose his own
terms upon an embarrassed Government, of strengthening the
Home Army and redressing the equation of linked-battalions out
of which an effective Reserve might grow, and of countering the
explicit technical arguments of the Indian Strategic Sub-Committee on Defence to which British politicians were all too
susceptible. In Wolseley's ideal constitution, a soldier would be
appointed as an apolitical, non-elective Minister of War, sitting
permanently in the Cabinet or whatever government was in
power, and charged to present annually to Parliament, and
therefore to the nation at large, an expert statement on the
national defences. [57] It would be superfluous to comment on the
naïveté of such a proposal, were it not seriously and insistently
made. No government – least of all a Victorian government –
could possibly contemplate abdicating such powers to a potentially rival Caesar: certainly not to one whose capacity for independent judgement was so evidently impaired.

What then accounts for Wolseley's seemingly uninterrupted
rise to the top of the military hierarchy? We must be careful not
to confuse rank with power. Ponsonby's remarks that he could
not see how any new Minister going to the War Office for the
first time could 'set himself up at once in defiance of Wolseley
fresh home from a campaign and with the whole business at his
finger ends' and that 'when Wolseley writes memorandums all
the War Office and Horse Guards tremble' [58] were probably on

the whole, even taking into consideration Ponsonby's radical biases and his like of soldierly decision, a fair representation of Wolseley-Ministerial relations before the fall of Khartoum. Certainly when it came to promising operations or reforms which would be both brisk and cheap, Wolseley could twist most Liberal Ministers — even whole Cabinets as he had done before Ashanti and Khartoum — round his little finger. His grasp of detail — whether the logistics of small wars or the intricacies of short-service — the formidable range of his experience, his shadowy influence over the Press struck them as a man with whom it would be dangerous to trifle and necessary to sup with a long spoon. For in these, the dark ages of British generalship which stretched back to the Crimean War, there seemed no acceptable alternative of comparable weight and stature. With all his faults, for all his critics said of him, Wolseley in 1881 still seemed the ablest general the country had produced without embarking on a major European war.

When in that year Gladstone and Childers tried to foist Wolseley upon the Queen and the Horse Guards as both Adjutant-General and a Peer, it provoked the most unholy row which dragged on in fits and starts for a full twelve months. They had attempted it partly to compensate Wolseley for not getting the Boer Command to avenge Colley's death at Majuba, but primarily to use Wolseley's prestige and expert knowledge to ram Childers' reforms down the throats of the military Lords such as Napier, Strathnairn and Sandhurst whom the Duke of Cambridge had marshalled against them. What the Duke feared most was not so much Childers' playing at Commander-in-Chief after all he had tried that in the Navy during Gladstone's first administration and come a cropper — but Wolseley's using the Lords as a forum from which to inflict his own wild schemes for army reform upon the public or to contradict or ridicule out of existence those of the Duke. Unseemly professional quarrels, which are normally the secret stuff of military politics, would become public and cause a loss of confidence in both Government and Crown. The Duke stood his ground. Threats of resignation were met with counter-threats; mutterings of dissolution with those of abdication. It was petty, silly and childish, and was only brought to some conclusion by the inexhaustible mediation of Granville and Ponsonby. [59]

Yet none of this was Wolseley's doing. Throughout the

longeurs of this extraordinary 'tempest in a teapot', Wolseley maintained a discreet reserve. It showed how controversial if not indispensable he was, and how closely matched were Government and Crown in their efforts to get their own way. At no time could either party – or indeed the mediators – produce a substitute candidate whose credentials satisfied the other or at least induced him to withdraw his resignation. In Wolseley's shadow stood 'our only other general', Roberts. But Roberts' outrageous handling of the Cabul reprisal executions, it was argued, was a shaky foundation for his relief march to Kandahar to which his slender reputation exclusively clung. [60] That operation had been shepherded by Stewart, his supreme commander, who (like Lindsay over Wolseley during the Red River Expedition) would have borne the final responsibility in the event of error or failure, and it was the exact counter-march to that conducted by Stewart one year earlier under more trying conditions from which Roberts undoubtedly profited. [61] He was distrusted by Gladstone and Ripon for his part in the Afghan War and the Simla Commission, was refused a seat on the Viceroy's Council and shelved in Madras. [62] He knew nothing of the British Army or European warfare and was reviled by Norman and the Duke as a grubbing opportunist, as dangerous and as unscrupulous as Wolseley. [63]

The Duke, advised by a knot of reactionaries to keep good men out, could only propose duds: stiff martinets such as Lysons, MacDonnell, Parke, Beauchamp Walker or Lord Alexander Russell whom Ponsonby had not even heard of and whose reputations did not reach beyond the walls of their offices. The Queen suggested Stephenson (whom Wolseley was later to supersede as Commander of the Gordon Relief Expedition) but according to Ponsonby he was 'not a big enough man' and anyway held 'peculiar views'. He was 'always a red-tapist and would stick like wax to the old system till the new was established – when he would be as devoted to that'. He was scarcely the man 'to work out reforms'. Ponsonby's own choice lay with Sir Lintorn Simmons, the retiring Inspector-General of Fortifications, who as Disraeli's closest technical adviser during the Eastern Question had developed a solid reputation within confidential circles as a hard-headed strategist, manipulating a vast network of military attachés and secret missions, composing muscular memoranda and finally accompanying the Prime

Minister to the Congress of Berlin. But it was an appointment that was only admissible in extreme circumstances. The Guards and the Line would object to an Engineer trespassing on ground traditionally their own. The Duke hated Simmons because he was too advanced, Childers because he was not advanced enough. Adye and Wolseley would be jealous, and Ellice and the Horse Guards furious with indignation. But he would pacify the Duke and was big and strong enough to keep Wolseley in line. 'At any rate,' concluded Ponsonby, 'it is a suggestion.'[64]

Indeed, fewer suggestions could have been better calculated to offend Wolseley: for Simmons represented all those solid implacable qualities of disinterested power and quiet achievement which Wolseley singularly lacked. Perhaps Ponsonby sensed this, for the suggestion was quietly but quickly allowed to drop. Instead other expedients were proposed – namely that Wolseley should become Permanent Under-Secretary at the War Office – but as this scarcely disguised the basic intention by putting Wolseley in mufti rather than uniform the Duke's main objections still applied. The imperatives of parliamentary supremacy, military efficiency and common sense alike dictated a settlement in Wolseley's favour and with an ill grace the Duke conceded, insisting to the end that Wolseley be forbidden to air his opinions on military matters and that the Government publicly reaffirm his own position as its principal official adviser.[65]

In somewhat more muted form this situation was to arise again over the question of the command of the Egyptian expedition. The Duke proposed Simmons; Childers preferred Wolseley.[66] 'Really,' wrote the Queen in disgust, 'as if there was *no man* in the Empire who could do *anything* but him.... . Only six months ago she was told he must be Adjutant-General, and now at the most critical moment he throws this up for the war command.'[67] Ponsonby retorted by reminding her that Wolseley was 'her senior and ablest tried officer' and that if large operations were contemplated no other was possible.[68] But the Queen was not mollified; for Wolseley's appointment was a disturbing magnet for his own cliquish nepotism. It was this, Ponsonby explained to his wife, which among other things accounted for Wolseley's success both as a commander and as a reformer, and for his mesmeric hold over Liberal governments which between 1868 and 1874 and between 1880 and 1885 had made that success possible in the waging of the Red River, Ashanti, Egyptian and

Soudanese campaigns. Ponsonby wrote,

> He does not inspire any love among those who serve under him, though I think they have confidence in him and I believe his Staff like him. He knows a good man and selects him and throws over all other considerations. Therefore his Staff are excellent soldiers. He has a talent for organisation and the energy to carry it through. He thoroughly believes in himself and this makes others believe in him and above all he is a lucky General. Of course this latest qualification is fanciful – but it is a useful fancy and has always backed him – tho' his enemies use it against him as much as his friends. He is hard and very likely unfeeling – but this is useful if unpleasant in a General. And he has the power of writing capital letters which please the receivers. [69]

As we have seen, all this was exploded by Khartoum, by the Indianisation of British strategic policy set in train by the Penjdeh crisis, and by the advent of Conservative governments, War Ministers, Indian generals and theorists who were no longer content to work or justify a system that had manifestly failed to cope with the insistent conditions and needs of Imperial defence, who could no longer afford to take Wolseley at his word and who now suspected that Wolseley may in the past have manipulated the Press, the politicians and the official histories to conceal his own professional blunders or those of his disciples (such as Colley at Majuba). [70] His staff was seen to be inefficient, riddled with nepotism and medal-hunters. A flawed strategy and bad organisation had compounded, or more likely brought about, his ill-luck. The shrill ideology of grasping success, of virtue triumphant, which suffused the ethics of the Victorian army had been proved false, or at least incompatible with the new cut and thrust of international politics and the co-ordinating machinery of massed warfare or strategic deterrence. Wolseley, not altogether understanding the deeper conditions which might have made it inevitable, so soon after his resounding victory at Tel-el-Kebir, stood bewildered and mortified by his failure and by the estrangement it brought him.

His letters and speeches, never dull, took on a sharper edge, and his toughness became a sort of bullying. All that Ponsonby claimed for him still remained essentially true, but it worked within decreasing limits. He found that he was no more able to influence policy or exact decisions as Adjutant-General between 1885 and 1890 than he had been while seconded to the India Office between 1876 and 1880. The real work of alerting the Government to the need for a comprehensive defence policy sub-served by efficient machinery for mobilisation and intelligence was performed by Brackenbury, Ardagh, Clarke and Hamley, whom Wolseley disliked and distrusted and who invariably came to swallow the Indian view that Russia could best be confronted – and if necessary decisively defeated – in Central Asia. With Cyprus and Egypt securely astride the Mediterranean corridor and with so much professional disagreement about the strategic value of Constantinople and the feasibility of long-range raids or risings in the Crimea or the Caucasus, the Foreign Office and the Cabinet refused to contemplate those Turkish and Persian alliances which alone would have made the Maurician strategy of sea-power which Wolseley inspired both possible and effective. [71]

Between 1889 and 1895, the higher structure of British military politics was almost continuously convulsed by a deadly game of musical chairs between the senior British and Indian generals for the key commands in India, Ireland, at Aldershot and at the War Office. How and why these appointments were finally settled is a long and complicated story that need not be told here, except to say that it represented a struggle between the Wolseley and Roberts schools for the supreme command of each other's armies and for the control of the strategic policies which directed them. [72] For the ultimate direction of British strategic policy, perhaps the most crucial exchange of all was between Brackenbury and Chapman, Director of Military Intelligence and Military Member of Council respectively of the British and Indian armies. Chapman had been one of the authors of the original memoran-dum which had sparked this whole controversy, [73] and when he took over Brackenbury's job as Director of Military Intelligence in 1891 he found as Adjutant-General, not Wolseley – with whom he might have had some trouble – but Buller, a stolidly unimaginative soldier, adaptable to whatever government was in power and without a flair for strategy, but who instinctively scouted the idea of any method or theory of Indian and colonial military co-operation which did not have Britain at its centre. [74] Wolseley had declined Stanhope's blandishments of India and accepted the honorific backwater of Ireland, traditionally reserv-

ed for retiring Indian generals, not so much to fight in the European war which then appeared to be imminent, but to be on the
ground when the Duke retired according to the provisions of the
Hartington Commission.[75] Wolseley therefore seems abruptly to
have played no further part in the debate in which he had been
passionately engaged, or in pressing upon Buller the War Office
viewpoint which Maurice and Brackenbury had formulated and
defended. And he probably assumed that Brackenbury was more
than holding his own in India.

But the Chapman letterbooks tell a different story: that as the
effects of Wolseley's departure, Mahan's books and the Franco-Russian alliance made themselves felt, the War Office, especially under Lansdowne's administration, rapidly came round
to the Indian argument.[76] In India, Brackenbury had been given
an uncomfortable reception, where, unlike Chapman at the War
Office, he found Roberts in undisputed control of a strategy and
a formidable array of technical committees that had been almost
ten years in the making. Since 1887, Roberts had quietly but insistently countered the arguments of Dilke and Maurice published in   *Blackwood's,* the *Fortnightly Review* and the *Nineteenth
Century,*[77] with secret memoranda circulated to friends in the
Cabinet, the Horse Guards, the Lords and the military clubs or
with inspired articles written by his junior staff. Mahan's *Influence
of Seapower,* published in 1890, had greatly fortified his views. If
Britain wished to retain her vast and widely scattered Empire, he
wrote to Lyall, she must send large reinforcements to Egypt and
India.[78] The paradox went something like this. Confronted with a
Franco-Russian alliance, Britain would be bound to fritter away
her forces in the local piecemeal defence of overseas colonies,
thereby crippling her capacity to field in Europe or Asia Minor
armies large enough to inflict decisive damage upon the combined conscript armies against which they would be arrayed. In
such a war, Britain could expect to recruit few if any reliable or
effective Continental allies, and her fragile seaborne armies
would meet with probable defeat and certain humiliation. In
Roberts' opinion, it was impossible to overrate the importance of
convincing British soldiers and statesmen that India was a Continental power and that the first principle of strategy, as of
politics, was to preserve territory and defend frontiers. And this
could only be done by sending massive reinforcements from Britain and the Colonies: that is converting the British Army and

the Colonial Militias into one gigantic Reserve for the Indian Army. The prime function of a maritime power was to establish and maintain naval supremacy and, where it counted, command of the sea. Britain therefore had a dual role: defence of India and command of the sea. He was not an alarmist, nor did he intend writing an Indian *Battle of Dorking*: but between people like Wolseley and Maurice who believed that Britain's true Imperial war policy lay in petty diversions in Europe, Asia Minor, Persia and the North Pacific, and others like Adye who saw no threat to India at all, it seemed impossible to bring the War Office to a sensible appreciation of the resources and the obligations of which India disposed.[79]

In respect of this, the abrupt and unexpected conversion of Brackenbury was to be crucial. The moment and the circumstances were recorded by Roberts in a letter to his confidant at the Horse Guards, General Sir Charles Brownlow.[80] They met, Roberts recorded, in solemn enclave on 20 June 1891. Durand and Collen, Foreign and Military Secretary respectively, were present. Roberts opened the questioning. What were Her Majesty's Government's strategic plans in the event of a war against Russia? Brackenbury replied: if against Russia alone, to form a Turkish alliance and to send expeditionary forces to Constantinople, Batoum and elsewhere in Eastern Europe. Roberts countered that Salisbury did not think such an alliance would be dependable, and he doubted whether the Ministry would adopt that policy. To this Brackenbury had no reply, as if unaware of Salisbury's ideas. To clinch matters, Roberts produced his own documentary evidence of Salisbury's views, namely the private letters exchanged between them. Brackenbury continued: if against France and Russia combined, to concentrate all troops for home defence. The Intelligence Department had proved to its satisfaction that invasion was possible since the Home Seas would be left unguarded while the Channel and Mediterranean Fleets were employed in blockading, hunting down and destroying the French Fleet in the Mediterranean. Roberts disagreed. He could not imagine that France would embark 100,000 troops without convoy protection, for even if the Royal Navy were decoyed or caught off guard, there were enough mines, fireships and torpedoes to wreak havoc upon unprotected wooden transports. Even if the French Army managed to land, it could neither penetrate inland nor retreat. Its advance would be blocked at every turn by regular troops and field-works and ravaged by guerillas. It would have no base on which to fall back, and its cross-Channel lines of supply would be severed by the returning Fleet. Clearly invasion was a convenient bogey of the War Office with which to rationalise its refusal to send reinforcements to India. Brackenbury seemed duly subdued, and did not argue that it was essential that the British Army be committed to the defence of India.

The turning point had been reached. Thereafter, nothing that Wolseley could do, no office that he could hold, could arrest the rapid and thorough Indianisation of British strategic policy. [81] Compared to most other contenders for the Commander--in-Chiefship in 1895, Wolseley was the closest thing to a military genius the age had produced, to whom it was only decent to offer first refusal. [82] But to offer an old and alienated man the position of *primus inter pares* with only vague powers of general supervision over powerful and quick-witted colleagues, a position of limited tenure and under threat of imminent abolition, was to confer no office at all. During the South African War, Wolseley found that in the crucial matters of Boer intelligence, strategic planning and the selection of higher commanders he was ignored or side-stepped as pointedly and as absolutely as he had ever been in the late 1870s and the late 1880s. By 1902, Wolseley, Wood, Buller and Butler — none of whom had ever served in India in a senior command — had been swept aside and their places taken by Roberts, Kitchener, Hamilton, Robertson and others who had. In that year it became official doctrine that 'in fighting for India, England would be fighting for her Imperial existence'. She would be compelled 'by the necessity for maintaining her prestige to apply her main strength across the Indian frontier'. As Russia could nowhere 'put effective pressure on England except in Afghanistan', it was there that 'the contest must be decided'. [83] As Field Marshal Sir William Robertson was later to testify in his classic work on *Soldiers and Statesmen,* it was a doctrine of astonishing persistence, affecting political calculations at least, long after the German menace had become more than evident. [84]

In this paper I have sought to show that Wolseley's decline was a function of the Indianisation of British strategic policy brought about by the conflict of interests, and systems of Imperial defence, implicit in the coincidence of the Soudanese and Penjdeh crises. It is, as I have tried to suggest, only a partial explanation but one which I believe to be crucial to an understanding of Wolseley's later career. It is clear that Wolseley was something more than the 'captain of a clique of self-advancers, trained in the tactics of the pamphleteer'.[85] But his strength did not lie in strategy or in War Office and Colonial administration, a role he detested unless accompanied by dictatorial powers within a specific and limited mandate. Perhaps it is significant that throughout the period of his decline he surrounded himself with decadent *litterateurs* such as Edmund Gosse, Andrew Lang and Alfred Austin. It is suggestible that in the long run Wolseley was no more to the British Army than they were to British literature? Or did Wolseley's tragedy exist, like Lear's and Tolstoy's, not because virtue had gone unrequited, but because somehow the man still seemed nobler than the forces which had destroyed him?

Notes

1. I am grateful to the Canada Council and to the RMC Research Fund for financial help in the preparation of this article. Two recent studies of the Khartoum Relief Expedition are Julian Symons, *England's Pride* (London, 1967) and John Marlowe, *Gordon at Khartoum* (London, 1973). For a much more revisionist assessment of Wolseley's career, see my introductions to *In Relief of Gordon: Lord Wolseley's Campaign Journal of the Khartoum Relief Expedition* (London, 1967); *The South African Diaries of Sir Garnet Wolseley, 1875* (Cape Town, 1971); *The South African Journals of Sir Garnet Wolseley, 1879-80* (Cape Town, 1973).
2. Wolseley to Hartington, 4 January and 6 February 1884; Wolseley to Cambridge, 20 January 1884, *Wolseley Official Papers*, War Office Library. (Hereafter cited as WOP.)
3. Same to same, 8 February 1884, *ibid.*
4. For a very frank assessment of the reasons for his supersession and Wolseley's chances of getting to Khartoum by the Nile, see Stephenson to his brother, 22 September 1884, *At Home and On the Battlefield: Letters from the Crimea, China and Egypt, 1854-88* (London, 1915), pp.324-7. See also Stephenson to Cambridge, 22 and 25 September 1884, *Cambridge Papers*, Royal Archives, Windsor. I am indebted to Her Majesty the Queen for gracious permission to consult the Royal Archives.
5. Wolseley to Hartington, 8 and 14 April 1884, *WOP*; Cambridge to Wolseley, 15 April 1884; Wolseley to Cambridge, 16 April 1884, *Cambridge Papers*, RAW. Since April Wolseley had been recommending the immediate despatch of a 'small cheap expedition' perhaps only to Dongola, commanded by Buller, which was not to relieve Gordon but merely cover his withdrawal. But Gladstone was suspicious of Wolseley's motives and feared that once launched the expedition would get out of hand. 'I can be no party to the proposed despatch, as a first step, of a Brigade to Dongola,' he informed Granville on 1 August, 'I do not think that the evidence as to Gordon's position requires or justifies, in itself, military

preparations for the contingency of a military expedition.' When Hartington's threat of resignation finally brought him to his senses, he was anxious that the expedition be kept to 'a minor effort' and under no circumstances should proceed beyond Dongola to Khartoum. 'Northbrook has promised to do all he can to allay Wolseley's ardour for an expedition,' Granville assured him, 'the temptation is great for a military man.' Gladstone replied that he relied on Hartingt on's explicit assurances 'that Wolseley is most anxious to avoid any expedition to Khartoum' but he did not really believe this. It was no use pretending that once Wolseley had reached Egypt he would not mobilise the biggest expedition he could and contrive to make its use appear necessary and inevitable. On 5 August, Ponsonby wrote to his wife that 'Wolseley writes to me keen on an expedition. He says he is against it – but that it is unavoidable and we had better face the difficulty than avoid it. And that we must at once prepare. If we only gaggle about it the expense will be double very soon.' *Ponsonby Papers*, Shulbrede Priory, Haslemere: *In Relief of Gordon*, pp.3-8, Granville to Gladstone, 31 July and 17 September 1884, *Gladstone Papers, British Museum Add. Mss.* 44177; Gladstone to Granville, 2 September 1884, *Granville Papers PRO 30/29/128*. See also A. Ramm (ed.), *The Political Correspondence of Mr. Gladstone and Lord Granville, 1876-1886* (Oxford, 1962), vol.II, pp.220,242-4. Hartington's detailed reasoning behind his selection of Wolseley to superintend the preparations for the Nile Expedition should one become necessary can be found in B. Holland, *The Life of Spencer Compton, Eighth Duke of Devonshire* (London, 1911), vol.I, pp.483-4.

6. See also Carnarvon to Wolseley, 28 August 1884, *Wolseley Papers*, Hove, warning Wolseley that the cabinet, in agreeing to his going to Egypt, might be using him for their own ulterior ends.

7. See D.W.R. Bahlman (ed.), *The Diary of Sir Edward Walter Hamilton, 1880-85*, (Oxford, 1972), vol.I, p.341, in which Gladstone is recorded as saying that 'Excellent as Wolseley is as a general, he has not shown himself either in South Africa or Cyprus a good civil administrator.' Gladstone had 'the highest opinion of Wolseley as a soldier but a very indifferent one of Wolseley's civil and administrative capacities'.

8. Ponsonby to his wife, 24 September 1884, *Ponsonby Papers*.

9. See my introduction to *In Relief of Gordon*.

10. Wolseley's campaign journal (Soudan), *PRO/WO 147/5*.

11. Ponsonby to his wife, 25 December 1882, *Ponsonby Papers*. Ponsonby was not alone in this opinion. At a party on 22 March 1885, Gladstone's private secretary heard 'E. Bourke inveighing against Wolseley and his tendency to job.' See Bahlman (ed.), *Hamilton Diary*, vol. II, p.820.

12. Diary of Colonel H.J. Crauford, Grenadier Guards, *Crauford MSS, 6710/48*, National Army Museum, Chelsea.

13. W. Porter, *History of the Corps of Royal Engineers* (London, 1889), vol. II. pp.66-87; Colonel H. E. Colville, *History of the Soudan Campaign* (London, 1889), Pt. II, appendix 47, pp.270-76.

14. Roberts to Grant Duff, 8 February 1885, *Roberts Papers, R97/2*, National Army Museum.

15. Adrian Preston, 'The Eastern Question in British Strategic Policy during the Franco-Prussian War, 1870-71', *Historical Papers, 1972*, Canadian Historical Association, pp.55-88; 'The Indian Army in Indo-British Political and Strategic Relations, 1745-1947', *United Service Institute of India Journal*, Oct-Dec 1970, pp.357-89; *British Military Policy and the Defence of India, 1876-80*, unpublished Ph.D. thesis, London, 1966.

16. See for instance, his memorandum 'Is an Invasion of India by Russia possible?', 31 December 1883, which was sent to Sir John Cowell, Sir Dighton Probyn, Sir Henry Rawlinson, Lord Northbrook, Sir Charles Dilke, Lord Lytton, Lord Salisbury and Lord Randolph Churchill, *Roberts Papers, R97/2*. See also his letter

to Hughes, 18 October 1883, in which he discusses the various choices open to him. Direct representation to the Cabinet would simply result in his memoranda being pigeon-holed. Articles published anonymously in the *Quarterly Review* would not carry the same weight as if signed; but if signed it would open him to censure and disavowal by the Government. Roberts therefore decided to send his papers privately to selected strategists and politicians known to be sympathetic to his point of view.

17. Roberts to Cowell, 28 December 1883, *ibid.*

18. Roberts to Grant Duff, 8 February 1835, *ibid.*

19. General Sir Ian Hamilton, *Listening for the Drum* (London, 1944), p.175; *The Commander* (London, 1957), pp.74-81.

20. Preston, *Defence of India*, pp.206-13.

21. Preston, *Wolseley's South African Journals*, pp.1-26.

22. Cambridge to Hardy, pte and strictly confdl. 2 April 1879; pte. 23 April 1879; pte and confdl. 16 September 1879; pte, 27 September 1879; pte, 16 April 1880, *Cranbrook Papers, T501/264*, Ipswich and East Suffolk Record Office; Haines to Cambridge, 8 January 1878, 14 January 1879, 4 February 1880; Cambridge to Johnson, pte, 12 April 1879; 6 June 1879; 18 July 1879; Hardy to Cambridge, pte, 2 April 1879; Johnson to Cambridge, 1 May and 15 May 1879; pte, 11 August 1879; pte and confdl, 4 February 1880, *Cambridge Papers and Army Papers, N35/India*, Royal Archives, Windsor.

23. Ripon to Hartington, pte, 26 July and 8 September 1882, *Ripon Papers*, printed, cf British Museum.

24. Wolseley to Bigge, 15 August 1899, *Royal Archives.*

25. Wolseley to Lady Wolseley, 6 July 1895, *Wolseley Papers*, Hove.

26. Brownlow to Roberts, 5 August 1888, *Roberts Papers, R/12.*

27. Note by Bigge, 6 August 1896, *Royal Archives, E/12.*

28. Brownlow to Roberts, 5 August 1888, *Roberts Papers, R/12.*

29. Salisbury to Ponsonby, 25 July 1885, *Royal Archives..*

30. Wolseley to Ponsonby, pte and confdl, 4 May and 5 May 1890; Ponsonby to Wolseley, 9 May 1890, *Royal Archives N/15.*

31. The subject is fascinating and can best be traced in the voluminous *Army Papers* in the Royal Archives.

32. Wolseley to Bigge, 26 October 1900, *Royal Archives E/33.*

33. Knollys to Bigge, 4 December 1898; Lansdowne to Bigge, confdl, 6 December 1898; Bigge to Lansdowne, 7 December 1898; Lansdowne to Queen Victoria, 8 December 1898, *Royal Archives W/14.*

34. Wolseley to Bigge, 14 December 1899; 9 and 10 January 1900; Wolseley to Queen Victoria, 9 January and 24 April 1900, *Royal Archives P/4-6.*

35. Napier to Dillon, pte and confdl, 6 July 1880, Letterbooks, *Napier Papers*, National Register of Archives, London.

36. Napier to Roberts, n.d., *Roberts Papers R/36.*

37. Napier to Dillon, n.d., *ibid.*; Cranbrook Diary, 8 November 1885, *Cranbrook Papers, T501/11.*

38. Wilson to his wife, 23 March 1885, C.W. Watson, *The Life of Sir Charles Wilson*, London, 1909, pp.341-2, *In Relief of Gordon*, 11 March 1885, pp.104-5.

39. A collection of these can be found in Wolseley's scrapbooks at Hove.

40. Brackenbury to Lady Wolseley, 16 September 1885, *Wolseley Papers*, Hove.

41. Review by 'Scrutator' (G.S. Clarke) in *The Times* of *The Soldier's Pocketbook.*

42. See Wolseley's extraordinary minute on Sir Andrew Clarke's Memorandum on the Suez Canal, n.d., *Wolseley Official Papers*: 'I have not taken A. Clarke's position upon any important matter. He was a shallow self-seeker and owed his position entirely to Childers. They had been in public life together in Australia and the common chaff as to how it came that the latter had murdered a man and that A.C. had seen him do it and threatened to preach on him if he did not help him

publicly in all possible ways. Whatever the lien was it was a strong one, for Childers was a clever fellow and must have recognised how shallow Clarke was and how absolutely untruthful and unreliable also.' See also Wolseley's poor opinion of Clarke, *In Relief of Gordon*, pp.110, 117-18, 148.

43. Ponsonby to his wife, 17 July 1885, *Ponsonby Papers.* 'The Queen told me that Wolseley was low when he talked to Her, his expedition was a failure. He had gone to rescue Gordon and his Garrison and had not done it. Checked by the Govt at home, delayed by Ministers and badly served at the critical moment by a good man but inefficient soldier, he missed his object by 48 hours. When he spoke of Gordon his voice broke. He told me he liked Hartington who backed him up, but some evil genius at home also neutralised what Hartington promised should be done.'

44. See my chapter on Wolseley and the Ashanti Campaign in *South African Diaries*, pp.75-113; W.D. McIntyre, 'British Policy in West Africa: the Ashanti Expedition of 1873-4', *Historical Journal*, V, 1962, pp.19-46; *The Imperial Factor in the Tropics*,1865-75 (London, 1967), pp.140-51, 174-7.

45. See Preston (ed.), *South African Journals*, pp. 1-24.

46. Wolseley to Lady Wolseley, 3 June 1895, *Wolseley Papers.*

47. Same to same, 3, 22 and 25 June 1895, *ibid.*

48. Same to same, 3 July 1895, *ibid.* in which he records a conversation with Sir John Ardagh, his Director of Military Intelligence and a former Military Secretary to Lansdowne in India who 'has no great opinion of Roberts and is aware of what a reputation he had in India for jobbery. But I hear on the best authority that Roberts and all his friends are moving heaven and earth to get Lansdowne, who of course knew him well in India, to make him Boss at the War Office when HRH goes . . . Roberts who does *not* and never did belong to the Queen's Army knowing nothing of it and will therefore be more amenable to political influence than I should be... . To you I confess I am down-hearted and feel before I am beaten as I have never felt before in any previous struggle of any sort... . I feel it is an arranged affair. Alas, alas, my life's vision and ambition is at an end. The wrench is hard to bear. But I lived through the fall of Khartoum and never allowed mortals to know how it affected me.'

49. Cambridge to Hardy, pte and strictly confdl, 2 April 1879, *Cranbrook Papers, T501/204.*

50. Wolseley to his wife, 6 July 1895, *Wolseley Papers;* Lady Wolseley to Bigge, pte, 21 December 1899; Bigge to Lady Wolseley, 26 December 1899, *Royal Archives W/15.*

51. Unpublished note, *Wolseley Papers.*

52. Wolseley's father had retired as a Major in 1832 and died in 1840 when Wolseley was seven years old. His mother was left with seven children to raise, all under the age of seven. Three made their careers in the Army, one founded the Wolseley Motor Car Company and one became a minor novelist.

53. Cross to Lansdowne, 20 March 1891, *Lansdowne Papers,* printed, British Museum; Kimberley to Ripon, pte and very confdl, 28 March 1884; Ripon to Kimberley, confdl, 21 April 1884, *Ripon Papers,* printed, British Museum.

54. Chesney to Blackwood, 19 August and 16 September 1881, *Blackwood Papers,* National Library of Scotland, Edinburgh.

55. Ripon to Hartington, pte, 2 and 14 February, 6 June, 15 July 1881 and 14 January 1882, *Ripon Papers.*

56. Lansdowne to Kimberley, 3 November 1892, *Lansdowne Papers;* Roberts to Lyall, pte, 22 June 1888, *Roberts Papers.*

57. F. Maurice and G. Arthur, *The Life of Lord Wolseley* (New York, 1924), pp.297-9.

58. Ponsonby to his wife, 6 October 1885 and 20 March 1890, *Ponsonby Papers.*

59. The whole dispute can best be traced in the Gladstone, Childers and Ponsonby Papers and in the Royal Archives.

60. John to Richard Strachey, 28 June 1880, uncatalogued *Strachey Papers,* India Office Library: 'Roberts (entre nous) had been making a great mess of political affairs in Kabul. We are now sending up Griffon as Chief Political Officer, and although nominally subordinate to Roberts, he will virtually be the head. Something of this sort ought to have been done long ago. There is not a man of sense among Roberts' advisers and nothing can exceed the stupidity he has shown in all non– military matters... . The belief in Roberts' strategical qualifications has evidently been terribly shaken.' See also Ponsonby to his wife, 4 March 1881, *Ponsonby Papers.*

61. Swaine to Bigge, 11 July 1895, *Royal Archives E/40.*

62. Hartington to Ripon, 11 January and 11 March 1881, *Ripon Papers.*

63. Johnson to Cambridge, most pte, 24 March 1880, *Cambridge Papers:* 'Roberts has personal interests and ambitions more than I can say. He is one of the most self-seeking men I have ever come across and would override everybody and everything that stood in the way of the attainment of his aim.'

64. Ponsonby to his wife, 21 May, 24, 25, 26 and 28 August, 17 and 18 September 1881, *Ponsonby Papers;* Ponsonby to Childers, 19 September 1881; Ponsonby to Queen Victoria, 17 September 1881, *Royal Archives E/25.*

65. Same to same, 11 and 12 November 1881, *ibid.*

66. Same to same, 6 July 1882, *ibid.*; Queen Victoria to Ponsonby, 19 September 1881, *Royal Archives E/25.*

67. Same to same, 21 July 1882, *ibid.;* Queen Victoria to Ponsonby, 19 September 1881, *ibid.*

68. *Ibid.*

69. Ponsonby to his wife, 4 November 1882, *ibid.*

70. Same to same, 13 May 1881, *ibid.*, in which he recorded a conversation with Haines, the retiring Commander-in-Chief in India, 'a good honest fellow...but not of the modern school. His voice got husky as I alluded to Wolseley. "He has the press in his hands and therefore they are all afraid of him. Colley made one of the greatest military mistakes ever committed and yet the press have dealt leniently with him because Wolseley held them back."

71. For the official side of the argument see H. Brackenbury, 'General Sketch of the Situation Abroad and at Home from a Military Point of View', 3 August 1886; J.C. Ardagh, 'The Defence of London', strictly confdl, 16 July 1868; L. Nicholson, 'Home and Colonial Defence', most confdl, 19 October 1886; J.C. Ardagh, 'The Defence of England', confdl, 17 April 1888; *Report of Committee on Army Mobilisation,* most confdl, December 1886; H. Brackenbury, 'The State of Preparedness for War', confdl, 14 April 1886; Wolseley to Permanent Under-Secretary of State, 8 May 1888, *Wolseley Official Papers.*
    The unofficial debate can be traced in the following: Sir Charles Dilke, 'The Present Position of European Politics', *Fortnightly Review,* CCXLI, 1887, pp.1-31, 161-95, 321-54, 473-98, 617-45, 785-834; 'The British Army', *ibid.,* CCLII, 1887, pp.741-82; 'National Defence', pp. 605-26. J.F. Maurice, 'The Balance of Military Power in Europe', *Blackwood's,* CXLII, 1887, pp.124-48, 291-316, 583-606, 870-90; 'The True Policy of National Defence', *Contemporary Review,* LIV, 1888, pp. 214-23; G.S. Clarke, 'Imperial Defence', *Edinburgh Review,* CCCXLVI, April 1889, pp. 552-91; E.B. Hamley, 'The Question of Imperial Safety', *Nineteenth Century,* XXIII, June 1888, pp.789-98; An Indian Officer (Ian Hamilton), 'Our True Policy in India', *Fortnightly Review,* CCLXV, pp.275-81; J.F. Maurice, 'A Reply', *ibid.,* pp.282-92.

72. I hope to treat this struggle in a fresh article, 'War Office Politics and the Defence of India Question, 1882-92.'

73. See the Memorandum, 'Is an Invasion of India by Russia Possible?', 31 December 1883, *Roberts Papers.*

74. Chapman to Buller, 3 November 1893; same to Brackenbury, 29 October 1892,

secret, 3 September 1893; same to Roberts, pte and confdl, 19 August 1892, pte and secret, pte and secret, 8 September 1892, *Chapman Papers, PRO/WO 106/16.*

75. Wolseley to Ponsonby, pte and confdl, 4, 5 and 9 May 1890; Ponsonby to Wolseley, 9 May 1890, *Royal Archives E/15.*

76. See note 74 above and Roberts to Napier, 8 February 1889; Roberts to Brownlow, 27 February 1889, *Roberts Papers.*

77. Roberts to Lady Dilke, 17 April 1887; Roberts to W.H. Smith pte, 31 January 1887. A copy of the letter to Smith was also sent to Lord Randolph Churchill, 31 March 1887; to Sir Henry Rawlinson, 6 March 1887; to Sir Richard Strachey, 2 April 1887; to Lord Napier, 12 May 1887 and to the Duke of Cambridge, 22 July 1887. See also Roberts to Marvin, pte, 4 January 1889; Roberts to Napier, 8 February 1889; Roberts to Dilke, 2 March 1889, *Roberts Papers.*

78. Roberts to Layall, 14 April 1891, *ibid.*

79. Roberts to Admiral Sir George Tryon, pte, 22 April 1891, *ibid.*

80. Roberts to Brownlow, pte, 20 June 1891, *ibid.*

81. See E. Peach, 'Great Britain in War against Russia and France Combined', 31 May 1901, appendix II; Short Summary of Official Decisions, Proposals etc. Relative to the Defence of India, 1885-93, *PRO/WO 106/48.*

82. Swaine to Bigge, 11 June 1895, *Royal Archives E/40;* J.C. Ardagh, Secret Memorandum, 6 August 1895, *Ardagh Papers, PRO/30/40.*

83. W.R.Robertson, 'The Military Resources of Russia and the Probable Method of their Employment in a War between Russia and England', secret, 17 January 1902, *PRO/WO/106/48/E3/1.* E.A. Altham, 'The Military Needs of the Empire in a War with France and Russia', secret, 10 August 1901, *ibid., E3/2.* Nicholson minuted to Roberts, 15 August 1901, that this was 'the first serious attempt to deal in a comprehensive manner with the problem of meeting the gravest military danger to which the Nation is exposed'. Roberts replied, 'I am in favour of permanently strengthening the British garrison in India to such an extent as may admit of an active military policy being promptly adopted in the event of complications arising with Russia beyond the North-West Frontier. Under such circumstances to continue ourselves to a purely passive defensive attitude would be most detrimental to our interests and prestige in the East. The scheme of operations...recognises the obligation to reinforce the garrison of India and lays stress on the importance of taking offensive action instead of confining ourselves to the passive defence of the United Kingdom.'

84. W.R. Robertson, *Soldiers and Statesmen* (London, 1928), vol. I, pp.1-44.

85. The phrase is George Orwell's, contained in one of his early war poems. He was not referring to Wolseley, but the words seemed so apposite to one side of Wolseley's case that I was tempted to borrow them.

British Civil-Military Relations on the North West Frontier of India*

W. MURRAY HOGBEN

Picking one's way through the jagged rocks and tribal incursions of the north-west frontier of British Indian history, one might well have encountered occasional British officers who seemed at home among the anomalies of their ambiguous position. These tanned and steely-eyed political officers of the Raj might often have been found exchanging ribald verses in local dialects with tall and bearded tribesmen whose hands roved ceaselessly between knifehilt to triggerguard. This everyday scene of imperial life was sometimes ended by the murder of a less-experienced political, or by a really unforgivable outbreak of tribal looting and killing in the sunlit valleys below the hills. Then, the surviving politicals would be linked in a temporary marriage of convenience with the military sent to punish the tribal offenders. And while it is a commonplace to say that civil-military relations have usually been troubled, it was especially true in the Indian case. There, the 'civilians' were mostly soldiers, and they had direct contact with the Viceroy over the heads of the commanders.

The Indian problem of 'political-military' relations is perhaps best epitomised in Philip Mason's little anecdote:

> There was a tale current in the folklore of Indian clubs and messes for which there was perhaps no historical authority but which did enshrine a truth. It concerned a Political Agent accompanying troops on a punitive expedition. After breakfast with the officers, he took his lunch in a haversack and disappeared; they did not see him again till evening when, sipping a pink gin by the light of a lantern carefully screened from snipers, he asked, 'And how did things go on your side today? Casualties on our side were half-a-dozen.'[1]

*I have two primary obligations to acknowledge at the outset: to the Canada Council for the doctoral fellowship which allowed me to gather the following material as part of my dissertation research, and to Professor A.P. Thornton for his generous advice and encouragement over the years.

The truth enshrined was, of course, that relations between these officers were frequently strained due to their quite diverging personal and professional outlooks. Naturally, not all members of the two groups disagreed on the handling of frontier campaigns, but when they did it revealed much about the peculiar role and nature of the politicals.

In the old Anglo-Indian terminology of British India, 'political' meant diplomatic, and referred to relations with the independent Indian princes and the various frontier tribes, as well as with some neighbouring countries. The term obviously originated in the days when politics and policy were matters discussed by princes in their courts, and not by later politicians in modern councils and legislatures. Hence, a 'political' was an officer, usually British, who was entrusted with such diplomacy in and around India. While dealings on an equal footing were gradually superseded by the system of indirect rule over the princes, the old terminology and outward courtesies lingered on. For these and other reasons the title of 'political' was 'a terse and slightly opprobrious name' – but one borne with a certain pride. [2]

While many British and Indians, officials and civilians, had various reasons for distrusting or resenting the politicals, [3] the source of the military's quarrel with the politicals was rooted in the past. As the East India Company had battled and intrigued its way across India its officers had wielded both pen and sword in their dealings with the rulers they encountered. Hence, in 1783 when the first Governor-General, Warren Hastings, had given his Secret, or Political, Department its first Secretary (or Foreign Secretary), [4] its role had included besides its diplomatic concerns, 'every military operation or movement of troops which is either ordered or undertaken'. [5]

Originally the realms of the rulers had been the frontiers of British power, but by the middle of the nineteenth century the Company and then the Crown had largely reached the eventual frontiers of British India. There, the politicals of provinces like Punjab or Bengal, or of the central Government of India, became more settled in their profession of frontier wardens. Meanwhile, their colleagues in the now isolated and increasingly harmless Indian states largely lost their military role. And while the north-east and eastern frontiers were sometimes troublesome, it was the north-west frontier that really worried or interested all concerned with questions of peace and war. This was because of the Russian threat, the instability of Afghanistan, and the endless hostility of the increasingly well-armed tribes adjoining India. As holders of the forward posts of British authority on the frontier, the politicals tried to keep the peace and uphold British interests by means of personal influence and sheer nerve. They were supported by the nearby local militias,[6] and by the usually more distant Indian Army forces. It was, in Lord Curzon's words, 'a question not of rifle and cannon but of character and all that character can do amid a community of free men' – the Pathan tribesmen.[7]

In this situation it was almost inevitable that the best of the politicals might develop a certain sympathy and understanding regarding the neighbouring tribes and their leaders. It was this sympathy that was so neatly evoked in Mason's introductory story. While this was harmless enough in time of peace, in time of war it became more of a problem.

During peace-time – a relative term on the frontier – there was less direct contact between the politicals and the military. But one of the chief features of frontier history was the unfortunate frequency of resort to the sword and gun in individual and group disagreements. Hence there were three Afghan Wars at forty-year intervals, and a host of punitive expeditions in the off years. On these occasions the military advanced to the fore, while the politicals acted as senior advisers because of their knowledge of the tribes, their leaders and their languages. And besides carrying on delicate diplomacy with their peace-time tribal acquaintances, the politicals organised local supplies of food, fodder, and transport animals for these campaigns. However, it was the diplomatic role of the politicals that was not always appreciated by the military. The sympathy of the politicals for the 'enemy' was often taken amiss.

Young Winston Churchill was an observer with the Malakand Field Force during the great 1897 frontier rising. His remarks on the activities of the handsome and talented political agent for Dir, Swat and Chitral, Major Harold A. Deane, are invaluable:

> The Political Officers who accompanied the force, with white tabs on their collars, parlayed all the time with the chiefs, the priests and other local notables. These political officers were very unpopular with the army officers. They were regarded as marplots. It was alleged that they always patched things up and put many a slur upon the prestige of

the Empire without ever letting anyone know about it. They were accused of the grievous crime of 'shilly-shallying', which being interpreted means doing everything you possibly can before you shoot. We had with us a very brilliant political officer, a Major Deane, who was much disliked because he always stopped military operations. Just when we were looking forward to having a splendid fight and all the guns were loaded and everyone keyed up, this Major Deane – and why was he a Major anyhow? so we said – being in truth nothing better than an ordinary politician – would come along and put a stop to it all. Apparently all these savage chiefs were his old friends and almost his blood relations. Nothing disturbed their friendship. In between fights, they talked as man to man and as pal to pal, just as they talked to our General as robber to robber.

We knew nothing about the police *vs.* the crooks' gangs in Chicago, but this must have been in the same order of ideas... .

However, they wanted to shoot at us and we wanted to shoot at them. But we were both baffled by what they call the elders, or as one might put it 'the old gang', and by what we could see quite plainly – the white tabs or white feathers on the lapels of the political officers. However, as has hitherto usually been the case, the carnivorous forces had their way. The tribes broke away from their 'old gang' and were not calmed by our political officers. So a lot of people were killed, and on our side their widows have had to be pensioned by the Imperial Government, and others were badly wounded and hopped around for the rest of their lives, and it was all very exciting and, for those who did not get killed or hurt, very jolly.[8]

A later example of the unusual friendships that grew up on the frontier was commented on by Lord Minto in a letter to the Secretary of State, John Morley. He was referring to the activities of the exceptionally able frontier political, Colonel George Roos-Keppel, Chief Political Officer with the expedition that suppressed the turbulent Zakka Khel Afridis in 1907. He wrote that 'by far the most striking characteristic of the expedition has been its political management by Roos-Keppel'.

Really the mere facts of his story are as thrilling as any novel. [General Sir James] Willcocks is immensely impressed with him and speaks with admiration of his courage when he insisted on going out alone to meet the Zakkas when their jirga came in from China and when no one's life was safe outside our own line of pickets. But Roos-Keppel's personal friendship with the very men against whom we were fighting is the most attractive part of the story. Though his own Khyber Rifles were full of Zakkas they insisted upon accompanying him to fight their own fathers and sons and blow up their paternal mansions, and I am told the first thing the jirga said to him when they met him was 'Sahib did we put up a good fight?' to which he answered 'I wouldn't have shaken hands with you unless you had'!

He added that Roos-Keppel had been very upset at the mortal wounding of one of the Zakka Khel leaders who had written from his death-bed to apologise for the opening attack. [9]

This kind of personal relationship of political and tribesmen did not end with the general loss of innocence in the First World War. Mason again recounts how during the inter-war period one frontier political could entrust his wife to the care of a convicted tribal murderer, another could accept the virtues of independent tribal life, while a third could be defended by a father against his son. [10]

A final example of the mixed loyalties of the politicals was recounted by the novelist John Masters in his autobiography of his years before the Second World War. His frontier experience centred on the Waziristan campaign against the Mahsuds in 1937-8. He admitted that the politicals would have been of no value if they had not thoroughly appreciated the views of tribesmen, 'but they often carried it too far'. A young political once came into their camp after a day's fighting, remarking that 'our chaps' had fought well even if outnumbered three to one. This momentarily confused the battalion commander who felt that the tribesmen had been the ones outnumbered. The political answered: 'Oh, I'm sorry. It's the tribesmen I was talking about.' Since Masters and his friends had lost casualties in the fighting they hardly appreciated this confusion. [11]

But it was not just this almost amusing confusion of loyalties that irked the military on frontier campaigns. It went much deeper and showed itself in a variety of incidents and indeed serious quarrels over the century following the First Afghan War of 1838-42. From that time onward the politicals were frequently blamed for military disasters on or beyond the Indian frontiers. It is quite probable that at least in this first case the fulminations of the military against the politicals were justified. After all, the politicals had never been to Afghanistan prior to the military intervention. However, because of the need for on-the-spot political decision-making, and perhaps because of personal ambition, the Foreign Secretary, Sir William Hay Macnaghten, was sent as Envoy to Kabul. Initially affairs had gone well. He had accepted the surrender of Dost Mohammed at Kabul, and saw the puppet ruler, Shah Shuja, placed upon the throne, supported by a British garrison. However, opposition developed and the political arrangements fell apart. Macnaghten and his young politicals were blamed for their inexperienced control of operations over the heads of the older and wiser commanders. [12] Macnaghten was soon murdered and the garrison, with all its dependents and camp-followers, were wiped out in the snows of the Khyber as it straggled towards India. [13] General Nott, the commander, had warned that the 'thousand and one politicals have bared the throat of every European in this country to the sword and knife of the revengeful Afghan and the bloody Balooch'. [14] The commander-in-chief, Sir Jasper Nicholls, blamed the Afghan disasters on both military errors and the inexperience of Macnaghten and his politicals. [15] A later military writer with frontier experience carried on the attack against Macnaghten citing the Duke of Wellington's strong criticism of political control over troops in the field. [16] Of course the military were not the only ones upset at the rout of the army. Punjab 'Paladins' [17] like Sir Henry Lawrence blamed the loss not on any system evolved by Macnaghten but on the general British policy of unrealistically trusting local rulers. [18] Another Punjab political, Herbert Edwardes, thought it was 'The old Indian story. Military defeated in an operation, and vexation vented on the "Politicals".' [19]

More than half a century later, at the conclusion of the great rising of 1897-8, a military writer stated the general case of the military this way:

A very curious and unique relic of bygone days is still

maintained on the frontiers of India. This is the recognition of a civil officer who under the title of 'Political Officer' accompanies all military expeditions. Even as late as the [Second] Afghan War, this official was not only entirely independent of the General Officer Commanding the field, but on his own responsibility entered into negotiations with the enemy, and corresponded direct with the Foreign Secretary [of India], and through him with the Viceroy, without any reference whatever to the officer responsible for the military operations. Such a system very naturally proved to be not only unworkable, but highly prejudicial to the successful working out of a campaign.

While reforms had partially 'mitigated the evil', this author and others would have preferred the use of military intelligence officers. [20]

Only a few years prior to this, the famous commander--in-chief, Lord Roberts of Kandahar, recalled that his father had resigned his command in the First Afghan War rather than follow the unwise instructions of his political adviser: 'History had vindicated my father's action, and clearly shown the disastrous result of placing the political over the soldier in war time.' While he admitted that it might be different in peace-time, the state of war presupposed the failure of diplomacy, although political advice was still necessary. [21]

But even when there were no major disasters to be debated, the association of the military and the politicals was rarely amicable. Roberts himself personified the attitude of the military. In 1891 he wrote a lengthy note for the current Viceroy, Lord Lansdowne, answering his own question: 'To whom should supreme control be entrusted in time of war — the Civilian [i.e. the political] or the Soldier.'[22] The note was also seen by the distinguished Foreign Secretary of the years 1885 to 1894, Sir Mortimer Durand. Durand said that while he generally agreed with Roberts' remarks, he had certain reservations too, and he defended Macnaghten's memory to some extent. [23] Indeed Durand and Roberts had first-hand experience with each other in political-military relations in the past.

During the Second Afghan War, Durand had been a junior in the Indian Foreign Office and had been sent to Kabul as Roberts' political secretary for some months. Durand had found the

military officers generally unsympathetic to political advice, and
he complained that while Roberts had listened patiently to his advice he had disagreed with Durand on almost all questions. If
Durand went so far as to press a point, Roberts did not appreciate
it. In the end most important matters were decided without the
knowledge of the handful of politicals.[24] Durand began to feel
that there was no sense of fair play at Kabul, and that the British
were becoming bullies just because they had recently lost a
fight.[25]

Perhaps one of the events that most upset the young and
idealistic Durand was Roberts' hanging of some hundred
Afghans at Kabul. The Viceroy, Lord Lytton, was appalled to
discover that only eleven of these had been directly involved in
the attack on the Residency where Major Louis Napoleon
Cavagnari and his escort had died. The rest appeared to have
been guilty of nothing more than resisting Roberts' advance – 'an
act of very questionable culpability'. Lytton also read the report
of Roberts' political committee (which excluded Durand) with
'blank dismay'.[26] Durand was soon returned to the Foreign
Office, and Lytton searched about for a more experienced
political adviser for Roberts. While the general was intelligent
and 'very quick to take a hint', he was 'without political experience', Lytton thought.[27] In the end he sent Lepel Henry
Griffin, chief secretary of the Punjab as Roberts' chief political
officer (CPO) for north Afghanistan. Griffin soon became, in
Lytton's words, 'a real danger to the Empire',[28] but that is
another story.

Griffin's equivalent to the south, at Kandahar, was Major
Oliver B.C. St John who was CPO under General Sir Donald
Stewart. Stewart was content to leave him in political control
while he himself marched north to relieve Roberts at Kabul.[29] But
while indications were that British interests were more endangered in the north, it was in the south that disaster struck.
There, Ayub Khan, rival of Abdur Rahman for the disunited
Afghan kingdom, routed a Bombay army at Maiwand in July
1880. This cost General Burrows more than a thousand
casualties, mostly in killed. The other half of his force that survived the flight to Kandahar was besieged and in a state of
shock.[30] St John, who had accompanied Burrows' force as CPO,
had tried in vain to rally the troops.[31] Subsequently, Roberts was
ordered south to relieve Kandahar, repeating in reverse Stewart's

earlier but less 'famous' march.

The Maiwand disaster was to lead to years of political-military ill-will, continuing in the Second Afghan War the tradition of putting the blame on the politicals begun in the First. This time it was St John who was in the centre of the controversy. Queen Victoria commented on the affair, saying that politicals were not the best advisers to the military.[32] Lord Ripon, the Liberal Viceroy who had intended to end the Conservative Lytton's frontier involvements, initially thought St John 'an advanced member of the forward school'.[33] But Ripon was wise enough to suspect that Burrows and his superior, General Primrose (Stewart's successor at Kandahar), were trying to place the blame on the politicals. Ripon thought St John 'a bold, ardent man' who had probably advised Burrows to strike at Ayub Khan's forces before the British themselves were cut off. Furthermore, St John had no authority over Burrows' actions, unlike the earlier years on the Afghan frontier. Also Ripon was anxious not to transfer political control from St John to Primrose, since Roberts' imminent arrival at Kandahar would allow this control to devolve on to him.[34] Ripon considered Roberts 'the worst of political officers' but one who had 'plenty of go in him'. Thus he was sure to defeat Ayub Khan at Kandahar,[35] which of course he did, and Afghanistan was then united under Abdur Rahman as Amir.

But if the fighting was over, the political-military quarrel was not. St John continued to write inflammatory letters from Kandahar,[36] while Ripon feared that any inquiry into the matter would be in vain.[37] He and Stewart defended St John on the grounds that his information had been correct up till the time of the battle, when Burrows' cavalry should have taken over this role.[38] But years later, when Roberts penned his note on the need for military dominance over the politicals in time of war, as had been in effect in recent years, he did not forget St John. He wrote that political domination, as had been in effect in the First Afghan War, or even equality, was highly dangerous and led to misunderstanding.[39] The sole exception to the new rule of military dominance, Roberts recalled,

> ...was made on Sir Donald Stewart's departure from Kandahar, when political and military authority was temporarily separated. Whether this would have anything to say to

the disaster at Maiwand it would be difficult to prove, but
it is significant that the only failure should have occurred
during the time when dual control was in force. [40]

Obviously there was no doubt in Roberts' mind as to the answer.
Roberts' inability to appreciate the political aspects of military
operations did not improve in the years after the Second Afghan
War. In 1885, Lord Dufferin had to be quite frank with the
Secretary of State, Lord Randolph Churchill, about the inad-
visability of appointing Roberts to a seat on the Viceroy's Council. Roberts did not have 'the political instinct', and even his
friends admitted he had 'made a mess of political affairs in
Afghanistan'. [41] Of course this did not prevent Roberts' becoming
commander-in-chief from 1885 to 1893. But even while holding
this high office he again showed his political shortcomings in
1888. He ordered General Sir John McQueen to advance against
the Chagarzais during the current Black Mountain expedition.
When McQueen questioned these instructions, supported by the
political officer and the Punjab Government, Roberts insisted it
was plain disobedience. Roberts said he would never again
employ McQueen militarily. Dufferin thought this unjustified,
that Roberts wanted McQueen 'to have a go at the Chagarzais…and wanted McQueen to trail his coat under their noses so
as to compel them to tread on it'. Thus Roberts had been angry
when McQueen suggested that this was provocation of a tribe
who had been promised freedom from interference, and with
whom they had no quarrel. [42] There were obviously dangers in
being a peace-maker if one wanted to get on in the army.

Another notable instance of the politicals being blamed for a
military setback occurred in 1894 when the Mahsuds attacked the
Wana garrison in Waziristan. This occurred during the attempt
to demarcate the boundary between Waziristan and Afghanistan.
Robert I. Bruce was the political agent for Waziristan and British
Joint Commissioner for the purposes of demarcation. He was a
disciple of the great and recently deceased Colonel Robert
Sandeman, the pacifier of Baluchistan. Sandeman's 'system' of
tribal management was somewhat controversial and required a
basis of hierarchical tribal loyalty, schemes for employing
tribesmen, tribal allowances for good behaviour, and extraordinary personal control. Bruce did not have all these at his
fingertips in Waziristan, and the Mahsuds were a highly in-

dividualistic group who rarely respected chiefly control or treaties. Therefore, during the demarcation, his 'system' failed. Bruce's inability to bring his subsequent negotiations with the tribe to a satisfactory conclusion led to the Government's planning of a punitive expedition. Its commander, General Sir William Lockhart, wanted to remove Bruce and assume dual political and military control himself.[43] Sir George White, Roberts' successor as commander-in-chief, supported Lockhart in this, rather than take the risk involved in a divided command. But the Viceroy, Lord Elgin, regretted the evident political--military friction and tried to uphold Bruce's position, at least as long as the negotiations lasted.[44] While he was sure that Bruce would co-operate with Lockhart should military operations begin, he was not so sure of Lockhart. The general would require more controlling, should he become his own chief political officer. This was not only because of Lockhart's questioned humanity, Elgin felt, but because he could not seem to give the tribesmen credit for any good motives at all. Personally, Elgin sympathised with the tribesmen's spirit of independence, and considered their opposition to British control little different to that which his fellow Scots had offered to Edward I, a sentiment that Minto was to echo some years later.[45] Therefore, Elgin tried to convince Lockhart that the Mahsuds were not just 'vagabonds' and that they should be left to manage their own affairs as much as possible.[46] But Lockhart complained that Bruce had not pressed the Mahsuds hard enough, did not know their dialect, and was wholly in the hands of an untrustworthy Native Adviser. Therefore, White successfully maintained that Lockhart be given dual control and be allowed to punish the Mahsuds whom Bruce had failed to win over.[47] Subsequently, after relatively little fighting, the tribe capitulated and agreed to the Government's terms in February 1895. Although Bruce was reinstated, Lockhart was the major winner in terms of promotion and rewards since 'his conduct of political affairs gave entire satisfaction to the Government of India', as his citation read.[48]

But hardly had one such disagreement been resolved than another one appeared on the jagged horizon of the frontier. Sir George Robertson, Resident for Gilgit, was besieged with his escort at Chitral fort in the spring of 1895.[49] They were under attack for forty-six days before being relieved by Colonel Kellys' expedition which crossed the hills from Gilgit. Then

Robertson joined the larger but slower Chitral Relief Force commanded by General Robert C. Low. Low was to undertake the
punishment of the erstwhile besiegers of Chitral fort, but he soon
complained that he did not want to share responsibility with
Robertson.[50] White acted as a peace-maker this time, and advised
Low not to try to displace Robertson, who knew the area well,[51]
but to refer all differences to the Viceroy.[52] But Elgin was no
more impressed with Low's political sense, and thought him
high-handed in his dealings with both Robertson and the tribes.
Elgin felt that unless a general was exceptional like Lockhart he
should only be given political control with great reservations. In
such a case, a general should receive his political instructions
directly from the Viceroy who was the only political equivalent
of the commander-in-chief. Elgin also hoped that after the
fighting was concluded he could 'bring the Foreign Office more
into prominence'. To keep himself better informed, Elgin sent
Colonel Algernon Durand along with Low, ostensibly just to
carry Elgin's congratulations, but also 'to keep his eyes open and
to give me all the news he can'.[53] Meanwhile, Robertson
temporarily left the frontier, suffering from a wound, and was
replaced as CPO by Major Deane, previously mentioned in
Churchill's story.

Deane's reputation as a political obviously depended on one's
point of view. One observer of the campaign suggested that
while the military usually considered the term 'Political' as 'one
of ill omen', the officers of the Chitral Relief Force had in Deane
'a guide, philosopher, and friend whose services throughout were
simply invaluable'.[54] The year after the Chitral troubles, Elgin
commended Deane as one who 'certainly has the knack of
managing these people'. Deane had co-operated well with
Lockhart who had political abilities of his own. Lockhart had
been given the Punjab command and was likely to become the
next commander-in-chief.[55] But unknown at the time was
Lockhart's violent dislike of Deane which developed for uncertain reasons.[56]

Within two years of the conclusion of the Chitral operations
another series of frontier incidents led to further punitive expeditions and accompanying disagreements. Initially, the Waziris
unexpectedly attacked Mr H.A. Gee, the touring political, and
his military escort at Tochi in June 1897. The commander of the
escort was killed and the other officers were killed or wounded.

It was suspected that a good political would not have been so caught off guard at the expense of the military. At any rate the Tochi Field Force was soon despatched there under General G. Corrie Bird. Elgin wanted to maintain direct control over political affairs as he had tried to do in 1894 with Low and Lockhart. He confided to the Secretary of State, Lord George Hamilton, that there was

> ...always a tendency even with the best and most considerate military officers to be a little hard on Civil Political Agents attached to these expeditions; and though I agree that the easiest way out of the difficulty is to make the General himself Chief Political Officer, still we have to get him into touch with the Foreign Department, and I am sure that this can best be done by the Viceroy in his character as head of that Department. [57]

Elsewhere on the frontier, trouble continued to brew. In late July 1897, the Mad Mullah led a sudden attack by the Swat tribes on the brigade camp that guarded the Malakand Pass on the road to Chitral. Deane, the responsible political, had been attempting to judge events when this outbreak occurred. The Malakand Field Force was then established under General Bindon Blood. Churchill's account of the military's view of Deane has already been noted, but Blood's antagonism was even more important. Blood wanted to be his own CPO, but Elgin thought it unfair to remove Deane from the Malakand. In the end Elgin reached a compromise with White whereby Deane was retained as CPO while the force was in his own area, after which Blood was to have dual control. In order to get to the root of the trouble, Elgin questioned both men. Deane denied the criticisms brought forward by Blood, and the latter only withdrew them on the advice of White, who now thought him in the wrong. [58] Blood's continuing animosity is well shown in his final report on the Force's activities:

> Major H.A. Deane...was in separate and independent charge of the political arrangements with the operations I have just described as far as Nawagai....He gave much assistance in arranging the collection of local supplies.

Surely this was damning him with faint praise! But Blood must have got on much better with Deane's successor beyond Nawagai, W.S. Davis. In the next paragraph Blood wrote that Davis 'carried out his duties to my complete satisfaction' and even his 'Native Assistant' was praised.[59] But Blood had his opponents in the matter, and not only the Viceroy and commander-in-chief suspected him, but the Secretary of State, Hamilton, also thought that Blood had misjudged Deane. However, he wondered if Deane might have been oversensitive since he had failed to predict the major rising at Malakand,[60] that had preceded the Tochi attack further south. Of course, behind all these disagreements must have been the fact that anyone with the strength of character necessary for this exacting political work may well have been a difficult man to work with.

In August 1897, the tribal revolt struck the centre of the frontier: the Khyber Pass and the Tirah, home territory of the Afridis. The Khyber had long been under the political control of Colonel Robert Warburton and his very able commandant of the Khyber Rifles, the Afridi levies, Honorary Colonel Aslam Khan.[61] Just before the rising Warburton retired from his post and Aslam Khan temporarily replaced him, while Captain Barton came in as the new commandant. In August, with trouble brewing in the Afridi Tirah, the Punjab's commissioner for Peshawar, Sir Richard Udny, ordered Barton to leave his Afridi levies in their isolated Khyber posts so that his continued presence would not require an expedition to be sent to his rescue. Then, robbed of their commander and under unusual stresses, the levies fought, or abandoned their posts in the face of the Afridi rising. To avenge the loss of the strategic Khyber, the Tirah Field Force of 44,000 men was set up under Lockhart.[62]

Warburton, Lockhart and other men had strong suspicions of the wisdom and loyalty of the veteran Afridi political, Aslam Khan. Lockhart investigated the case and only dropped his doubts once they were proven groundless.[63] Lockhart and the military were also opposed to the policies of Udny whom they criticised for not having warned them in time of the coming Afridi outbreak in the Khyber.[64] When Udny was made CPO, the debate over political-military relations and Udny's subordination to Lockhart led Elgin to warn Hamilton not to believe some newspapers which had

...a dead set against Political Officers, and Udny in particular.... The relations between military and civil officers are apt to become strained at these times, and much that is unfair, if not untrue, is said on both sides. [65]

In turn, Hamilton sympathised with Elgin in his difficulties with the two groups of officers. He was sure that the military were not in fact reliable when it came to non-military subjects. [66]Later he suggested that it was all very well for Lockhart and other commanders to march through tribal territory and come away with an impression of tribal tractability. It was quite another for the politicals who had to operate there on a daily basis without military forces. Lockhart, he felt, was not a good judge of politicals and their work. [67] This, of course, could be said of most military officers.

By the spring of 1898 the last resistance of the tribes involved in the rising was crushed. Lockhart hurried off to leave and fame in England, while Deane was duly elevated to the comfortable Kashmir Resident's post in 1900. The following year Lord Curzon gave him the headship of the North-West Frontier Province which he had just created to separate the frontier from the Punjab's apparently unsatisfactory handling of frontier affairs. There, Deane's reputation and health suffered a gradual decline until his death in 1908. [68]

In the same year before Deane's death, the redoubtable Roos-Keppel and his very able assistant, Sahibzada Abdul Qaiyum, successfully managed the political side of the Zakka Khel Afridi campaign of 1908. General Willcocks, the commander, had been very satisfied with the political activities of both men. During the First World War 'R.K.' and 'A.Q.' largely managed to keep the lid on the ever-bubbling tribal cauldron. The first of the post-war frontier campaigns was the short but important Third Afghan War. The Afghans crossed the Indian frontier in May 1919, just when Roos-Keppel was about to retire after many years on the north-west frontier. Since Roos-Keppel was therefore needed to hold down his frontier province, Lord Chelmsford gave the job of CPO with the forces to another frontier officer, John Maffey (the late Lord Rugby), who was currently acting as the Viceroy's private secretary. Maffey accompanied the troops through the single month's campaign and then assisted the Foreign Secretary, Sir A. Hamilton Grant, with the peace negotiations. These were not made easier by the lack of a resounding British victory. Presumably it was a point well worth making when Chelmsford reported to Secretary of State Edwin Montagu that 'both Army and politicals have worked together in perfect harmony'.[69]

Skipping over the frontier campaigns that followed the First World War for several years, one finds that political-military relations had not noticeably improved. Lieutenant-General G.N. Molesworth, made Deputy Director of Operations and Intelligence on the General Staff in India in 1936, found the old differences even at headquarters. While the civil and political attitude could be epitomised as 'let's wait and see', the military were all for nipping any trouble in the bud before matters got worse. During the serious Mahsud War of 1937 the only resolution of the clash of views had been the granting of both military and political control to the General Officer Commanding Northern Command, over the head of the Chief Commissioner of the NWFP, a senior political and civil officer.[70]

During the same campaign, a long-debated issue again arose: the question of the use of aeroplanes against the tribesmen. The rule of the day was that the local political officer in an area to be punished by bombing had to give the tribesmen twenty-four hours notice while an aeroplane dropped leaflets, all of which allowed the tribesmen and their families and animals to take shelter in caves. It was very unsatisfactory as far as the military were concerned.[71]

But it was not only the apparent sympathy of many politicals for 'their friends the enemy', nor the question of the accuracy of information, nor the apportionment of blame that marred political-military relations on the frontier in time of war. There were also certain other factors that did not help matters. Churchill had noted in the Malakand that

Just when we were looking forward to having a splendid fight and all the guns were loaded and everyone keyed up, this Major Deane – and why was he a Major anyhow? so we said – being in truth nothing better than an ordinary politician – would come along and put a stop to it all.[72]

Stopping the expected fighting was one thing, but that this was done by a former soldier was quite another! Indeed, one probable reason for the strained relations on the frontier was that most of the politicals encountered by the military were former soldiers who had escaped from military duties by way of the Staff Corps of the Indian Army to the political service. At least two-thirds of this service had military backgrounds, while the remainder came from the Indian Civil Service. The 'military politicals' tended to be found in even higher proportions than their ICS colleagues on the frontiers due to the nature of their former experience and outlook. Expressing a military view at the time of the First Afghan War, General Nott wrote:

> If a man is too stupid or too lazy to drill his company, he often turns sycophant, cringes to the heads of departments and is often made a Political, and of course puts the government to an enormous expense, and disgraces the character of his country. [73]

While these words may have been unduly influenced by the unfortunate events of that earlier war, they were echoed eighty years later by another military writer who explained that

> Because...the avoidance of war, rather than the discomfiture of foes, is so often the prime object of our operations, political officers accompany the force, and it has usually been their duty to say when the ways of peace have failed, and to loose the dogs of war. They must therefore of necessity have a somewhat prominent position with the force they accompany. But as they are often drawn from the junior ranks of the army by chance, or by family influence rather than ability, their position does not make them popular. [74]

While there may have been some truth to these allegations, they hardly did justice to the political service, many of whose best men were former soldiers. Their lot was not an easy one, as one noted frontier political wrote in ringing terms:

> The day has passed and their work will soon be forgotten, but they were, with very few exceptions, a goodly company who carried out a delicate, difficult, and often hazardous task as well as any men could have done, who lived

hard and sometimes died hard, who were patient, firm, ruthless, or kindly as occasion warranted, and who were above all rulers undeterred by criticism and false report. They made their mistakes and they often disagreed, not only with their friends the enemy, if one may call them so, but also with their Government and among themselves...[75]

And while young Churchill agreed with the diplomatic role of the politicals, he did not appreciate their information-gathering which could be better done by the army. However, he regretted that his discussion of the subject might wound the politicals,

those gallant men who take all the risks of war, while the campaign lasts, and when it is over live in equal peril of their lives among the savage populations, whose dispositions they study, and whose tempers they watch. I am glad to have done with it.[76]

But still, the old rivalry lingered on. Even during the Second World War, Lord Wavell once asked lightly about the politicals: 'Isn't that the Service staffed with civilians [the Indian Civil Service] who don't want to work and soldiers who don't want to fight?'[77] And no doubt the politicals must have often looked down their noses as their less interesting and enterprising former comrades-in-arms marched up the hill and down again.

Adding to the mutual hostility must have been rivalry for recognition and rewards. Medals and promotions were usually earned through successful combat alone. However, the natural role of the politicals was to keep the peace while the military preferred a little fighting to keep the troops in shape and to insure a chance of glory on occasion. Of course generalisations are dangerous here as elsewhere. But because of these inevitable attitudes, it was the concern of some Viceroys like Elgin to see that the allocation of rewards was not based 'solely on the butcher's bill'. Therefore, he said, good political work that obviated the need for expensive punitive expeditions should also be recognised.[78] Similarly, Curzon felt the need to reward Roos-Keppel in 1899 for 'the most brilliant little feat that has been performed on the frontier in many a day', a small preventive strike against some troublemakers.[79] Keeping the peace had to be made to bring rewards not only to peaceful tribes but to active politicals.

Before drawing any conclusions about the relations between politicals and soldiers, it should be remembered that the issue was not purely a local one, but was debated in such widely separated corners of the Indian sphere as Tibet and Mesopotamia. During the 1904 Mission (or Expedition) to Lhasa, Colonel Sir Francis E. Younghusband, the noted political and explorer, carried on a long paper war with, and over the head of, Colonel J.R.L. Macdonald, the commander of the Mission's enlarged escort. The point at issue was which of the two was to have control over the Mission's movements, and when. [80] In Mesopotamia, Colonel Sir Percy Z. Cox, the famous Persian Gulf Resident, quarrelled with General F.S. Maude over the conduct of the ill-fated Indian expedition during the First World War. But these are matters quite beyond the immediate subject.

Having scrambled up and down the disputed peaks of Indian frontier history with the best of the politicals and soldiers, certain conclusions can be made as a result of this exercise. Obviously, throughout the century political-military relations were frequently troubled. On the other hand, in war-time the early military predominance of the politicals, or even their complete equality, had never survived after the disasters of the First Afghan War. Politicals still retained their independence of the commanders, could negotiate with the tribesmen at will, or discuss matters with the Viceroy and Foreign Secretary; and by 1891 a system was established whereby the Viceroy would not be kept too long in the dark as to the political aspects of military operations, which gave the politicals a certain initiative. [81] But in many cases the question of divided command (so-called) was effectively solved by the granting of dual control over political and military matters to the commanders of expeditions, especially if they showed a certain political wisdom. Generally in war-time, as Masters put it,

> All the politicals took one pace sideways and one pace backward and, instead of telling their military opposite numbers what to do, assumed a knowledgeable air and advised them of the probable political effects of the action they intended to take. [82]

And, of course, the military would have preferred military intelligence officers for information gathering. They also considered negotiation as a method to be employed only when the enemy had been defeated, and not before that. Indeed, the military would have preferred more decision in these eventual defeats, followed by the occupation and pacification of tribal homelands. Hence the politicals seemed to be standing in the way of this happy solution to the tribal problem. However, there was a chance that the military would have 'solved' the tribal question much as their counterparts did in the American west. Then the only good Indian might have been a dead one.

Because of these diverging attitudes, the management of the tribes was left in peace-time to the politicals who maintained relations with the tribes and watched for immediate or distant threats to the Pax Britannica. They did this through a rough system of indirect rule, although it was not as neat and free from loopholes – and indeed the active use of some force – as the system employed in the Indian states. Both in the states and on the frontiers the politicals tended to preserve the ways of the past in what they thought were the interests of their political charges. This was natural enough perhaps, in a service whose work was based on treaty relations – however tenuous or unequal – and on the maintenance of the *status quo*. Hence they accepted and even upheld tribal codes of life and death on the frontiers, as they supported the decaying splendour of the maharajahs in their states. There is ample evidence of a basic conservatism among the politicals, and they had many critics, both British and Indian. Philip Mason, whose anecdote opened this essay, said in defence of the politicals that their role was unlike that of the regular District Officers of the ICS. They were not supposed to interfere too actively in the affairs of the Indian states (nor of the tribes for that matter). While there were great men among them, 'theirs was not a training to prepare men for revolution'. He added:

If there was more consciousness among them of all the coloured diversity of India, of the poetic reality of a past living in the present, there was perhaps less awareness of the political reality of a future clamorous for recognition. It was, in short, more common among political officers than in the administrative service to find a tendency to complacency with things as they were, a certain cynicism as to political progress.[83]

Significantly, 'political' in the twentieth century was used increasingly in terms of Indian aspirations and methods, and not of diplomacy with somehow isolated leaders in their palaces or forts. What ideas of eventual Indian political or social progress the politicals did hold tended to be expressed in paternalist terms. However, there were some who mixed their concern for the tribes with certain modernising ideas. For example, Roos-Keppel managed successfully to press the daring introduction of non-British officers to the political service, something opposed throughout the nineteenth and early twentieth century. [84] And Denys Bray, a former frontier political, and later Foreign Secretary from 1920 to 1930, talked about road-building and the employment of Mahsuds as tribal levies as civilising influences that would eventually bring results:

> It may be thought visionary to talk of the civilization of the Mahsud. But you must take long views on the frontier. Civilization, after all, has succeeded often enough with material far more unpromising and intractable than the Mahsud, who, for all his barbarity and ignorance, is a man of magnificent virility and courage and with no small share of natural wit and intelligence. [85]

In other words, the civilising mission was to be tried with the Mahsuds of Waziristan, who might well respond since they were such fine men! It was this kind of warm paternal humanism that so irritated the military and complicated their task of defeating the tribesmen in war-time. The politicals were trying to win the peace and not the war, and perhaps deserve a certain respect. It was a difficult situation where the tribesmen were never reluctant to defend their houses and way of life against the dangers of the Pax Britannica.

Notes

The primary material in these notes comes largely from the collection held by the India Office Library, London. These are indicated by the following prefixes:
  MSS Eur. E 264 – Chelmsford Collection;
  MSS Eur. F 111 – Curzon Collection;
  MSS Eur. F 130 – Dufferin and Ava Collection;
  MSS Eur. D 727 – Durand Collection;
  MSS Eur. F 84 – Elgin Collection;

MSS Eur. F 132 – Lyall Collection;
MSS Eur. E 218 – Lytton Collection;
MSS Eur. D 573 – Morley Collection.
Therefore I should like to thank the Librarian, Mr S.C. Sutton, and his staff, and especially Mr Martin Moir, for their kind assistance to me when I was gathering material for my Ph.D. thesis.

The bound papers of the First Marquess of Ripon in the North Library of the British Museum are indicated by the initials BM. I must also thank the British Ministry of Defence for access to the papers of Lord Roberts of Kandahar in the Army Museum's Ogilby Trust, indicated by the initials AMOT.

1. Philip Woodruff [pseud. for Philip Mason]. *The Men Who Ruled India* (London, Jonathan Cape, 1953-4), II. p.153.
2. W. Murray Hogben, 'The Foreign and Political Department of the Government of India, 1876 to 1919, a study in imperial careers and attitudes' (unpublished thesis, University of Toronto, 1973).
3. Sir William Kerr Fraser-Tytler, *Afghanistan, A Study in Political Development in Central and Southern Asia* (London, Oxford University Press, third edition, revised 1967), p.269n.
4. William Foster, *A Guide to the India Office Records, 1600-1868* (London, HMSO, 1919, reprinted 1966), p.43.
5. Indian Institute of Public Administration, *The Organization of the Government of India* (London, Asia Publishing, 1958), p.37.
6. See Thomas D. Farrell, 'The Founding of the North-West Frontier Militias', *Asian Affairs* (June, 1972), pp.168-75.
7. Lord Curzon's speech in the House of Commons, 15 February 1898, cited in David Dilks, *Curzon in India*, 2 vols, (London, Rupert Hart-Davis, 1969-70), vol. 1. p.62.
8. Winston S. Churchill, *My Early Life, A Roving Commission* (London, 1930; New York, Scribners, 1958), pp.131-2.
9. Minto to Morley, 23 March 1908, MSS Eur. D 573/14, General Willcocks, commander of the Zakka Khel Field Force was given full political control, with Roos-Keppel accompanying as CPO. The latter was also put in command of the 'flying column' during the operations, co-operating with Willcocks' main force. For details of the Government's largely political instructions to Willcocks, and for Roos-Keppel's political report following the operations, see Indian Army, Intelligence Branch, *Frontier and Overseas Expeditions from India* (Calcutta, Superintendent of Government Printing, 1908), vol.II supp. A, pp. 8-9, 32-8.
10. Woodruff [Mason], *The Men Who Ruled India*, II, pp. 292-4.
11. John Masters, *Bugles and a Tiger, cf A Volume of Autobiography* (New York, Ballantine, 1968), pp. 191, 188-9.
12. Lt.-Gen. Sir George MacMunn, *Afghanistan, From Darius to Amanulla* (London, G. Bell, 1929), pp. 133-6.
13. Patrick A. Macrory, *The Fierce Pawns* (Philadelphia, Lippincott, 1968), or under British title, *Signal Disaster* (London, Hodder and Stoughton, 1966); and J.A. Norris, *The First Afghan War, 1838-1841* (London, Cambridge University Press, 1967).
14. Cited in MacMunn, *Afghanistan*, p. 139; and in Macrory, *The Fierce Pawns*, pp. 329-30.
15. Cited in MacMunn, *Afghanistan*, p. 154; and in Macrory, *The Fierce Pawns*, pp. 329-30.
16. Major A.C. Yate, *Lieutenant-Colonel John Haughton* (London, John Murray, 1900), pp. 31, and 37-8.
17. Sir Olaf Caroe, *The Pathans: 550 B.C. – A.D. 1957* (London, MacMillan, 1965), pp. 329-45.
18. Cited in Sir Herbert B. Edwardes and Herman Merivale, *Life of Sir Henry*

Lawrence (London, Smith, Elder, 1873), p. 313.

19. *Ibid.*, p. 233.

20. Capt. and Brevet-Major G.J. Younghusband, *Indian Frontier Warfare* (London, Kegan, Paul, Trench, Tribner, 1898), pp. 246-7; also Yate, *John Haughton*, p. 38; and Winston S. Churchill, *The Story of the Malakand Field Force* (London, Longmans, Green, 1898), p. 277.

21. Lord Roberts, 'To whom should supreme control be entrusted in time of war – the Civilian or the Soldier?', memo, 4 May 1891, Simla, AMOT, vol. VI, part II, pp. 869-71.

22. *Ibid.*

23. Durand to Roberts, 8 May 1891, MSS Eur. D 727/4; Yate also admits that Gen. Elphinstone was 'a broken down General', but saves his real fire for Macnaghten: Yate, *John Haughton*, p. 38.

24. Brig.-Gen. Sir Percy Sykes, *The Rt. Hon. Sir Mortimer Durand* (London, Cassell, 1926), p. 111.

25. Durand to Layall, D.O., 13 December 1879, MSS Eur. F 132/40.

26. Lytton to Cranbrook, 5 December 1879, MSS Eur. E 218/3/4.

27. Lytton to Cranbrook, 31 December 1879, MSS Eur. E 218/3/4.

28. Lytton to Ripon, 8 June 1880, MSS Eur. 218/518/6.

29. Stewart to Lady Stewart, 16 March 1880, cited in G.R. Elsmie (ed.), *Field Marshal Sir Donald Stewart* (London, John Murray, 1903), p. 315.

30. Ripon to Hartington, 25 November 1881, BM, B.P. 7/3.

31. St John to Lyall, 1 August 1880, enclosed with Ripon to Hartington, 16 August 1880: see also Hartington to Ripon, 10 December 1880, BM B.P. 7/3.

32. Lucien Wolf, *Life of the First Marquess of Ripon,* 2 vols. (London, John Murray, 1921), II, pp. 26-31.

33. Ripon to Hartington, 26 July 1880, BM, B.P. 7/3.

34. Ripon to Hartington, 9 August 1880, BM, B.P. 7/3.

35. Ripon to Hartington, 1 August 1880, BM, B.P. 7/3.

36. Ripon to Hartington, 16 August 1880, with both St John to Lyall, 1 August 1880, and 21 September 1880, BM, B.P. 7/3.

37. Ripon to Hartington, 16 August 1880, BM, B.P. 7/3.

38. Ripon to Hartington, 14 November 1880, BM, B.P. 7/3; Yate mentioned the inaccuracy of political information in the First Afghan War, and said that it was analogous with Burrows' situation at Maiwand in the Second: *John Haughton*, p. 31 n.

39. Roberts, 'To whom should supreme control be entrusted...' memo, 4 May 1891, AMOT, vol. VI, part II, pp. 869-71, paras. 2-6.

40. *Ibid.*, para 9.

41. Dufferin to Churchill, 30 July 1885; and Churchill to Dufferin, 8 September 1885, MSS Eur. F 130/2.

42. Dufferin to Cross, 3 December 1888 (extract to Lansdowne), MSS Eur. D 558/2.

43. Caroe, *The Pathans,* pp. 375-6, 398-401; and (the late Sir) Evelyn [B.] Howell, *Mizh, A Monograph on Government's Relations with the Mahsud Tribe* (Simla, Government of India Press, 1931), p. 15; and White to Elgin, 20 November 1894, MSS Eur. F 84/65.

44. Elgin to Fowler, 20 November 1894, MSS Eur. F 84/12.

45. John Buchan, *Lord Minto: A Memoir* (London, Thomas Nelson, 1924), p. 235; and Minto to Morley, 1 March 1906, MSS Eur. D. 573/7.

46. Elgin to White, 22 November 1894, MSS Eur. F 84/65; and see Elgin to Fowler, 5 December 1894, MSS Eur. F 84/12.

47. White to Elgin, 17 December 1894, MSS Eur. F 84/65.

48. Elgin to Fowler, Memo on Queen's Birthday Honours, 1895, MSS Eur. F 84/13.

49. See Sir George Robertson, *Chitral, The Story of a Minor Siege* (London, Methuen, 1898, reprinted 1900).

50. Low to White, telegram 26 April 1895, enclosed with White to Elgin, 29 April 1895, MSS Eur. F 84/66.
51. White to Low, telegram 27 April 1895, enclosed with White to Elgin, 29 April 1895, MSS Eur. F 84/66.
52. White to Elgin, 29 April 1895, MSS Eur. F 84/66.
53. Elgin to Fowler, 1 May 1895, MSS Eur. F 84/13.
54. Capt. George John Younghusband and Capt. Frank [Francis] E. Younghusband, *The Relief of Chitral* (London: MacMillan, 1895, reprinted 1897), p. 85.
55. Elgin to Hamilton, 11 August 1896, MSS Eur. F 84/14.
56. See Curzon to Hamilton, 9 May 1900, MSS Eur. F 111/159; and Hamilton to Curzon, 30 and 31 May 1900, MSS Eur. F 111/159.
57. Elgin to Hamilton, 20 July 1897, MSS Eur. F 84/15.
58. Elgin to Hamilton, 6 January 1898, MSS Eur. F 84/15.
59. Churchill, *Malakand Field Force*, p. 336, paras. 66-7.
60. Hamilton to Elgin, 28 January 1898, MSS Eur. F 84/16.
61. Col. Sir Robert Warburton, *Eighteen Years in the Khyber, 1879-1898* (London, John Murray, 1900).
62. Indian Army, Intelligence Branch, *Frontier and Overseas Expeditions from India* (Simla: Government Monotype Press, 1908), II, pp. 70-3.
63. Elgin to Hamilton, 24 March 1898, MSS Eur. F 84/16; Lockhart to Elgin, 24 January 1898, MSS Eur. F 84/72; Elgin to Hamilton, 27 January 1898, MSS Eur. F 84/16; and Lockhart to Elgin, 27 January 1898, MSS Eur. F 84/72.
64. Indian Army, Intelligence Branch, *Frontier and Overseas Expeditions*, II, p. 69.
65. Elgin to Hamilton, 27 October 1897, MSS Eur. F 84/15.
66. Hamilton to Elgin, 19 November 1897, MSS Eur. F 84/15.
67. Hamilton to Elgin, 29 April 1898, MSS Eur. F 84/16.
68. Hogben, 'The Foreign and Political Department of the Government of India', pp.372-6.
69. Chelmsford to Montagu, 28 May 1919, MSS Eur. E 264/5.
70. Lt.-Gen. G.N. Molesworth, *Curfew on Olympus* (Bombay, New York: Asia Publishing, 1965), p. 114.
71. *Ibid.*, p. 118.
72. Churchill, *My Early Life*, pp. 131-2.
73. Cited in Macrory, *The Fierce Pawns*, p. 331.
74. MacMunn, *Afghanistan*, pp. 132-2.
75. Fraser-Tytler, *Afghanistan*, p. 271.
76. Churchill, *Malakand Field Force*, p. 277.
77. Sir Olaf Caroe, 'The Indian Political Service', review of Sir Terence Creagh Coen, *The Indian Political Service* (London, 1971), *Asian Affairs* (June, 1971), p. 204.
78. Elgin to Hamilton, 9 June 1898, MSS Eur. F 84/16.
79. Curzon to Hamilton, 9 March 1899, MSS Eur. F 111/158.
80. Peter Fleming, *Bayonets to Lhasa* (London, Rupert Hart-Davis, 1961).
81. Durand to Elgin, 2 August 1895, MSS Eur. F 84/67.
82. Masters, *Bugles and a Tiger*, p. 188.
83. Woodruff [Mason], *The Men Who Ruled India*, II, pp. 270-1.
84. Hogben, 'The Foreign and Political Department of the Government of India', pp.280-319.
85. Denys Bray, 5 March 1923, contained in C. H. Philips *et al* (eds.), *Select Documents on the History of India and Pakistan*, (London, Oxford University Press, 1962), IV, *The Evolution of India and Pakistan, 1858 to 1947*, pp. 495-6.

Sir Arthur Currie and Politicians: A Case Study of Civil-Military Relations in the First World War

A.M.J. HYATT

Addressing members of the Civil Servants Research Institute of Canada in 1924, the Principal of McGill University, General Sir Arthur Currie suggested that many difficulties had been created during the past war when Canadian political leaders ignored sound military advice on military questions. Public reaction to the speech was slight, but Sir Robert Borden, then living in retirement, was convinced that Currie was preparing to begin a political career. Either unaware of, or unconvinced by Woodrow Wilson's statement that being President of the United States was relatively simple after having been president of a great university, Borden recorded that Currie would find the organising of a government 'a harder task than he did the leading of the Canadian Corps in France or than he does the heading of McGill University'.[1]

We will never know if Borden was correct, for Currie in spite of many suggestions that he ought to enter politics refused to do so. Indeed he reacted vigorously and negatively whenever the suggestion was put to him. He had refused Mackenzie King's offer to make him Canada's first High Commissioner in Washington in 1923,[2] and he rejected at least once Arthur Meighen's persuasion that he should become a politician.[3] When a friend pressed him to run for Parliament in 1924, he replied:

> You would have me believe that all my friends on the coast consider that I am sinking into oblivion. What would you have me do? Get up on the housetops every morning like a noisy rooster? ... I have had from here just as much encouragement to go into political life as anything you have suggested, but I am not particularly interested.[4]

Shortly after Sir Robert Borden speculated on Currie's political aspirations, the former corps commander was asked directly about his difficulties during the war with British professional soldiers. His reply provides an important clue to his

attitude towards politics. 'My fight', he wrote, 'was not with
regular officers at all. It was with Canadian authorities in
London.'[5] Even earlier, immediately after the war in fact, Currie
had shown considerable sympathy for the plight of British
soldiers, particularly Sir Douglas Haig, in dealing with
politicians. 'Much has been written', Currie had recorded,

> ... and much has been implied concerning his [Haig's]
> troubles with ... the politicians. He had to withstand from
> them much criticism and much interference, but he never
> complained bitterly about these things, but always held out
> with the greatest patience for what he knew to be right.[6]

Perhaps this observation indicates only that Currie's memory,
like the recollection of almost any man, could play tricks. Certainly during the war he disagreed vigorously with the British
Commander-in-Chief, and on at least one occasion he sought the
help of Sir Robert Borden when in disagreement with Haig. But
it also suggests that there may have been more friction between
Currie and Canadian politicians than appeared on the surface. In
other countries, after all, conflicts between soldiers and civilians
produced profound difficulties. In a short essay it is impossible to
investigate thoroughly Canadian political-military relationships
in the First World War, but aspects of Currie's attitude towards
Canadian politicians can be explored briefly.

Probably few historians would quarrel seriously with the assertion that the First World War was Canada's greatest collective
experience.[7] And probably the most significant aspect of that experience was the resulting 'fundamental change in the
Anglo-Canadian relationship'.[8] Civil-military relations, and
particularly the relationship of the Canadian Corps Commander
with his political superiors, forms part of this fundamental
change. The position of the Corps Commander *vis à vis* his own
government, in the first instance, was made precarious because of
the peculiar status of Empire or Colonial forces. For all military
matters, Canadians were theoretically under the command and
control of the appropriate British Commander-in-Chief. The
nature of 'military' was often the question. Combat was clearly
military. But what of promotion, equipment, pay and other administrative issues? When the Canadian Minister of Militia's
representative in England attempted to have all Canadian bat-

talion commanders in France promoted to the rank of colonel, and the Canadian minister approved this step, the War Office quickly recognised that a routine administrative question could have 'military' implications.[9] On the other hand, the individual commanding a Dominion force had always been obliged to keep his own government informed on all matters pertaining to the welfare of soldiers as well as his military superiors. William Otter had discovered during the South African War that the task of commanding such a force could be exceedingly distracting. 'I had to serve two masters,' Otter wrote, 'one in the form of the general commanding ... to whom I had to make daily reports, returns, etc., and the other our own Department at Ottawa, which required even more similar information.'[10]

In the First World War the task, if anything, became even more demanding. Not only were the numbers involved much greater and Canadian attention more concentrated on the activity of the expeditionary force, but from the beginning of the war until late in 1916 the Canadian Department of Militia and Defence was under the control of Sam Hughes, one of the most extraordinary ministers of the Crown in Canadian history. Although he had resigned from office before Currie took command of the Canadian Corps, Hughes' administrative methods were often bizarre and the legacy of his administration was substantial. As a result of Hughes' activity, the Corps Commander in France had to deal not only with British military authorities, and with the direct communications of Sam Hughes, but also had to endure a six-way split of authority in England.[11] Partly to overcome this administrative jungle, the Ministry of Overseas Military Forces of Canada (OMFC) had been created, and it was the establishment of this overseas branch of Canadian government which precipitated Hughes' resignation. Thus, from December 1916 until the end of the war there were only two departments of the Government charged with the administration of Canadian military affairs. Theoretically there should have been little difficulty since the Ministry of Militia and Defence dealt only with those forces in Canada and the Ministry of Overseas Military Forces of Canada dealt only with those forces overseas. As a matter of practice, the system, complicated by other administrative appendages and the personalities of those in positions of authority, worked less smoothly than the theory would suggest. One of the appendages, for example, was the establishment of a Canadian representative to British General Headquarters in France. For two years this position was held by Sir Max Aitken. [12] In January 1917, however, a Canadian Section was formed at GHQ which, in the words of the Canadian Official History,

> ... provided a direct channel of communication between the Ministry, O.M.F.C. and G.H.Q., as well as a channel between these bodies and the heads of Canadian formations in the Field. Under direction from the O.M.F.C. Ministry it was responsible for supervising the various Canadian Administrative Services and Departments in the Field, and *was empowered to take executive and administrative action regarding the control of personnel of the Canadian Forces in the Field.* [13]

In other words, there existed in France an administrative body which could take 'executive action' in regard to the formations under the direct control of the Corps Commander. Given such organisation, misunderstandings were almost bound to occur. While the creation of the OMFC was an enormous organisational improvement from that which existed in the first years of the war and while for smaller semi-autonomous units in France (for example the Cavalry Brigade, railway or forestry units) it provided necessary direct access to the Canadian Government, nevertheless the administrative system remained sufficiently complex, from the Corps Commanders' point of view, to present real irritants.

In the South African War, Otter had complained that he worked for two masters. By late 1919 Currie was in direct contact with Sir Edward Kemp, then Minister of the OMFC. The Minister of Militia and Defence, General S.C. Mewburn, worked closely with the Corps Commander on questions related to demobilisation. Currie also communicated with Sir George Perley, the Canadian High Commissioner in London and the former Minister of the OMFC. In addition there were visits from, and communication with the Prime Minister. For all 'military' matters of course, he was still responsible to a British chain of command. Currie, it seemed, worked for several masters. The administrative structure at the very least provided ample opportunities for friction between the soldier commanding the Canadian Corps and his civilian masters.

However, the system alone did not account for Currie's attitude towards politicians. Probably the influence of Canada's first war-time Minister of Militia, Sam Hughes, cannot be over-emphasised as a factor in the growth of Currie's suspicion of and disdain for politicians. Much of Hughes' career has been outlined in the Canadian Official History and in Mr Swettenham's account of the Canadian Corps and does not need to be repeated.[14] It is sufficient to note that Currie entered the CEF as one of Hughes' appointments, and that he initially was grateful to Hughes.[15] Hughes' continuous interference in the affairs of the Canadian Corps, his support of the Ross rifle, his role in discrediting General Alderson, and his promotion of friends and relatives did much to mitigate Currie's sense of debt to the Minister. By the time that Borden demanded Hughes' resignation, Currie could share the sentiment of a 1st Division diarist who observed 'there is a new contentment among us all ... now that the inevitable has really happened. . . . Sir Sam has lost his job. . . . I do not like to kick a man when he is down, but I am willing to break nine toes in kicking Sam'. [16]

However, Currie soon discovered that Hughes' removal from office by no means wiped out his influence on the Canadian Corps. One of Currie's first tasks as Corps Commander was to appoint his successor to command the 1st Canadian Division. The first choice of the politicians for this position was Sam Hughes' son, Garnet Hughes, who was insufficiently qualified for the post in Currie's view. Currie chose General A.C. Macdonnell of the 7th Canadian Infantry Brigade, a pre-war professional soldier whose promotion to brigadier Sir Sam had opposed. [17] 'I refused', Currie later wrote,

> to accept command [of the Corps] ... on any condition which I thought would embarrass me. Their main condition was that I should accept as my successor in the 1st Division Major General Garnett [sic] Hughes ... who was then in England commanding the 5th Division. I was importuned, coaxed, threatened and bullied. I was told that Garnett Hughes would have to get the 1st Division, that there was a combination in England and Canada for him that neither I, or any man could beat; that his father wanted him to get the position and that God help the man who fell out with his father. [18]

There were, of course, many other factors which complicated
the selection, not least of which was the insensitivity of the
British War Office in announcing Currie's appointment without
first checking with the Minister of OMFC, Sir George Perley.
Perley had not only to insist on the right of the responsible Canadian Minister to approve such an appointment, but he was embarrassed by a promise previously given to his own Chief of
Staff, Major-General Richard Turner, that Turner should be considered for the position of Corps Commander. Perley recognised,
however, that Turner was 'rather out of touch with the front'
and knew that Currie was 'considered most suitable for the
corps'. Perley solved this dilemma with a compromise. He would
keep Turner in England, but give him additional power, including 'a certain measure [of] authority over administrative
matters at the front particularly on lines of communication'. [19]
This solution would later cause trouble when Currie discovered
that significant appointments and promotions were arranged
within the Canadian Corps without consulting him. At the time,
however, the most frustrating fact seemed to be that both the
Prime Minister and Sir George Perley favoured the appointment
of Sam Hughes' son to the 1st Division. Borden wired Perley indicating that 'if Garnet Hughes is acceptable for Division Commander, I would like to see him appointed but [I] leave the question to your judgement'. [20] Currie came to regard the pressure on
him to accept Garnet Hughes as unwarranted interference from
politicians, a view which was strengthened during the summer of
1917 by other events.

Currie's reaction to the conscription crisis has also been outlined elsewhere and this too, perhaps wrongly, strengthened his
view that Canadian politicians were prepared to sacrifice the interests of the Canadian Corps to political exigencies back home.
To him it seemed that 'as the need for reinforcements steadily
grew, the government inexorably postponed or whittled away
the promised provision of men ...that the politicians were
prepared to postpone a solution almost indefinitely. They seemed
more concerned with foisting incompetent subordinates upon
him, and with using his name in electioneering than in fulfilling
their responsibility to the Canadian Corps'. [21] This view may have
been one-sided, even naïve, but given the pressures under which
the Corps Commander operated in 1917 it was understandable.

While Currie resented the fact that his name was used in the conscription election, his main problem, a lack of reinforcements for the Canadian Corps, was solved by his reorganisation of the Corps in early 1918. Basically Currie looked at every issue from a military point of view. For him it was axiomatic that more casualties would result when an understrength unit was sent into action than would be the case if the same unit went into the same action at full strength. It was precisely this point of view which made him advocate conscription when he thought it would provide sufficient numbers of men to keep the Corps up to strength, and this point of view which made him lose interest in conscription when it was clear that it would not provide the men he needed. It was this point of view which prompted him to introduce the reorganisation of the Canadian Corps in 1918. After the reorganisation, it was his military point of view which brought about his most vigorous controversy with his military chief Sir Douglas Haig, and which made him seek the aid of his civilian leader Sir Robert Borden.

The episode came about as a result of the German attempt at a gigantic breakthrough in March of 1918. In the short run, the Germans were spectacularly successful – in four days they advanced fourteen miles, the greatest advance on the Western Front since 1914.[22] Throughout the German offensive, which extended into June of 1918, the greatest Allied need was for additional soldiers to contain the German drive. Again and again, Haig was forced to make hasty emergency dispositions to meet fresh German threats. Not unnaturally, the Commander-in-Chief made heavy demands on Canadian formations and man-power. On 23 March the 2nd Canadian Division was placed under command of GHQ Reserve and the 1st Division was moved to First Army Reserve. Three days later the 3rd and 4th Canadian Divisions were detached from Currie's command and his headquarters, without forces under its control, was sent into reserve. 'Under the pressure of circumstances', Currie recorded, 'the four Canadian Divisions were to be removed from my command, placed in two different Armies ... and under the command of three different Corps.'[23]

Currie recognised that in such a crisis desperate redispositions of force had to be made, but he was also of the opinion that the military results achieved from a piecemeal disposition of the Corps would be less than if it could be engaged as a collective unit. All of his reorganisational efforts had been towards strengthening the Corps rather than individual divisions. To his own officers he frequently remarked that a corps with four divisions was the logical tactical organisation for success. This was based on his conviction that the division was 'too small an organization to get the full benefit of artillery' and other support.[24] He made these views known to his army commander, General Horne, and to Haig's Chief of Staff, and suggested that the Canadian Corps should be reunited as quickly as 'the tactical and administrative requirements of the moment' allowed.[25]

Currie insisted that he did not wish to embarrass Haig 'in the slightest degree' by his request. But, he added, when separately employed, Canadian divisions do not achieve the success they should:

> From the very nature and constitution of the organization it is impossible for the same liaison to exist in a British Corps as exists in the Canadian Corps. My staff and myself cannot do as well with a British Division in this battle as we can do with the Canadian Divisions, nor can any other Corps staff do as well with the Canadian Divisions as my own.
>
> I know that necessity knows no law and that the Chief will do what he thinks best, yet for the sake of the victory we must win, get us together as soon as you can.[26]

Within twenty-four hours of sending this message, the 3rd and 4th Divisions were back under Currie's headquarters. By 8 April, the 1st Division had also returned. But the quick reunion had not been the result of Haig accepting Currie's logic. Currie had sent a copy of his letter requesting the return of Canadian divisions to Sir Edward Kemp, who in turn relayed a copy of its contents to Lord Derby, the British Secretary of State for War.[27] Derby then informed Haig that it was 'the Canadian Government's desire' that the Canadians fight together. Haig later admitted that it was this communication which caused the Corps' reunion.[28]

Engaged in a life or death struggle with Ludendorff's offensive, Haig had little time to digest Currie's request. He strongly resented the pressure to reunite the Canadian Corps which came through political channels. Currie's army commander, General Horne, took a similar view and made it plain that he objected to 'any reflections on the fighting ability of British Divisions'.[29] Currie was being critical of British forces. He had already noted in his diary that 'many British troops are not fighting well. This is what I expected ... would be the case.' [30] But he was not critical of British forces because they were British, his opinion was based on military considerations, specifically his opposition to the nine battalion division which the British had adopted and he had rejected in his January reorganisation. This distinction was lost on Horne. Sir Arthur was angry when Horne proved so obtuse, doubly so because he shared with most British senior officers a resentment towards Lloyd George's diversion of troops to other theatres. [31] He was even more annoyed that his British commander did not understand that he was not trying to use political pressure, but had informed his minister routinely of the situation.

Picqued by the interview and Horne's failure to comprehend his position, Currie reflected, 'they do not want the truth, they want camouflage and they're getting it. O God, how they are getting it and how the British people are getting it in all the balderdash being published in the Press.' [32] Meanwhile, Horne reported to Haig that he though Currie was 'suffering from a swollen head' which in turn provoked Haig. 'Currie', Haig wrote,

> wishes to fight only as a 'Canadian Corps' and gets his Canadian representatives in London to write and urge me to arrange it. As a result the Canadians are together holding a wide front near Arras, *but they have not yet been in the battle!* The Australians on the other hand have been used by divisions and are now spread out from Albert to Amiens ... [33]

It is hard to know exactly what Haig meant by his italicised phrase. If he thought the Canadians would be hurt by missing the fighting he certainly misunderstood soldiers. If he kept the Corps out of battle as punishment for Currie's stand, he was being less vindictive than Lord Beaverbrook's pen sketch of the Commander-in-Chief indicates and even less inventive than Liddell Hart suggests. Beaverbrook described Haig as 'frank, truthful, egotistical, self-confident and malicious'. [34] Liddell Hart wrote that he possessed a 'calm unimaginative acceptance of whatever fate may have in store'. [35]

After experiences in another war and in United Nations Forces, General E.L.M. Burns saw the episode as a 'continuing difficulty'. The Canadians, he observed, 'their sentiments of nationality greatly intensified in the war, [wanted] … to fight all together in a homogeneous Canadian higher formation; and the British commander, faced with a very difficult tactical problem … [wanted] to solve it by moving the most conveniently placed divisions to meet the threat.'[36] There can be little doubt that Canadian sentiments of nationality were indeed 'intensified in the war'. Equally, there is no doubt that Currie could and did on other occasions, particularly after the war, write and think in nationalistic terms. But this was not his argument at the time. He was prepared to have the Corps split in an emergency, but he believed that better military results could be obtained if it were reunited as quickly as possible. Ironically, the Canadian Prime Minister did not learn of the episode until 3 May. He then wrote in purely nationalistic terms that 'any proposal to break up the Canadian Corps would have the most unfortunate effect upon public opinion'. [37] Shortly afterwards, the Prime Minister had an interview with the Corps Commander during which Currie was able to make his criticisms of the British military system explicit. Borden came away from this interview convinced that the Allied defeats were due to 'lack of organisation, lack of system, lack of preparation, lack of foresight and incompetent leadership'. [38] The interview strengthened his conviction in 'the higher quality and character of the Canadian war effort'. [39]

What Borden failed to recognise was that Currie's criticism was mainly with the officers who surrounded Haig and specifically that it was directed against the British tactical system on the Western Front, not the British strategy of fighting on the Western Front. Whether this misunderstanding was the Prime Minister's failure to understand, or the Corps Commander's failure to explain, matters little. Currie unquestionably shared Borden's 'earnestness' and his belief in the efficacy of the Canadian Corps. But his experience with Canadian administration did not make him believe without reservation in the 'higher quality and character of the Canadian war effort'. [40]

Two factors added to Currie's mistrust of Canadian politicians. First, he was most bitterly attacked in Parliament by Sir Sam Hughes in late 1918 and 1919. At the time of these attacks, no replies were immediately forthcoming from members of the Government. Shortly after the Corps Commander's return to Canada, Hughes reviewed Currie's war-time record in Parliament. A record, in Hughes' words, which made Currie a 'coward, unworthy of association with his fellow-man and woman'. He accused Currie of wasting Canadian lives. 'Were I in authority', the ex-minister declared, Currie 'would be tried summarily by court martial and punished so far as the law would allow ... you cannot find one Canadian soldier returning from France who will not curse ... [his] name.'[41] When this speech was made the Prime Minister was out of the country, but no other member of the Cabinet immediately spoke out for the Corps Commander. Eventually, when Borden returned, he did make a strong statement on Currie's behalf,[42] but similar statements issued much sooner by a member of the Government would have helped. Hughes, after all, was a politician. He had been a member of the Government. The Prime Minister, even after Hughes' resignation, had tried to have his son promoted to command of a division in the Corps. It seemed that Hughes was able to destroy Currie's reputation from the protected walls of Parliament without being challenged by any of those politicians Currie had served for four years. The Corps Commander could hardly be expected to accept this without feeling betrayed.

Secondly, Currie was very much disillusioned during his term as Inspector-General of Militia after the war. When he took the job of Inspector-General, Currie had hoped to initiate a thorough reorganisation of both the Militia and the permanent force in Canada. It would be incorrect to say that he had a master plan for such reorganisation, but he did have a plan for creating the plan. During the war Canadian success had been achieved in large measure because of the quality and efficiency of Canadian planning. Currie had never hesitated to put ideas of his own forward, but there was never anything sacred about such notions. His staff had been given a very free hand in criticising his plans and initiating their own ideas. Currie hoped to follow the same procedure in peace-time. He believed that the key to successful military reorganisation was to have an efficient staff organisation and a small but well-organised permanent force and he planned to build this around a nucleus of officers who had served in the Canadian Corps. Thus, the first step in reconstruction was to persuade the best officers of the Corps to remain in the permanent force. Many good men came with Currie, but he was surprised by the official resistance to this idea.[43] Several positions which he wanted to fill with veterans were blocked by pre-war permanent soldiers who had spent the entire war in Canada, and there was considerable opposition to opening jobs by pensioning off the incumbents.

By statute the permanent force of Canada was fixed at ten thousand all ranks – more than sufficient for the kind of role that Currie visualised. The trouble was that he was prohibited by the Government from recruiting more than five thousand men. Numbers were even further restricted by the failure to build proper accommodation for the permanent forces. 'We have tried our best', Currie noted, 'to make what we have into a well-balanced force, ... yet I cannot get the government to provide such necessary organization as a Signal Corps.' [44]

Currie also wanted to reorganise the Militia. In this regard his main idea was to rectify the difficulties which had been created by wholesale mobilisation of new battalions during the war. In short, he hoped to return to some rational form of Militia organisation. At the same time he wanted to ensure that each battalion of the CEF would be perpetuated by a Militia battalion. He was astonished to find that the notion of perpetuating CEF battalions was vigorously opposed in the corridors of Ottawa's bureaucracy. Some people, he remarked, want to forget 'that there was such a thing as the Canadian Corps as soon as possible'. [45]

But other matters were incredibly hard to proceed with. Currie's frustration and disappointment increased daily. Even such a simple act as sending an official letter of thanks to British officers who had served with the Canadian Corps during the war seemed impossible to accomplish. Currie, of course, could and did communicate directly with these officers as former Corps Commander, but he wanted some official recognition of their service by the Canadian Government. He suggested to the Prime Minister in the spring of 1919 that such letters would be a gracious act, and he provided Borden with a list of British officers to whom the letters should be sent. Despite repeated reminders from Currie, they were never written. [46] Currie found the disparity between commanding a unit in war and serving in the Canadian forces in peace to be enormous. Disheartened by his failure to get through the endless red tape and bureaucracy of Ottawa, he observed that 'when conducting affairs in the field you simply went ahead and did what you thought was right and did it at once'. But as Inspector-General there seemed to be 'no

freedom of action: financial considerations, political considerations, personal considerations and all sorts of other things
retarding what one considers progress'. [47] This statement by the
Inspector-General may seem like the perennial cry of men of action who become deskbound, but it also accurately represents the
difficulties faced by the Chief of Staff following a war.

Currie in fact had no quarrel with political issues taking
precedence over military questions. As a pre-war Militia officer
he knew that a certain amount of politicking and political influence was inevitable in military affairs in Canada. What he objected to was the notion that every decision on military matters
would be made in light of the political circumstances of the moment. 'In these days', he wrote, 'Governments ... do not lead the
people, they simply try to guess what the people want and
govern their policy and action accordingly.' [48] He was
particularly offended by the suggestion repeatedly advanced that
his own position of Inspector-General was, after all, a reward for
services previously rendered, and that he should keep his mouth
shut and be thankful.

As already indicated, Currie's method of making changes was
to encourage subordinates to put forward their own ideas and to
insist on criticism and comment from his staff. Invariably he insisted that his own ideas be subjected to the same critical analysis.
One idea, however, he was prepared to push above all others. He
had suffered, and he believed that all Canadian soldiers had suffered, throughout the war from the confusion which resulted
from divided authority and bifurcated chains of command. Even
after the reorganisation which established the Overseas Military
Forces of Canada, Currie always had had to deal with two
government departments. In peace-time the responsibility for the
defence of Canada rested with the Department of Militia and
Defence and the Department of Naval Service. In addition, an
Air Board had been created, and in April 1920, a order-in-council authorised the formation of the Canadian Air Force. Currie
had strongly advocated the creation of an independent air force
during the war, but it required little imagination to foresee that
there could easily be three departments and three Government
Ministers responsible for defence matters in the future. He believed that such division could only be inimical to the development
of all Canadian armed forces. It would foster rather than reduce
wasteful competition among the services for funds and un-

necessarily duplicate many services. More and more it seemed that much of the difficulty he encountered as Inspector-General stemmed from the overlapping bureaucracy in Ottawa which controlled various aspects of defence. Currie was convinced that a single Ministry of Defence which would be responsible for Navy, Militia and Air Services was the best possible solution to the difficulty. He placed his arguments directly before the Prime Minister and the Minister of Militia, and campaigned for a single Defence Department. [49]

There is no record of vigorous opposition to Currie's sugges-tion, which can perhaps be interpreted either as an indication of its importance or as a measure of the low priority which military matters had in the postwar period. In either case, no action was taken and the idea was killed by gentle neglect – or so it appeared for a time. In the words of Professor Eayrs, 'Currie's retirement from the armed forces deprived them of the principal advocate of a unified administration.' [50] In April 1920 Currie was offered the position of Principal and Vice-Chancellor of McGill University. Although he had doubts about his training and abili-ty to handle the job, his hesitation was only momentary. The frustrations and disappointments of peace-time military service, no doubt, hastened his decision. The first Canadian general in the Canadian Forces left the army at the age of forty-five feeling that his major suggestion for reform had been totally ignored. Reflec-ting on this fact, he observed to a friend,

> ... from the attitude of the people generally, and that of the Government in particular, I have come to the conclusion that it would be a long time before these ideas would result in anything practical. In a way it is a relief to get away from here. I always disliked intensely holding a Government position. There were many you know, both in Govern-ment, and outside of it, who considered that I was given the position of Inspector-General, as a reward, and I never relished being placed in such a position. [51]

In spite of the relief which he felt at leaving the service, Currie did not give up in his attempt to have a unified administration created. As soon as Mackenzie King replaced Meighen as Prime Minister, Currie wrote to him again outlining the advantages which would accrue from a unified administration. It is impossi-

ble to determine the extent to which Currie's advocacy of un-
ification influenced the decision, but it is a matter of record that
in 1922 the Department of Defence was created. However,
Currie's letter to Prime Minister King was as close to engaging in
politics as the former Corps Commander was to come.

Conflicts between soldiers and politicians during the First
World War produced profound problems for democracies.
Indeed, it is not too much to say that the modern conception of
civil-military relations owes a great debt to the experience of that
war. While Clemenceau's observation that 'war is too important
to be left to soldiers' has been accepted as perhaps the chief lesson
of 1914-18, most students now recognise that friction between
soldiers and politicians in the war was far more complicated than
simple differences over military strategy between professionals in
uniform and others in 'frock-coats'. Robert Blake suggested that
there were three major issues between government leaders and
soldiers in Britain; genuine differences of opinion on strategy,
real difficulties of communication between soldiers and politicians, and good old-fashioned conflicts between Liberals and
Conservatives, all of which 'disturbed relations between the
Government and the High Command during the First World
War'.[52] Less has been written on the relationship of soldiers and
politicians in the British colonies, perhaps because historians have
concentrated on the more important relationship evolving
between the British and Colonial Governments. But there were
also important differences between colonial soldiers and their
governments.

Fortunately, in Canada these conflicts were neither as profound
nor as tragic as those which occurred in Britain. If Currie's case is
typical, neither politicians nor soldiers were blameless, but one
may believe that the soldiers have been the more misunderstood.

Notes

1. Public Archives of Canada (cited hereafter as PAC), Borden Papers, 'Memo re
   General Currie's Remarks to the delegates to the Tax Conference and Civil Servants Research Institute of Canada, September 11th, 1924'.
2. PAC, Currie Papers, Currie to King, 1 September 1923.
3. Roger Graham, *Arthur Meighen: A Biography* (Toronto, 1963), II, p. 265.
4. PAC, Currie Papers, Currie to Richardson, 6 January 1924.
5. *Ibid.*, Currie to Nelson, 9 December 1925.
6. *Ibid.*, Currie to Beattie, 8 February 1920.

7. W.A.B. Douglas, 'Why Does Canada Have Armed Forces?', *International Journal*, vol. XXX (Spring, 1975), p. 263.
8. Robert Craig Brown, 'Sir Robert Borden, The Great War and Anglo-Canadian Relations', in John S. Moir (ed.), *Character and Circumstance: Essays in Honour of Donald Grant Creighton* (Toronto, 1970), p. 201.
9. Colonel G.W.L. Nicholson, *Canadian Expeditionary Force 1914-1919: Official History of the Canadian Army in the First World War* (Ottawa, 1962), p. 203.
10. Desmond Morton, *The Canadian General, Sir William Otter* (Toronto, 1974), p. 180.
11. Nicholson, *Canadian Expeditionary Force*, p. 205.
12. A.J.P. Taylor, *Beaverbrook* (New York, 1972), p. 87. Taylor claims that in this position Beaverbrook was 'a go-between who could write his own instructions'.
13. Nicholson, p. 357. Emphasis added.
14. See John Swettenham, *To Seize the Victory: The Canadian Corps in World War I* (Toronto, 1950).
15. Hugh M. Urquhart, *Arthur Currie: The Biography of a Great Canadian* (Toronto, 1950), pp. 108-9.
16. PAC, Creelman Papers, Diary, 19 November, p. 77. Somewhat later the same writer observed that 'with Sam out of the way, promotion is likely to be according to seniority and ability, which is all that anyone can ask for'. *Ibid.*, xx, 8 December 1916, p. 78.
17. House of Lords Library, Beaverbrook Papers, Hughes to Aitken, 28 May 1916.
18. PAC, Currie Papers, Currie to McGillicudy, n.d.
19. PAC, Perley Papers, Perley to Borden, 9 June 1917.
20. *Ibid.*, Borden to Perley, 13 June 1917.
21. A.M.J. Hyatt, 'Sir Arthur Currie and Conscription: A Soldier's View', *The Canadian Historical Review*, vol. L (September 1969), pp. 293-4.
22. Hanson W. Baldwin, *World War I: An Outline History* (New York, 1962), p. 141.
23. A.W. Currie, 'Interim Report on Operations 1918', in *Report of the Minister of Overseas Military Forces of Canada, 1918*, p.12.
24. Interview with General A.G.L. McNaughton, 27 March 1963.
25. Currie, 'Interim Report', p. 112.
26. PAC, Kemp Papers, Currie to Laurence, 27 March 1918.
27. *Ibid.*, Kemp to Derby, 29 March 1918.
28. Robert Blake (ed.), *The Private Papers of Douglas Haig 1914-1919* (London, 1952), p. 319.
29. PAC, Currie Papers, Currie Diary, 11 April 1918.
30. *Ibid.*
31. *Ibid.*, 1 March 1918.
32. *Ibid.*, 14 April 1918.
33. Blake, *Private Papers*, p.p. 303-4.
34. *Men and Power, 1917-1918* (London, 1956), p. xvii.
35. *Reputations, Ten Years After* (Boston, 1928), p. 290.
36. 'Douglas Haig's Diary', *Canadian Army Journal* (July 1953), p. 108.
37. Henry Borden (ed.), *Robert Laird Borden: His Memoirs* (Toronto, 1938), II, p. 77.
38. PAC, Borden Papers, Secret Memorandum, 15 June 1918.
39. Robert Craig Brown, 'Sir Robert Borden, The Great War and Anglo-Canadian Relations', p. 209.
40. *Ibid.*
41. House of Commons, *Debates*, 4 March 1919.
42. *Ibid.*, 7 July 1919.
43. PAC, Currie Papers, Currie to Farmar, 5 January 1920.
44. *Ibid.*, Currie to MacBrien, 12 April 1920.
45. *Ibid.*, Currie to Farmar, 5 January 1920.
46. Urquhart, *Arthur Currie*, pp. 282-3.

47. PAC, Currie Papers, Currie to Paterson, 24 February 1920.
48. *Ibid.*, Currie to Radcliffe, 6 July 1920.
49. *Ibid.*, Currie to Meighen, 5 August 1920, Currie to Guthrie, 5 August 1920.
50. James Eayrs, *In Defence of Canada: From the Great War to the Great Depression* (Toronto, 1964), p. 225.
51. PAC, *Currie Papers,* Currie to Urquhart, 7 June 1920.
52. Blake, *Private Papers,* p. 34.

The Royal Naval College of Canada, 1911-22

G. WILLIAM HINES

> There shall be an institution for the purpose of imparting a complete education in all branches of naval science, tactics and strategy.
> Such institution shall be known as the Naval College of Canada, and shall be located at such place as the Governor in Council may determine. [1]

On 12 January 1910, the Liberal government of Sir Wilfrid Laurier introduced into the House of Commons a Naval Service Bill, providing for the creation of a Canadian navy through the purchase of several warships and through the recruiting and training of Canadian naval personnel. It was evident at the time that Canada would have to rely on Britain to furnish officers for her new naval force until she could supply her own; and it was obvious, too, that, so long as such a state of affairs continued to exist, Canada could never aspire to complete sovereign control of her own navy. To reduce the presence and influence of a British officer corps in her naval service, Canada required some means of obtaining an adequate number of well-trained *Canadian* naval officers in as short a period as was practicable. The Liberals were quick to recognise the significance of this requirement. Thus, one section of the Naval Service Bill advocated the foundation of a Canadian naval college 'to train the lads who would later on become officers in the proposed Canadian ships', [2] in the expectation that the college would eventually supply enough Canadian officers to obviate the need for British personnel. [3] With the passage of the Liberal naval legislation through the Commons on 20 April 1910, the establishment of the suggested naval college was assured; and on 7 January 1911, it was officially proclaimed the Royal Naval College of Canada* by the Director of the Naval Service, Rear-Admiral C.E. Kingsmill. [4]

---

* Hereafter RNCC.

It was intended by the Government that the RNCC should commence operations early in 1911. First, however, several considerations had to be resolved. Not the least of these was the question as to where the new naval college should be located. In the course of the parliamentary debate on the Naval Service Bill, it had become clear that Laurier would model the college after the Royal Military College at Kingston;[5] and, accordingly, the suggestion that the two institutions be situated side by side in Kingston was not, perhaps, a surprising one.[6] But Laurier himself seems to have favoured Halifax as the site for the RNCC almost from the start.[7] As early as June 1910 Admiral Kingsmill was investigating the problem of temporary quarters for naval college cadets and staff in Halifax.[8] Kingston, it would appear, was never seriously examined by the Liberals as a prospective location for the college, if only because better, cheaper, and more immediate facilities for RNCC personnel accommodation were available in the form of the old naval hospital at Halifax. From January 1911, therefore, until its destruction in December 1917, the latter became a 'temporary' site for the naval college.

There remained the problems of selecting cadets and staff for the RNCC. At the time of the discussion of the naval service legislation in the Commons, the conditions of cadet entry into the proposed college had not yet been determined; Laurier and Frederick Borden, the Minister of Militia, could say only that such conditions would presumably be identical with those governing entry into the Kingston military institution.[9] Not until 26 September 1910 did an Order-in-Council set out the requirements for cadet admission to the naval college. Applicants for cadet vacancies would have to be British subjects between fourteen and sixteen years of age; they would write a common competitive examination and then pass into the college in order of achievement up to the number of vacancies available, provided that they could successfully pass a medical fitness test. Beyond these qualifications, and unlike the case affecting the cadets at the Royal Military College, the RNCC cadets would have to serve for a length of time in the new Canadian navy following their graduation. Sir Frederick Borden explained the distinction:

The Royal Military College was established at a time when there was no permanent force at all in Canada. The object was very largely to give an opportunity for military training and a course of teaching which would fit young men to enter civil life, or the engineering professions, and at the same time give them instructions in military matters which would be of use when they became part of the active militia. An arrangement was also made with the imperial authorities by which six or seven commissions were given every year to the best men coming out of the Royal Military College. The position now is entirely different. We are starting with a permanent militia, we have no officers at all, and this course is to be limited to the preparation of cadets for the naval service and that only. [10]

In return, the Government bound itself to provide commissions and appointments for naval college graduates with appropriate qualifications.

With no naval officers of her own, Canada had to turn to the Royal Navy for officers to fill the principal service positions at the RNCC. The result was that, late in 1910, three retired British naval officers found their way to the new Canadian naval college – Lieutenants R.A. Yonge and Edward A. E. Nixon and Commander Edward H. Martin. The Royal Navy also supplied the college's Director of Studies, Naval Instructor Basil S. Hartley, and certain other subordinate members of the RNCC's teaching staff. Three Canadian civilians, Lorne N. Richardson, Albert G. Hatcher, and John J. Penny, rounded off the college's academic community as the masters respectively of mathematics, sciences and languages." Of the RNCC's original staff, Nixon, Richardson, Hatcher and Penny were to remain with the college until its closing in 1922, and Hartley until 1921, thereby ensuring a continuity of educational and administrative policy and a staff identification with all aspects of RNCC life that benefited the cadets of every term from the first to the last.

Before outlining the history of the naval college during its years of operation, the issue as to who actually commanded it throughout those years should be resolved. From 1 October 1910 until 31 December 1917 Commander Martin was the Captain--in-Charge of the Halifax Dockyard and Senior Naval Officer, Halifax, in which capacity he was also the officer-in-charge of the RNCC. During the same period Nixon was Martin's deputy, and, from January 1918 to June 1922, himself the officer--in-charge of the naval college. The evidence is clear, however,

that, while Martin was nominally in command of the college
from 1911 to 1917, it was Nixon who acted as its actual
administrator.[11] Rear-Admiral F.L. Houghton, a cadet at the
RNCC from 1913-15, recalls that the boys rarely caught sight of
Martin, and were invited to tea with him just once in their $2\frac{1}{2}$
years at the college.[12] The true state of affairs respecting the
college leadership, in fact, is effectively summarised by Commodore G.M. Hibbard, a classmate of Houghton's, in his statement that 'to all intents and purposes, we considered Commander
Nixon to be the moving spirit of the college'.[13] For most of the
cadets who attended the RNCC at some stage in its existence,
Nixon, quite simply, seems to have been the very personification
of the college – the driving force behind it, and the apostle of the
standards by which all the boys lived.[14]

Since Nixon commanded the RNCC during its entire history,
an understanding of his nature is essential to a proper appreciation of the college itself. Born in Ireland in 1878, he had joined
the Royal Navy in 1892, and subsequently served in the North
Atlantic, East Indies, and Mediterranean before applying for service at Canada's new naval institution. With his application
accepted, he had promptly retired from the Royal Navy.[15]
Nixon's appointment to the RNCC, therefore, marked a significant departure from his former naval way of life; and it seems
evident that, from the start, he intended to employ his position to
make a success of his new charge. Certainly it could not have
prospered as it did without his efforts on its behalf.

'Decisive in action, frosty in manner, sardonic in humour', as
Rear-Admiral P.B. Brock, RN, a cadet from 1917-20, describes
him,[16] Nixon was always by far the most impressive figure
among the RNCC staff members for the cadets. This was due in
part, of course, to the position of authority which he occupied
and to his own strong belief in rigid naval discipline. 'He was a
strict disciplinarian, a physical fitness fanatic, and a strong
believer in naval tradition', observes Admiral Houghton; 'under
his piercing eyes and bushy eyebrows, our little lives were
ordered from day to day.' To Rear-Admiral H.F. Pullen, a cadet
at the RNCC from 1920-22, 'he seemed of another world, barely
mortal', while Captain B.D.L. Johnson, a classmate of Pullen's,
remembers how it was said that Nixon 'could look one in the
eyes and tell if one's shoes were properly polished'.[17]

Beyond the natural awe and respect in which he was held by

the cadets by virtue of his rank and authority, however, the Commander was also greatly admired by them for his personal code of ethics and obvious love for the naval college. The morality to which he expected all cadets to adhere became, in many cases, the object of their emulation in later life. 'Throughout my service life', insists Vice-Admiral H.G. DeWolf, a cadet from 1918-21, 'I was influenced in thought and action by the question "what would Commander Nixon think?" "Would Nix be pleased?" ' At the RNCC, DeWolf believes, 'I gained a moral outlook or philosophy, and an appreciation of right and wrong, good and bad, fair play, etc. under Commander Nixon's guiding influence, which has served me well, and which I have felt no urge to change.'[18] Not that it was always easy for the cadets to live up to Nixon's high standards. As one cadet from the 1914-17 period recalls:

> Commander Nixon, not really understanding Canadian Sports, had an idea that when an ice-hockey player was awarded a penalty of two minutes in the penalty box for tripping, etc. ... he had brought dishonour on the Navy and therefore could never play on the team again. Hence the Naval College team was rapidly denuded of players!

Where the manly sports were concerned, however, the Commander was of a different fibre:

> Once a year an Assault-at-Arms was held. This was a show to which Senior Officers' friends were asked, and was akin to a spectacle in a Roman Arena, inasmuch that no cadet could give in, no matter how much blood was shed. Commander Nixon always said:- 'Box On' when appealed to. I think this was to impress his guests of our bravery. Nowadays, I am told, boxing has been abolished at Service Colleges, in case the Boys' beauty might be marred. I don't imagine this gory spectacle did us much good in any case.[19]

Conditions in the RNCC sick-bay, according to the same writer, were made so tough by Commander Nixon to prevent malingering 'that cadets were literally scared to go sick'. Altogether, the Commander was indeed the most unforgettable character for most of the cadets, as he was for Admiral DeWolf; and the latter

accurately sums up Nixon's impact on the naval college boys
when he attributes to Nixon 'an equally profound influence on
most of his cadets'[20] as he had on DeWolf himself.

1911–14

Despite its unfinished condition, the naval college opened for the
first time on 19 January 1911, when twenty cadets entered its
doors – the successful applicants from the thirty-four who had
written the RNCC admission examination the preceding
November.[21] Like their successors, the first cadets received a
systematic and intensive instruction in navigation, seamanship
and pilotage, engineering, applied electricity, physics, chemistry,
mechanics, mathematics, English, history (including naval
history), geography, French and German.[22] Seamanship was
clearly the most important teaching subject, comprising, in the
words of Admiral Houghton, 'knots and splices, bends and
hitches, rope and wire splicing, navigation and pilotage, ship
handling, ship construction, engineering and practical shopwork,
sailing and boatwork, and much more'. In seamanship instruction, recalls Commodore Hibbard, the sailing of service craft
played a big part – and with both Commander Nixon and the
college itself in possession of yachts, opportunities for cadet practice were frequent and welcome.[23] Academic choice for the boys,
however, was non-existent, Admiral Houghton remembers: 'you
jolly well had to learn everything they taught you or you were
OUT'.[24]

What 'spare' time the cadets possessed was taken up largely
with sports and recreation. There were never enough cadets in
residence at the same time to play rugger, but soccer, ice and
ground hockey, boatwork, boxing, wrestling, gymnastics,
baseball, fencing, lawn tennis, cutlass and rifle drill, and gunnery
were all popular among cadets and staff.[25] Extra curricular
activities included an official dance each term to which the cadets
could invite Halifax girls, and work on behalf of the cadet
college magazine *Sea Breezes*, first published in 1914.[26] In general,
however, remembers a contemporary cadet, there was little time
for favourite activities since 'these were established for you'.[27]

Discipline and punctuality at the RNCC were from its opening the orders of the day as far as the boys were concerned. Inside
as well as outside the college they never moved anywhere except

at the double, as a boy laboratory assistant at the college from 1911-16, Frank Hall, has testified:

> It was an amusing thing to watch the cadets in the morning just before the 9 o'clock gong. They would be gathered at the foot of the main staircase, brushing each other's uniforms for the last speck of dust, with one eye on the clock and the moment the gong rang there was a thunder of feet up the stairs to the dormitory for inspection by the commanding officer. For a few minutes there would be a silence, then a sharp command, a stamp of feet, and another thunderous rush of bodies down the stairs and to the study rooms, or perhaps to the engineering shops. . . . [28]

'I'm sure', contends Admiral Houghton, 'the strict routine inculcated in us all a lifelong respect for punctuality.' [29]

With a highly diversified curriculum, both academic and recreational, a superb commander, superior instructors, a promising career for its graduates, and government financial support, the RNCC was apparently off to a sound start with excellent prospects for further expansion. Recognition of the merits of the naval college was reflected in its early enrolment, which included the sons of a number of prominent and upper-class families. The interest of the latter, in fact, was essential to the very survival of the college, given the high fees and expenses entailed by attendance at the RNCC – so high, indeed, that a member of Parliament with a son at the college could feel himself justified in complaining about the cost. [30] Notwithstanding the growing interest in it, however, the college found its existence endangered within just two years of its inception.

This first crisis for the RNCC began with the advent of a Conservative government from the election of 1911. The new Prime Minister, Sir Robert Borden, was not inclined to pursue Laurier's naval policy as manifested by the enactment of the Naval Service Bill in 1910. As time passed, therefore, 'the Naval College was [placed] in an anomalous position, training lads for a Navy which was not being built and which was being allowed to disappear quietly'. [31] By the beginning of 1913, with the first cadet term ready to graduate from the college, it was evident that the Canadian cruisers to which they should have been attached for further instruction were in fact in no fit condition to receive them.

The problem was resolved temporarily when the British Admiralty agreed to accept the RNCC cadets concerned for further training on HMS *Berwick* for the period of a year. This, however, was merely a stopgap measure, recognised as such by all involved: and the naval college's future remained obscure. In September 1913 Admiral Kingsmill outlined the nature of the current problem to G.J. Desbarats, the Deputy Minister of the Naval Service:

> The original suggestion was that after completing a year's training [in the *Berwick*], those who were to qualify for Engineers should return to the Naval College and the others continue serving at sea. This scheme was proposed when it was understood that Canada's Dockyards would have advanced, that we would be building ships in Canada and that we would have sea-going ships of our own in which to further train these young Officers. As these plans have not materialised, I would suggest that the Admiralty be asked to allow these young officers to continue serving in one of the ships of the Imperial Service until they have completed their time for examination for the rank of Lieutenant, or until some further decision is arrived at by the Government as to their ultimate career.

The 'extraordinary condition of affairs now existing', Kingsmill warned, jeopardised the future careers of the cadets concerned, who had, after all, enlisted with the prospect of a solid naval occupation before them. 'I think that the least that can be done for them', he concluded,

> is to give them a chance to enter the profession for which they were designed and complete their training in such a way that they may, if they wish, qualify for the Imperial Service, and that arrangements may [so] be made with the Admiralty.[32]

In a memorandum of 29 September to J.D. Hazen, the Minister of Marine and Fisheries, Desbarats relayed Kingsmill's observations, and added:

> The various arrangements by which these young Canadians

are serving or being trained in Imperial ships have been made in a temporary manner and as expedients adopted to meet the pressing needs which arose from time to time. These arrangements do not correspond to any definite policy and there is a certain amount of restlessness and dissatisfaction among these young men on account of the uncertainty as to their prospects and as to the future which is before them. This uncertainty is having a very bad effect on the Halifax College, only four cadets having entered at the last term.

If, Desbarats noted, a Canadian navy or Coast Defence force was still to be created as Laurier had envisioned, 'then it would be well to continue the training of the Canadian cadets and Sub-Lieutenants[33] with a view to their taking service in the Canadian vessels'. However, he concluded:

If, on the other hand, it is not proposed to have a Canadian Navy or Coast Defence vessels manned by a Canadian organization, the wisdom of continuing indefinitely the training of a distinct corps of Canadian Naval Officers may well be doubted. The young men who are now training on Canadian lines should at a certain point by absorbed into the Imperial Service or discharged to Civil life. [34]

On the basis of these representations, Borden's government was compelled to examine the entire basis of the RNCC's existence. In December 1913 it was decided that the transformation in Canadian naval policy effected by the Conservatives had undermined the original *raison d'être* of the naval college, and that it should therefore be reconstituted by the Department of the Naval Service on a different basis. The new objective for the RNCC's instruction, Desbarats informed the Under-Secretary of State for External Affairs, would be

... to give boys an education in nautical subjects, including marine engineering, seamanship, navigation, pilotage and nautical surveying as well as in mathematics and scientific subjects, and thus train them for
(a) the Royal Navy   (b) the Hydrographic and Tidal Surveys
(c) the engineeering and scientific professions.

Those boys not entering the Royal Navy would complete their education in a university. [35]

By the end of January 1914 Hazen was referring in Parliament to these suggestions in response to criticism that the career prospects of the naval college cadets had been sacrificed by the Conservative government. [36]

The proposed arrangements were finalised when Britain's Admiralty agreed in April to accept up to eight RNCC cadets annually for sea training, provided that the two-year course of academic instruction at the naval college was extended to three to improve the cadets' readiness for their Royal Navy service. Simultaneously, the Department of the Naval Service resolved to inform new cadets entering the college in 1914 'that they were no longer obliged to serve in the Canadian navy and that the Canadian Government would not guarantee that they would receive Naval commissions'. [37] On 18 April 1914 a new Order-in-Council revised the conditions of cadet entry into the naval college in accordance with the agreement with the Admiralty, adding that, upon graduation, cadets would have to join the Canadian Naval Reserve. [38] Hazen announced the RNCC changes in the Commons on 5 May 1914. [39] It was quite true, he informed the Prime Minister in June, that uncertainty as to the future of the Canadian navy and as to the cadets' training for service in that navy had resulted in a comparatively low enrolment in the naval college over the past several years. However,

> ... now that these points have been cleared up it is hoped that there will be a good attendance at the College both by lads wishing to join the British Navy and by lads wishing to enter a technical profession and to enjoy the advantages of the technical, moral, and physical training which are given at the Halifax College. [40]

Such did matters stand with the RNCC at the outbreak of the First World War.

1914-17

Hazen's expectations notwithstanding, the naval college did not experience a substantial increase in its cadet enrolment during the first three years of the war. The principal reason for this may have been the fees charged the boys, which remained very high – some $450 for their first year and $325 their second and third years, exclusive of transportation costs to and from the college several times a year for cadets living outside Halifax. West Coast cadets were particularly hard hit by the latter expense, as one from the 1914-17 term remembers:

> The cadets from Halifax [paid] a ten cent fare to attend the College, while those from B.C. paid up to $150 each way, and there was always the question of going home for the bi-annual leave. The then Minister at Ottawa was most unsympathetic, and replied to one parent who asked for Government assistance with rail fare, that *He* only wanted *Gentlemen* as *Officers*. He didn't seem to understand one could be a gentleman, and still have no money. [41]

Whatever the factors responsible, new cadet enrolment in 1914 amounted to just eight, in 1915 to six, and in 1916 to fourteen – of which total one was discharged from the RNCC, three were withdrawn, and one went AWOL to fight with the Army in France. Not until 1917, when twenty new cadets entered the naval college, was there a resurgence of its former popularity; and the increase can be attributed, at least in part, to the impatience of young boys to join the war. Meanwhile, the RNCC experienced its first cadet losses due to the war late in 1914, when four graduates of the first college term of 1911 – Cann, Hatheway, Palmer and Silver – went down with H.M.S. *Good Hope* during the battle of Coronel. They were the first battle casualties of the Royal Canadian Navy. [42] One other first-term graduate, Maitland-Dougall, was killed in action while in command of HM Submarine *D-3* in March of 1918.

Throughout the 1914-17 period, the RNCC academic curriculum remained essentially unaltered from its pre-war state; but college sports were revolutionised with the introduction of rugby in the fall of 1916. From the time the cadets were awakened at 0635 until 'lights out' at 2100, recalls one contemporary, life resembled that of Trappist monks. So heavily regimented were the wartime cadets, in fact, that the annual social highlights for the 'inmates of the Naval College' amounted to just 'one heavily chaperoned picnic in the Summer and one ditto dance in winter'.[43] In sum, the RNCC facilities were very good, approximating, it has been suggested, those of the Royal Naval colleges within the restrictions of a much shorter course and mediocre facilities.[44]

This latter short-coming, coupled with the rise in naval college enrolment in the autumn of 1917, came to cast an unfavourable light on the suitability of all existing RNCC facilities. Small and of a makeshift character,[45] these had barely been adequate for their purpose at the opening of the college in 1911; and by late 1917, they had become entirely inappropriate to the existing personnel requirements. As the Director of Studies argued in a memorandum to Captain Martin in October of 1917, the current classroom accommodation had always been made to serve 'in the hope that something better would be soon forthcoming'. A new classroom had alleviated the situation only slightly; the others remained 'insufficient in number, size, and natural light and in some cases defective in ventilation and heating'. More modern facilities should be constructed, he submitted, 'now that the future of the College seems secure'.[46]

Prophetic words, indeed. For the year 1917, in retrospect, marked the peak of the college's fortunes, presenting it at first with its highest level of success, and then reducing it to the poorest state of its existence. Less than two months after Hartley's comments, the RNCC was demolished in the great Halifax Explosion, and compelled to seek new facilities at another location. Thereafter, the security of its existence was never firmly re-established; and within five years, it was to close, the victim of reduced government appropriations.

1917-22

On the morning of 6 December 1917, cadet term examinations were to begin. Just before nine o'clock − when a good many boys were still trying to cram a last few points[47]− one cadet noticed a ship on fire about half a mile from the college. At five past nine, the cadets dispersed to their various gunrooms to prepare for inspection, a number lingering to observe the fire in the harbour. Three minutes later, the burning ship exploded in Canada's greatest disaster of the century.

The air was filled immediately with flying glass splinters and other debris, and almost all the RNCC cadets and staff members

were injured to some extent by them. In the instance of the
junior cadets, whose gunroom faced away from the direction of
the explosion, the injuries proved comparatively minor, appear-
ing at first to be 'much worse than they actually were'. [48] The
seniors, however, exposed as they were by their gunroom to the
full force of the explosion, suffered much more seriously; several
were badly scarred for life; and one could not rejoin his term until May of the following year. The staff fared worst of all – one
petty officer was blinded, and Nixon himself was gravely
wounded about the head:

> My head was the only part of me that was damaged. I was
> thrown against an ordinary wooden door which was shut,
> and door and I came down together. At first they had to
> devote most of their attention to saving my eyes, which
> they did successfully. My other little cuts became badly in-
> fected and I developed erysipelas, like a lot of other people
> . . . . [49]

It was a small miracle that no one was killed. But the College
itself was so badly damaged that it eventually had to be condemned. As Admiral Brock described it at the time:

> The building was a horrible mess. The floors were covered
> a foot deep with plaster, glass, woodwork, papers, and
> countless fragments no longer recognizable. Window panes
> and sashes had been blown in and small fragments of glass
> were scattered everywhere. [50]

In the new wing at the north end of the naval hospital, the roof
was lifted clear away from the north wall and the floor
collapsed. [51] Not the least impressive feature of the damage was
the huge section of boiler-plate from the exploded ship which fell
through the college roof into the study where the cadets would
have been writing their exams a few minutes later. [52]

Within a few days of the Halifax Explosion, the uninjured
RNCC cadets were all sent home on leave over Christmas while
the Government pondered the fate of the institution. With the
naval hospital unfit for habitation and the city devastated, the
first priority was to settle upon some location other than Halifax
where the cadets might resume their studies in the forthcoming

term. Thus, only a few days after the explosion, Admiral Kingsmill and the Department of the Naval Service were examining the feasibility of boarding the RNCC cadets temporarily with their counterparts at the Royal Military College in Kingston.

As early as 17 December, Kingsmill himself visited RMC to ascertain whether suitable accommodation for the naval college cadets could be found there. At the time of his visit, a new cadet dormitory was in the last stages of construction, and Kingsmill quickly seized upon the idea of utilising this structure for his purposes. Although the Admiral was privately convinced that 'the instruction in engineering [at RMC] will not be of such high standard as that obtained at Halifax', [53] he informed Colonel Perreau, Commandant of the military college, on 24 December that the matter had definitely been settled: the RNCC cadets would be going to Kingston for the spring of 1918. [54]

Perreau confessed himself delighted, promising Kingsmill that all at RMC would do everything to make the temporary attachment of the naval cadets a pleasant one – the more the two services could be brought together in such fashion, in fact, the more admiration and respect they would acquire for one another. [55] He would even ensure that the RNCC cadets had their own drill shed. [56] But the key to the understanding about the prospective naval-military partnership at RMC lay in the word 'temporary'. Accommodation for the naval cadets, Perreau informed the Admiral, would be available only until 1 August 1918, after which he would require their dormitory space for his own new recruits. [57]

Obviously, therefore, the RNCC cadets would be tolerated officially at RMC for just a few months. This left Kingsmill with the unenviable task of selecting in a short time a new site which the naval college might occupy late in 1918. As early as the tenth of December, he had been considering this problem when he asked Nixon whether he could look after Esquimalt Yard as well as the college – a query that indicated a possible RNCC move to Esquimalt. This location he referred to again in January 1918, in a memorandum to the Minister of the Naval Service. At the same time, Halifax remained a viable site for the re-establishment of the college, since the naval hospital was still standing with walls and roof apparently in good condition. [58] Finally, there was the alternative of Kingston itself, an option which Kingsmill himself preferred 'because it was more or less central in geographical location, close to the Government in Ottawa, and positioned on the natural naval training site of Lake Ontario'.[59] Thus, after eight years, the prospect that the naval college might be situated in Kingston had been resurrected for consideration.

By mid-February 1918, sketch plans had been prepared for C.C. Ballantyne, the Minister of the Naval Service, by the Department of Public Works, calling for a naval college with double the capacity (104 cadets) of the old institution (45 cadets) at an approximate cost of half a million dollars. A crossroad in the development of the RNCC had been reached; advice was needed, the Minister informed Borden on 13 February, on whether to rebuild the college on such an expanded scale or to restrict it to its current, more limited dimensions. Ballantyne himself considered the education provided by the RNCC excellent, and favoured the expansion of the naval college 'for the purpose of furthering the cause of scientific education and of providing a certain number of young Canadians with an opportunity of entering the Naval Service'. He noted too that the new college would also reduce the *per capita* operational cost from $3,-000 to $3,500 to just $2,000. However, he refused to put forward a recommendation to such effect without the Prime Minister's concurrence in the projected rebuilding scheme. The latter replied that he tended to support the Minister's proposal for the RNCC reconstruction at Halifax, but that inability to determine a naval defence programme and financial stringencies would together make it necessary to discuss the issue in Council.[60]

In the next two months, Kingsmill's own preference for Kingston as the new site for the naval college – a preference assisted immeasurably by the fact that the RNCC cadets and staff were already situated in that city – appears to have gained ground with the Department of the Naval Service in Ottawa, if only for reasons of expediency. By May, Colonel Perreau had become aware of rumours that the RNCC might erect additional temporary buildings and remain billetted with RMC for an indefinite period. He was greatly alarmed by such a prospect. In a memorandum of 28 May to the Secretary of the Militia Council, Perreau insisted that the continued presence of the naval college cadets at RMC into a second term of instruction would entail a considerable reduction in admissions to RMC itself. Worse, that presence would also create serious friction between the naval and military cadets at the college, since tension was inevitable if the interests of the military institution were to be so seriously threatened. If the naval college must remain in Kingston, he asserted, then let it be located at a site other than the grounds of RMC [61] Perreau's forceful presentation swung the Department of Militia and Defence behind his plea, in opposition to the interests of the Naval Service. On 8 June the former informed him that a meeting of 3 June between the Minister of Marine, the Minister of Militia and Defence, the Adjutant-General, and the Master-General of the Ordnance had resolved the problem of selecting a new site for the RNCC by deciding upon Esquimalt as its new home. [62]

During this same interval, the naval college cadets were boarded alongside their military counterparts; and, for most, the experience did not prove particularly pleasant. One RNCC cadet of the period recalled in 1955 that, understandably perhaps, the naval college boys were inclined to feel that they were on sufferance [63] – and it was probably axiomatic in any event, asserted a second in 1965, that unwanted guests did not bring out the best in anyone. [64] Despite the fact that their new accommodations at RMC were far superior to those furnished by their old quarters in Halifax, the RNCC cadets found themselves unable to enjoy a situation in which they possessed little in common with the military cadets who surrounded them. With the naval and military cadets eating separately and with their respective periods of instruction rotated [65] there were few opportunities for intermingling among them – and, in any case, different service training backgrounds and loyalties and substantial differences in ages between the RNCC and the more senior RMC cadets conspired to produce a mutual antipathy between them. 'Unless we happened to know a gentleman cadet privately, we never mixed with them', recalls Admiral Brock; [66] so that, if there was no direct friction between the naval and military cadets, then neither was there any direct contact between them.

The military college cadets particularly resented the fact that the RNCC visitors were occupying their newest, and best, residence in single rooms while they themselves were doubled up in the older buildings. [67] In time, many of them came to term the naval college boys 'water babies'. The latter, unimpressed with the bearing of the RMC cadets, were quick to respond with such expressions as 'Bullocks', 'Turkeys', 'Flat Feet', and, sar-castically, '*Gentlemen* Cadets'.[68] When it was rumoured for a time in April that the RNCC cadets would be spending their next term in Kingston, Brock remembers how he, with Kingston relatives, was 'very pleased, but the others were not and used much forcible language'. And, when, finally, it was resolved that the RNCC would not remain at RMC after all, rejoicing among the naval college cadets was widespread. 'I do not think that there was anyone else in the College who was even moderately sorry at leaving Kingston.'[69]

The move of the RNCC to Esquimalt in September, 1918, proved popular among the cadets, who found the climate much more to their liking than that of Halifax had been. Their new liv-ing quarters in the Esquimalt Naval Dockyard were not ready when they arrived, so for the first few weeks of the autumn term, they had to make their home in HMS *Rainbow*. Thereafter, college life settled quickly into its former Halifax routine. The calibre of academic instruction remained first class – equal to un-iversity teaching, in the opinion of one contemporary cadet – although classroom facilities, as at Halifax, were simple and bare-ly adequate to their task.[70] Rugby, in its turn, remained the established RNCC sport at the new location, with games being organised five or six times a week; after the demise of ice-hockey because of the warmer climate, it was rivalled only by boating in popularity. Morale at the naval college was high, enrolment was up, and the future of the RNCC again appeared promising. By May, 1919, Ballantyne was asserting that a new naval college would eventually be built at Halifax.[71] And the excellence of the RNCC was formally brought to the attention of the Department of the Naval Service by Admiral of the Fleet Viscount Jellicoe of Scapa in his report on his *Naval Mission to the Dominion of Canada* late in 1919:

> In setting up the Royal Naval College in 1911, and com-mencing the entry and training of officers on similar lines to those obtaining in England, Canada prepared a sound foun-dation for the provision of executive officers for a future navy. The value of such a step is apparent when it is realiz-ed that by this means Canada has trained 25 Lieutenants ranging in seniority up to $2\frac{1}{2}$ years, 15 Sub-Lieutenants, and 12 Midshipmen, whilst in addition there are 46 cadets under training.[72]

But the storm clouds of economic retrenchment were gathering again to menace the continued existence of the naval college. On 22 October 1920 the Naval Committee met in Ottawa to examine the question of its future. There, it was observed that, for some years to come, only six appointments annually in the Naval Service could be afforded naval college graduates, at the exorbitant cost of an estimated $30,000 each for their training. If, however, the RNCC were closed and the cadets for whom appointments could be found assigned directly by arrangement with the British Admiralty to Royal Navy training vessels, a saving in the vicinity of $170,000 per annum would be achieved. The other alternative was to permit the naval college to operate on a more economical basis by effecting reductions in its staff. On 28 October these considerations were forwarded to the Minister of the Naval Service, who decided to keep the RNCC open for the present. But the following day, Commander Nixon was requested by the Naval Secretary to proceed to Ottawa to advise the Department on what economies might be effected in the operation of the naval college. [73]

The writing was on the wall; and, significantly, the cadets themselves were beginning to reveal their awareness of it. Up to the end of 1918, all RNCC graduates had chosen a naval career. But, commencing in 1919, several turned to civilian professions following their graduation, taking advantage of the opportunity afforded by McGill University and the University of Toronto to enter as second-year students. In the autumn of 1919, one cadet entered McGill; seven more followed in the autumn of 1920, and three entered the University of Toronto in the autumn of 1921. [74] By September of that year, too, if the experience of L. C. Hyndman, a cadet at the time, is any judge, it was evident to the naval college boys that they would be unable to continue in the naval service beyond the following June. [75]

Such, indeed, was the case; the 1921-2 term proved the last year of operation for the naval college. Rumours about its impending closing had been circulating since 1921; and on 3 April 1922 the Naval Secretary informed Nixon that the college would probably have to be closed shortly owing to reduced appropriations for the Naval Service for 1922-3. [76] This decision was confirmed by the new Director of the Naval Service, Commodore Walter Hose, on 1 May, with Hose adding that a scale of gratuities for the RNCC staff had been forwarded to the Minister for approval of Council. Nixon himself, stated Hose, would not be employed further by the Department after the termination of college operations.[77] On 22 May George P. Graham, the Minister of the Naval Service, outlined the situation to the Commons. There was little point, he insisted, in permitting existing RNCC cadets to complete their three-year course of instruction when no employment could be found for them in either the Canadian or British navies upon their graduation. A complement of sixty-five officers, instructors and civilians were currently engaged in training just forty-two cadets—and to what purpose if no naval careers existed for them?[78] Sentiment was not enough to justify the college's continuation. If the cadets were to be trained only for further university education, then they should commence their studies in the university itself and not in a naval college.

To its credit, the Department did its utmost to provide for the further civilian education of the naval college cadets. Thus, Desbarats despatched letters to the Deans of the Faculties of Applied Science at McGill University, the University of Toronto, Queen's University (19 May) and the University of British Columbia (2 June), asking that they accept second-year RNCC cadets into the first year of their Applied Science programmes. By 9 June, all had consented to do so;[79] and most of the cadets ultimately took advantage of this arrangement.

The RNCC closed its doors for the last time on 16 June 1922. 'How very sad it is', complained Hartley to Nixon,

> that the thing started with such infinite labour, watered and weeded with tears and care for eleven years and which had sprung up into the thriving plant bearing such noble fruit should be cut down by a damned upstart of a worm [Hose].[80]

Despite Hose's promise to Nixon that all the naval college staff members would be provided for, only the officers received gratuities from the Department, as Nixon noted bitterly the following year.[81] He himself died just two years after the closing of the college. For the next twenty years, until the opening of the Royal Canadian Naval College in September 1942, in response to the wartime demand for trained officers, Canadian naval cadets would be instructed in the ships and establishments of the Royal Navy.[82] Forty years later, the last ex-cadet on active duty with the RCN (R.A. Wright) retired as a Rear-Admiral.[83]

Assessment

During its years of operation from 1911-22, the Royal Naval College of Canada cost the taxpayers an estimated total of $1,453,000.[84] For this expenditure, it was able to graduate 150 cadets, almost half of whom subsequently pursued naval careers. Sixteen of the RNCC graduates ultimately achieved the rank of commander, 20 of the rank of captain, 6 that of commodore, 14 the rank of rear-admiral, and 5 that of vice-admiral and Chief of the Naval Staff. One, P. W. Brock, became a rear-admiral in the Royal Navy.[85] Thus, almost one in six of the naval college cadets rose to hold flag rank; and the fact that most of the senior officers who directed the Royal Canadian Navy in the Second World War and in the immediate post-war years were RNCC graduates must attest favourably to the calibre of the institution. Other cadets attained prominence in legal, political, engineering and related civilian fields.

More than anything else, the cadets appear to have benefited from the high sense of strict, but equitable discipline, of comradeship, and of proper behaviour that the college instilled in them. This discipline was of the sort, recall Commodore Hibbard and Admiral Houghton, which promoted self-respect and teamwork and a personal belief that under no circumstances must the RNCC be let down. Throughout their later careers, many cadets sought to subscribe to the code of conduct that Commander Nixon inspired in them all.[86] L. C. Hyndman summarises the principal virtues of the cadet training at the naval college:

> Aspects which impressed me most could probably be said to be discipline, order, decisiveness, decency, fair treatment, and fair punishment, respect for established authority when properly exercised, precision, organization, punctuality, tidiness, cleanliness, and like qualities.[87]

If the cadets tended to be unimpressed by anything in their RNCC experience, it was perhaps by the hazing of junior by senior cadets practised there. In his 1918 diary, Brock set down several aspects of the hazing system:

> We were always to run past the seniors' gunroom, to give way to them on all occasions, to wait until they had all

entered the messroom before going in ourselves, and to let them have the seats in the bootroom. We had to stand at attention in their gunroom and run their errands for them. [88]

A harmless enough arrangement, it would seem; 'fagging duties were trivial, and physical punishment (a few cuts with a cane) was at best nominally based on some disciplinary offence'. [89] Harmless, that is to say, if Hyndman's recollection was true that 'the majority of seniors were generously disposed toward juniors although necessarily insistent that their reasonable commands be obeyed and no nonsense'. [90] Where the system ceased to have any merit, however, occurred when seniors abused their privileges respecting the junior boys. Ex-cadets recall how hazing could be excessive, even savage, with the least able (and therefore the most punished) junior cadets the worst bullies in their senior years. For at least one naval college cadet, the hazing became 'a really black mark against the RNCC, probably carried out in accordance with old customs by unthinking young men'. [91]

In the years immediately following their graduation from the naval college, those cadets bent on pursuing a naval career were required to serve in warships of the Royal Navy. It is interesting, therefore, and a valid test of the adequacy of the RNCC's system of instruction, to observe how the Canadian midshipmen compared to their British counterparts in the execution of their shipboard duties aboard British vessels. Commodore Hibbard remembers how the Canadian midshipmen in HMS *Erin* were often given preference over their British colleagues of equal seniority; in fact, their captain recommended their early promotion to Sub-Lieutenant. For Admiral Houghton, there was no trouble in holding his own with his Royal Navy opposite numbers in naval knowledge and in general education. 'Our professional competence', he recalls in retrospect, 'was certainly equal to theirs; and in some ways, I believe we were a bit more sophisticated and surer of ourselves.' Commander Pressey notes simply that he was treated by the British officers 'like one of their own'; while another cadet insists that, after his experiences at the RNCC, his treatment in the Royal Navy was actually luxurious. Although Admiral Pullen was the lone Canadian midshipman among 1,100 officers and men on HMS *Hood*, he was able to hold his own with his British colleagues and 'was never made to feel inferior to them'. [92] And Admiral DeWolf describes his own experience in HMS *Resolution*:

> We were received kindly enough – though we joined an
> already overcrowded gun-room. There were four
> Australians, a New Zealander, and a South African already
> there, and the Colonial influence was strong! We were a
> year older than the R.N. midshipmen of our seniority, on
> the average, and generally stronger, and made a major con-
> tribution in the athletic field. This undoubtedly helped us in
> our relation with the ship's officers. We were considered
> 'quaint' – but good! I think the only thing we lacked in
> comparison with our R.N. contemporaries was an un-
> derstanding of big-ship routine, and we soon learned this
> the hard way! ... I would say that we were given the same
> consideration by the R.N. Officers as was given their own
> midshipmen.[93]

Admiral Brock notes that a Royal Navy captain was willing to
recommend him for transfer to that navy in 1921, immediately
after his graduation from the RNCC, and that without his Canadian naval college background, he could not have made the transition. In his view, too:

> The short answer to the value placed by the R.N. on my
> R.N.C.C. background is that the 1st class certificate I got
> there counted exactly the same for my seniority as a Lieute-
> nant as if I had got it at R.N.C. Dartmouth.[94]

How valuable was the RNCC background of the cadets to
their later naval careers? One remarks that 'no Naval Education
ever helped make money, except through the marriage route – I
ended up about where I expected'. Admiral Pullen believes that
his RNCC experience had nothing to do with his advancement
in the pre-war Royal Canadian Navy – but notes that 'certainly
there was a common bond with our seniors who were all ex--
cadets RNCC'. For Captain B.D.L. Johnson, 'my RNCC education was sufficient to serve me on my life's path when
supplemented by the College of Hard Knocks'; and in the opinion of Admiral DeWolf, his naval college background was
'most assuredly' beneficial to his advancement in the service.
Commodore Hibbard contends that the training at the RNCC

was eminently suitable for naval service and civil career alike; and Commander G.M. Mitchell also maintains that anyone who attended the naval college 'could not but be helped in the development of any career'. Captain J.R. Mitchell may well sum up best the advantages of an education at the RNCC for later life:

> The education, academically and physically, was of such a nature that any young man who was fortunate enough to be able to be part of it could not help but be improved, and benefited no matter what career he followed. [95]

The naval college, wrote Admiral Kingsmill to Nixon in 1920, 'is the only part of the Naval Service that I regret ceasing to have anything to do with'; and his son remembers well his distress at the news that it would be closed. [96] Most of the RNCC cadets were similarly chagrined, and are inclined to agree with Hyndman that the closing of the college was a distinct loss, not only to the naval service, but to Canada itself. It was a stupid thing to do, observes Admiral Pullen – even if, as Commander G.M. Mitchell points out, the Royal Canadian Navy was so small and costly at the time that 'there was not much else that could be done'. [97] One cadet observes that he has been looking askance at politicians ever since the closing of the RNCC, for the simple reason that the Royal Military College did not close up as well. Perhaps Admiral Houghton's remarks are a fitting epitaph for the naval college:

> During the College's twelve years of existence, it gave excellent early training to 148 young Canadians, some 60 of whom were still serving in 1939; and the majority of these formed the professional nucleus of a Service which in four years grew to *sixty* times its pre-war size and became, in numbers of men and ships, the third largest Navy in the world. If that isn't a credit to our early training I don't know what is. [98]

Notes

1. Gilbert Norman Tucker, *The Naval Service of Canada*, 2 vols. (Ottawa: King's Printer, 1952), 1, Appendix 5, p. 382. Section 32, subsections 1 and 2 of the Naval Service Act of 1910.

2. From a lecture from C.C. Ballantyne, Minister of Marine and Fisheries, to Robert Laird Borden, Prime Minister, 13 February 1918. Borden Papers. File No. M.G. 26 H2(f), vol. 316, pp. 130063-9, in the Public Archives. The object of the College, asserted Sir Frederick Borden in Parliament in 1910, was simply 'to fit young men for service as officers in the navy'. Canada, Parliament, House of Commons, *Debates,* vol. 93 (19 April 1910), col. 7489–90.

3. See Tucker, p. 152.

4. File R.G. 24 vol. 5596 (N.S.S. 23-1-1), 'Miscellaneous Data and Correspondence Relating to Royal Naval College of Canada', in the Public Archives.

5. Laurier in the House of Commons, *Debates,* vol. 93 (4 May 1910), col. 8840.

6. Mr. Edwards in the House of Commons, *ibid.* (19 April 1910). col. 7488. This suggestion was to be made again after the destruction of the RNCC in December 1917. See further.

7. Laurier, *Debates,* col. 7487.

8. Memorandum prepared by Kingsmill for the Deputy Minister of Marine and Fisheries, 14 June 1910, in File No. R.G. 24 vol. 5596 (N.S.S. 23-1-1), Public Archives.

9. House of Commons, *Debates,* vol. 93 (19 April 1910), col. 7489. Nor had conditions been determined in May. Laurier, *Debates* (4 May 1910), col. 8840.

10. *Ibid.* (19 April 1910), col. 7489.

11. This is the opinion of the Naval Historian in agreement with the views of the CNS of the time. Memorandum on 'Photographs of Commanding Officers - RNC of C, etc.' to the Commodore, RCN Barracks, Halifax, from the Naval Secretary, 25 July 1952, File 1700-120/2 vol. 1 (N.S. 1788-110/1) in the Directorate of History, Department of National Defence.

12. Letter to the author.

13. Letter to the author.

14. Vice-Admiral H.G. DeWolf, Rear-Admiral H.F. Pullen, R. Wolfenden, letters to the author.

15. Personal information supplied by Captain C.P. Nixon, RCN (Ret.), Commander Nixon's son.

16. Letter to the author.

17. Letters to the author.

18. Letter to the author.

19. Letter to the author.

20. Letter to the author.

21. Report of the Department of the Naval Service for the fiscal year ending 31 March 1911, in File No. 1700-120/2 vol. 1 in the Directorate of History, DND. See also Commander E.H. Martin to Kingsmill, 18 January 1911, in File No. R.G. 24 vol. 5596 (N.S.S. 23-1-1) in the Public Archives.

22. For the curriculum see the speech of J.D. Hazen, Minister of Marine and Fisheries, in the House of Commons, 27 March 1915, *Debates,* vol. 120, col. 1615.

23. Letters to the author.

24. Letter to the author.

25. Admiral Houghton, Commodore Hibbard, Commodore J.C.I. Edwards, Commander A.R. Pressey, letters to the author. Also *Sea Breezes,* vol. 1, No. 1 (December 1914).

26. Admiral Houghton, letter to the author. He was the first editor-in-chief of *Sea Breezes,* and observes that, as far as he can remember, the idea of an RNCC magazine was his.

27. Letter to the author.

28. Frank Hall, 'Memories of the Naval College', letter to the editor in *The Crowsnest,* vol. 12, Nos. 7 & 8 (May-June 1960), p. 36.

29. Letter to the author. See also Commodore A.M. Hope, 'The Royal Naval College of Canada', *The Crowsnest,* vol. 12, No. 3 (January, 1960), p. 6.

30. L.J.M. Gauvreau in the House of Commons, *Debates*, vol. 113 (30 January 1914), p. 330.
31. C.C. Ballantyne to Borden, 13 February 1918, Borden Papers.
32. Memorandum from Kingsmill to Desbarats, 5 September 1913, Borden Papers, File No. M.G. 26 H 1(a) vol. 126, pp. 67842-43.
33. These were the Canadian naval officer trainees recruited before the RNCC was opened.
34. Memorandum from Desbarats to Hazen, 29 September 1913, Borden Papers, File No. M.G. 26 H 1(a) vol. 126, pp. 67836-40.
35. Letter from Desbarats to the Under-Secretary of State for External Affairs, 12 December 1913, File No. R.G. 24 vol. 5596 (N.S.S. 23-21-1 vol. 1), 'RNC of Canada. Reconstitution, General Proposals', Public Archives.
36. House of Commons, *Debates*, vol. 113 (30 January 1914), cols. 229-31.
37. W. Graham Green, Secretary to the Admiralty, to the Under-Secretary of State, Colonial Office, 21 April 1914, in File No. R.G. 24 vol. 5596 (N.S.S. 23-21-1 vol. 1), Public Archives; Hazen in the House of Commons, *Debates*, vol. 116 (5 May 1914), col. 3254; Ballantyne to Borden, 13 February 1918, Borden Papers.
38. *The Canada Gazette*, vol. 47, No. 43 (25 April 1914), p. 3749.
39. *Debates*, vol. 116 (5 May 1914), col. 3254.
40. Hazen to Borden, 6 June 1914, Borden Papers, File No. R.G. 24 vol. 5596 (N.S.S. 23-21-3 vol. 1).
41. Letter to the author.
42. Tucker, vol. 1, p. 221; Letter from the Naval Secretary to Lt.-Cdr. Bruce N. Wright, RCNR (ret.), 16 February 1960, in the Directorate of History, DND.
43. Letter to the author.
44. Tucker, p. 156.
45. Ballantyne to Borden, 13 February 1918, Borden Papers.
46. Hartley to Martin, 15 October 1917, File No. R.G. 24 vol. 5596 (N.S.S. 23-1-1), Public Archives.
47. From the contemporary diary of P. W. Brock, now in the possession of the Library of the Royal Military College of Canada.
48. *Ibid.*
49. From Nixon's account of the explosion at Halifax, preserved in the Nixon Papers in the Directorate of History, DND.
50. Brock diary.
51. From *Sea Breezes*, vol. 1, No. 4 (December 1917).
52. Lt.-Cdr. P.W. Brock, RN, 'The Senior Service at R.M.C. – 1918', *R.M.C. Review*, vol. 15 (June 1934), p. 50.
53. Kingsmill in a memorandum to the Minister of the Naval Service, 19 December 1917, in File No. R.G. 24 vol. 5596 (N.S.S. 23-23-1 vol. 1), 'R.N.C. Transfer of RNC to Kingston. General Correspondence', Public Archives.
54. Kingsmill to Perreau, 24 December 1917, in R.M.C. File No. 6-1-41 in the possession of the Library of the Royal Military College.
55. Perreau to Kingsmill, 26 December 1917, R.M.C. File No. 6-1-41.
56. Perreau to Kingsmill, 28 December 1917, *ibid.*
57. Perreau to Kingsmill, 29 December 1917, *ibid.*
58. Desbarats to Acton Burrows 7 January 1918, in File No. R.G. 24 vol. 5635 (N.S.S. 37-25-4 vol. 1), Public Archives.
59. Kingsmill to Nixon, 10 December 1917, Nixon Papers; Kingsmill to the Minister of the Naval Service, 8 January 1918, in File No. R.G. 24 vol. 5596 (N.S.S. 23-23-1 vol 1). Public Archives.
60. Ballantyne to Borden, 14 February 1918; Borden to Ballantyne, 16 February 1918, Borden Papers.
61. R.M.C. File No. 6-1-41.
62. Major-General Elliot to Perreau, 8 June 1918, *ibid.*

63. Captain H. Kingsley to E.C. Russell, Naval Historian, 30 January 1955, enclosed in the latter's memorandum to the Chief of Naval Personnel, 3 February 1955, in File No. 1700-120/2 vol. 1 in the Directorate of History, DND.
64. 'P.W.B.' in a book review of D.M. Schurman's *Education of a Navy, Naval Review* (October 1965), p. 381.
65. Kingsley to Russell, 30 January 1955.
66. Brock, *R.M.C. Review*, p. 52.
67. Col. Perreau, Memorandum to the Secretary of the Militia Council, Ottawa, 28 May 1918, R.M.C. File No. 6-1-41; Brock, *R.M.C. Review*, p. 52; Commander G.M. Mitchell, letter to the author.
68. Brock, *R.M.C. Review*, pp. 51, 52; Admiral DeWolf, letter to the author.
69. Brock diary.
70. Admirals DeWolf, Pullen, Mr L.D. Hyndman, letters to the author.
71. House of Commons, *Debates,* vol. 136 (27 May 1919), col. 2850.
72. p.28.
73. Memorandum to the Minister, 28 October 1920; J. R. Hemsted to Nixon, 29 October 1920; Nixon Papers.
74. File No. 1700-120/2 vol. 1 in the Directorate of History, DND.
75. Letter to the author.
76. Memorandum from A. Woodhouse to Nixon, 3 April 1922, File No. R.G. 24 vol. 5596 (N.S.S. 23-1-11 vol. 1), 'R.NC General Series. Scheme for Demobilization, 1922', Public Archives.
77. Hose to Nixon, 1 May 1922, Nixon Papers.
78. Graham in the House of Commons, *Debates,* vol. 153 (22 May 1922), cols. 2048-49.
79. File No. R.G. 24 vol. 5596 (N.S.S. 23-1-11 vol. 1), Public Archives.
80. Hartley to Nixon, 19 June 1922, Nixon Papers.
81. Nixon to G.P. Graham, 4 April 1923, Nixon Papers.
82. Tucker, vol. 1, p. 349; vol. 2, p. 257.
83. *The Crowsnest*, vol. 14, No. 5 (March 1962), p. 3.
84. Tucker, vol. 1, p. 324.
85. From statistics in the possession of the Directorate of History, DND.
86. Impressions derived from letters to the author from Vice-Admiral DeWolf, Rear-Admirals Houghton and Brock, Commodores Edwards and Hibbard, Captains J.R. Mitchell and Kingsley, J. McAvity, C.G. Kingsmill, and others.
87. Letter to the author.
88. Brock diary.
89. Brock, letter to the author.
90. Letter to the author.
91. Letter to the author.
92. Letters to the author.
93. Letter to the author.
94. Letters to the author.
95. Letters to the author.
96. Kingsmill to Nixon, 7 April 1920, Nixon Papers; C.G Kingsmill, letter to the author.
97. Letters to the author.
98. Letter to the author.

The Reconstitution of the Territorial Force 1918–1920

PETER DENNIS

While the Continental powers of nineteenth-century Europe relied upon a system of conscription to bolster the ranks of their regular military forces, Britain was content to muddle along with an ill-coordinated assortment of Volunteers, Yeomanry, and Militia that theoretically stood behind the Regular Army. There was no clearly understood and generally accepted method of mobilising this manpower, but in the era of small colonial wars that added to the Empire and gladdened the hearts of Englishmen in the latter half of the century, this seemed of little account. Not until one 'small war', against the Boers in South Africa, unexpectedly ballooned into a much more serious struggle, did the whole structure of Britain's military power come into question. By then, or shortly afterwards, the emergence of Germany as a naval power lent an added sharpness of focus to the invasion scares that had been rife from the end of the nineteenth century. In this context the Volunteers could lay claim to a real and significant role in military planning: they would repel any invasion force that managed to slip past the shield of the Royal Navy while the Regular Army was fighting to defend the Empire or assisting any allies that Britain might have. But, as the most recent historian of the Volunteers warns, 'It would be a mistake and an injustice ... to take them too seriously.' Despite the claims they often made, they remained partly, and often poorly, trained amateurs, whose most serious shortcoming, perhaps, was their lack of any specified place in the military establishment. [1]

An attempt was made by the Liberal Secretary of State for War, R.B. Haldane, to remedy the faults exposed by the South African experience. In creating the Territorial Force in 1907, Haldane sought to bring into existence a National Army based on the Volunteers and the Yeomanry. (The Militia insisted on retaining its own units – which had not functioned as such for years, was abolished, and reconstituted as a Special Reserve of the Regular Army, charged with continuing what it had done best for some time, supplying recruits for the Regulars.) Complete success in achieving his ideal was denied him, for whereas Haldane conceived of the Territorial Force as the second line of the Regular Expeditionary Force, available for overseas service, the Volunteer interests had wielded sufficient influence to prevent an obligation for overseas service being included in the terms of enlistment. The Volunteers, now transformed into Territorials, could still think of themselves as training primarily for home defence.[2]

When war broke out in 1914, Kitchener, hastily made Secretary of State for War, jettisoned Haldane's system of expanding the military forces of the nation by means of the Territorial organisation, for he distrusted and despised anything to do with amateur soldiering. Instead he raised his own 'New Armies', while allowing the Territorials to continue to recruit and to serve overseas, where they fought with skill and courage, and belied the reputation that had followed them from their Volunteer days.[3]

At the end of the war the future of the Territorials posed a considerable problem to the War Office and the Government. In view of their fighting record and sterling example of voluntary military service, especially in the early months of the war in support of the British Expeditionary Force and, shortly afterwards, in relief of the Regular garrison in India, the Territorials felt they were entitled to a fair consideration in post-war military planning, and not simply to be cast away or relegated to the status of a tolerated but not much encouraged force. The Government was not unsympathetic to their claim, but to move beyond this and to articulate a realistic and useful role for the Territorial Force proved an exacting task. The immediate solution was not wholly satisfactory.

The difficulty lay in the changed situation that now faced British military planners. A primary role for the Territorials as home defence troops seemed to be ruled out by post-war conditions. The defeat of the German Army and, more significantly, the scuttling of the German fleet at Scapa Flow, laid to rest the invasion scares that had swept Britain before the war. Now it hardly seemed necessary to maintain an army at home to guard against invasion forces that eluded the Royal Navy and threatened a country devoid of Regular troops. A 'bolt from the blue' was all but impossible, and remained so in the authorities' eyes until well into the 1930s, when air power made the problem of a system of home defence independent of the protection afforded by the Navy a question of paramount importance. [4]

Nor was the Territorial Force suitable for garrison duties in the Empire. Some Territorials had been sent out to India during the war, but it was doubtful whether the conditions that had pertained in the early stages of the war would apply in future contingencies. It had been possible to replace Regular Army garrisons in India with Territorial troops because the likelihood of serious trouble there was small. The sub-continent seemed relatively quiet, and Britain's long-standing rival, Russia, was now an ally. By 1919 the situation was very different: the nationalist movement in India was demonstrating for far-reaching political concessions, and the Bolshevik government in Russia had swung the focus of Britain's military concern away from Western Europe once more to the east. Throughout the 1920s it was the Russian threat to Britain's imperial interests that loomed most menacingly in the eyes of British planners; not until 1933 did the Chiefs of Staff shift their emphasis back to Europe and warn of the dangers of the resurgence of German power. [5]In these circumstances the Territorial Army, with its partially trained forces, could not be relied upon to provide immediate relief for regular garrison troops and to release them for more important duties elsewhere. It was equally difficult to use the Territorials as peace-time garrison troops, for that entailed long-term duty that was inappropriate for part-time volunteers. There had been loud criticism of the War Office decision to send Territorials to India during the war, and when there seemed to be an unwarranted delay in bringing them home, ill-feeling grew, [6] compounded by the belief that their services had not been appreciated either by the War Office or the country at large. [7]

Haldane's concept of the Territorial Army as the basis for the expansion of the military power of the nation, the means by which the Regular Expeditionary Force was to be supported in the field, appeared to have no immediate relevance to the situation in 1919. The German Army was crushed, there seemed to be little likelihood that a major expeditionary force, requiring massive reinforcements, would be needed for some time, if at all. The Empire, including the newly-won, and shortly thereafter mandated, territories, promised to be a source of continual strife for years to come. But the potential enemies there, Russia excepted, were classed as undeveloped aggressors: against them the

Regular Army would be capable of holding its own.

The prospects of a vigorous revival of the Territorials after the ravages of the war did not, then, appear to be especially hopeful. Yet the Territorial Army was not without its supporters, and as with the Volunteers, its political influence was considerable. Its own members made it a body whose opinion could not easily be ignored. In the House of Commons a number of MPs, who comprised the back-bench Army Committee, were or had been Territorials, and even those who were not had to pay some attention to local feelings of pride over the achievements of the Territorial units within their constituencies; while in the House of Lords the Territorials found a natural well of sympathy in the magnates who played an important part in the County Territorial Associations. With opinion such as this behind it, and with the widespread realisation that Britain's unpreparedness in 1914 had put her in a perilous position, the Territorials were strongly placed to bring their claims to the attention of the Government.

During 1919 the War Office grappled with the problem of how to reconstitute the Territorial Army. With the impending demise of the Military Service Act, voluntary service again became the only means of expanding the Regular Army, but since it seemed unlikely that the Army would be involved in a major war in the foreseeable future, the inherent deficiences of the Territorials as a genuine second line dominated discussions. The resolution of these difficulties owed as much to expediency as to carefully considered judgement, and was to create further difficulties in the 1920s and 1930s, when the climate of government and public opinion was much less sympathetic to problems bearing on defence.

In February 1919 the Director-General of the Territorial Force, the Earl of Scarbrough, submitted proposals to the Army Council for the reconstitution of the Territorial Force. Favourable conditions prevailed, he suggested, for laying the foundations of a part-time second line simultaneous with the establishment of a volunteer regular first line. There was a large pool of trained manpower which had either just completed or was about to complete its engagement, and which might well be prepared to undertake further service if sufficiently attractive terms were announced. The general feeling of comradeship that had developed during the war could be exploited by the War Office and

channelled into a newly-constituted Territorial Force. Scarbrough recognised that the main questions to be decided dealt
with the obligations and conditions of service. Once these had
been settled recruiting could open before the interest in part-time
soldiering faded away among the trained man-power that was
most useful to the War Office. If speedy agreement was not
possible, however, he still thought it wise to set up the essential
framework and to take applicants' names, with the necessary
safeguards and guarantees in case the final conditions did not
satisfy those who initially indicated their willingness to serve. [8]

While these proposals were being considered within the War
Office, Churchill, Secretary of State for War, was coming under
pressure in the House of Commons to provide specific details
regarding the reconstitution of the Territorial Force, the acceptance of which in principle he had already made known. He was
warned that any undue delay in announcing his proposals would
result in a serious setback: once the initial interest had been lost, it
would be very difficult to get it back. [9] This became a frequent
criticism levelled against the War Office in the following
months, as Parliament and the Territorials awaited the
Government's plans. But, as Churchill replied to his critics, the
reconstitution of the Territorials had to be carried out within a
much wider context, the readjustment of Britain's military
organisation to the new conditions of the post-war world. Until
the overall problem had been appreciated, there could be no steps
taken that might prove to be of a mere stop-gap nature. [10]

The chief objections to Scarbrough's proposals from the
General Staff quickly emerged. It was unanimously agreed that
no case could be made for reconstituting the Territorial Force except on the basis of a foreign service obligation, that the
Territorials would undertake to serve overseas in the event of a
'national emergency'. But what constituted a 'national emergency' was difficult to define. In a major crisis it was understood that
general conscription would be imposed; the grey area covered
the 'moderate wars' in the Empire and its bordering territories
that appeared all too possible. It was doubtful if the ranks of the
Territorial Force could be filled if there was an obligation to
serve in imperial wars that did not warrant general conscription,
especially since in such circumstances the primary requirement of
the Regular Army would be for drafts to maintain the strength of
regular units. [11]

One of the strongest fears of the Territorials had always been that the Regular Army and the War Office would ignore the integrity of its units and merely draw on the Territorials for draft-finding purposes. Scarborough suggested that the imperial service pill might be sweetened by linking it with a guarantee that if the Territorial Force was embodied for overseas service, it would proceed and operate in its original units, compulsory transfers being permitted only in extraordinary circumstances and then only as a temporary measure.

While this might have calmed the worst fears of the Territorials, it created serious problems for the War Office. [12] If it promised to maintain the integrity of Territorial units, the usefulness of the Territorial Force as a means of supporting the Regular Army in a moderate war would be severely circumscribed, if not destroyed. Yet to make such a pledge would undercut the efficiency of a wider mobilisation scheme under general conscription, by creating a special class of soldiers. Without such a pledge, however, recruiting might be so impeded that the new Territorial Force might be still-born. The problem appeared to be insoluble, especially when there was a common feeling among those who studied Scarbrough's proposals that no commitments should be entered into that would subsequently tie the hands of the War Office, even if this entailed a delay in reaching a final decision, with the risk that the current interest in the Territorials might have waned by the time the conditions were established.

Despite these reservations it was agreed that the Force should be reconstituted. A sub-committee in the War Office, chaired by the Adjutant-General, Sir George Milne, submitted its proposals at the end of March. It recommended the reconstruction of the Force on the pre-war basis of fourteen infantry divisions and fourteen mounted brigades, raised and administered by the County Associations. While recognising that the precise terms of service would take some time to be formulated, it pressed for the immediate appointment of divisional and brigade staffs so that applications for enlistments (as opposed to enlistment itself, or attestation) could begin as soon as possible.

The thorny problem of conditions of service was to be resolved by an uneasy compromise: Territorials would be liable for overseas service once – but not before – general conscription was introduced. When that situation arose they would proceed

overseas with their own units but then would be available for
service as the War Office saw fit. No pledge would be given to
maintain the integrity of units, although every effort would be
made to do so.

The compensation for these burdens lay in the liberal pay scales
and concessions that the sub-committee proposed, namely, that
while in camp Territorials would receive the same pay and
allowances as corresponding ranks in the Regular Army in addition to an annual bounty, and that a legal obligation be imposed
on employers to allow their employees any additional leave
necessary to enable them to attend the annual fifteen days' camp.
These were expensive and not entirely satisfactory proposals. If
adopted they would commit the War Office to maintaining a
well-paid force that would not fit easily into the military requirements of the country. The sub-committee also recommended that, to assuage a strong sense of grievance many Territorials
had, some form of special recognition be given to those
Territorials who, when serving in August 1914, had volunteered
for overseas service, whether or not they had actually served
overseas.[13] This referred to the case of those Territorials who had
been willing to serve outside Britain but had been held back in
training positions, thus making themselves ineligible for the
coveted medals awarded for overseas service, medals which had
come the way of most conscripts later in the war but had been
denied those who arguably showed a greater sense of patriotism
and sacrifice.

On the basis of Milne's report, Churchill addressed a meeting
of Territorial representatives on 1 April 1919. His position was
not an easy one, for in summoning the representatives to meet
him when he had only the most general proposals to lay before
them, he opened the door to the airing of all the grievances, real
or imaginary, that the Territorials felt they had suffered. If that
happened the co-operation that was necessary for the successful
reconstitution of the Force could be destroyed. He was therefore
generous in his praise of the Territorials' achievements during the
war, quick to acknowledge the error that Kitchener and the
government had made in by-passing Haldane's scheme for the
expansion of Britain's military power in time of emergency, and
open in admitting that the international situation did not yet permit a final decision to be reached on the precise terms of the
reconstitution. Delivered in that vein, his remarks were well

received.

He proposed that the pre-war organisation of the Territorial Force into fourteen infantry divisions and fourteen mounted brigades be adhered to, and that immediate steps be taken to begin appointing divisional and brigade staffs. Suitably qualified Territorial Officers would be eligible for commands at the brigade level. This settled another Territorial grievance. Haldane's undertaking that Territorials would be considered for senior commands had never been honoured in spirit: though they may have been considered, very few were ever appointed. Enlistment in the ranks was for the moment to be restricted to men who had already served in the Regular or Territorial Army. Once accepted for service in the new Territorial Force they would be paid when in training at the same rates that applied to the Regular Army. These proposals were well calculated to appeal to the Territorials' wish to be taken seriously as a military force, and to be treated in the same way as the Regulars. In return Churchill made it clear that the new terms of service would involve a major departure from the pre-war system: men would be enlisted under a foreign service obligation, which would not be put into effect until a general service act had been passed and conscription imposed on the nation as a whole. Secondly, while promising to do everything possible to keep units intact when they were sent overseas, he warned that the War Office would be unable to give a firm guarantee to preserve the integrity of Territorial units. He concluded by suggesting a further meeting in the near future when the exact terms had been finalised, after the Territorial Associations had been able to sound out local opinion. [14]

A month later Churchill again met the Territorial representatives. He was still unable to give them the promised details, yet urged the necessity of a speedy revival of the Territorial movement. The latter was hardly a novel suggestion to his listeners, but what perhaps did give rise to some concern was Churchill's emphasis on the ability of the Territorial Force, in the absence of the Special Reserve that provided drafts, to 'secure the Regular Military Forces of the country that amphibious and world-wide mobility on which the security of our Empire depends'. [15] This implied a role for the Territorials, not as a genuine self-contained second line, but as a body to raise reinforcements for Regular units. The April promise to maintain the integrity of Territorial units as far as possible seemed to have been pushed aside. In fact, as the War Office worked on the pamphlet describing the conditions of service, reservations about the scheme that Churchill had outlined grew. Again, as with Scarbrough's original proposals in February, there was a unanimous opinion that no pledge on the integrity of units could be given, since the primary need of the Regular Army was for drafts over and above what the Regular Reserve could provide. By now it was accepted (at least for the moment) that enlistment in the new Territorial Force had to be on the basis of a foreign service commitment. For its part, the War Office wanted that to be the only commitment. It was reluctant to be encumbered by obligations that would restrict its ability to use the Territorial Force when, where and how it saw fit: notwithstanding the mounting criticism over the delay in publishing its precise proposals, the military members of the War Office felt that the scheme was being drawn up with undue haste.[16]

The tension between Churchill's public commitment to reconstitute the Territorial Force and the reservations of his professional military advisers came to a head in August 1919, when the Cabinet imposed stringent limits on defence expenditure and laid down that future service estimates were to be based on the assumption that no major war would occur within ten years and that no expeditionary force would be required.[17] The 'ten year rule' led the Chief of the Imperial General Staff, Field Marshal Sir Henry Wilson, to denounce the whole concept of a Territorial Force. As he forcefully explained to Churchill in October, the circumstances under which he had originally given his approval, albeit reluctantly, to the reconstitution of the Territorials, had now so changed that no serious case could be made for it. Dire predictions of civil unrest in Britain in 1918 and 1919 fortunately had not materialised, and there was no longer any doubt, as there had been earlier, about the stability of the Regular Army. What was causing increasing anxiety was the problem of finance. It was surely wrong, Wilson argued, to allot funds to the Territorial Force before the much more pressing needs of the Regular Army had been satisfied. This was especially so when a reconstituted Territorial Force would not fulfil the draft-finding requirements of the Regular Army in a moderate war, i.e. one that did not warrant the introduction of conscription. He warned:

Remember that it may be politically wise, politically ex-
pedient, even politically necessary to re-create the old
Territorial Force, on this subject I express no opinion except that in our present financial state such a course may
conceivably cause the loss of a portion of our Empire. If
with all the facts before them, the Cabinet decide on this
course I have absolutely nothing further to say. [18]

Churchill's publicly announced deadline of 1 October as the
date by which final proposals would be unveiled had passed, and
still no agreement had been reached. In answer to the criticism
that the bounties to be offered were excessively liberal, the
Quartermaster-General had suggested that an additional burden
in the form of a liability to be called out in aid of the civil power
might be imposed on the Territorials. [19] Churchill had seized on
this and instructed the War Office to draft the necessary changes
in the attestation forms, even though this was as controversial a
proposal as the foreign service obligation, and one that had not
been foreshadowed in the original announcement in April. [20]
Haldane had calmed the fears of the Labour movement by giving
a specific pledge that the Territorials would not be required to
aid the civil power in the event of strikes or other disturbances, [21]
and Scarbrough admitted that the inclusion of such an obligation
would probably have serious effects on recruitment among trade
unionists and hence be self-defeating. [22] Further study of the
proposal revealed its disadvantages and it was shelved, but not –
in Churchill's mind – dropped.

Instead, in an attempt to reconcile Wilson's basic objections
with Churchill's pressing need to reach agreement, Scarbrough
produced an unwieldy compromise. Given the military situation
and the Cabinet decision on defence expenditure, it would be an
unjustified 'extravagance' to establish a Territorial Force solely
for home defence. If the Territorials wished to be taken seriously
as a military force, it could only be on the basis of a foreign service obligation, which most seemed willing to accept. Then the
Territorials would be a genuine line. Territorial fears that the
general service obligation might be too suddenly implemented
would be put to rest by the creation of a 'special class' of
Territorials. These would be men who accepted an obligation
similar to that of the Regular Army Reserve in that they could be
called out on the proclamation of an emergency and used as

drafts for Regular units. In return for this additional obligation
they would receive a larger bounty. This 'special class', Scarbrough suggested, would act as a 'visible buffer' between the
Regular Army and the rest of the Territorials, and would add
weight to the Government's undertaking, in lieu of a firm
pledge, that transfers from Territorial units would only be made
as a temporary measure. Scarbrough claimed – on what basis it is
difficult to say – that this would replace a costly and inefficient
system of reserves with a 'single, simple and inexpensive
organization closely assimilated to that of the Regular Forces'. [23]
In fact, the two-tier system would divide Territorial units into
those who had pledged and those who had not, for although the
'special class' would be supernumerary to the establishment of
each unit, training would be undertaken in common and an un-
healthy rivalry would probably develop. As for the claim that
the new organisation would be inexpensive, the cost of the
reconstitution scheme as a whole had been one of the main stick-
ing points. The Financial Secretary of the War Office, Sir
Charles Harris, was strongly critical of the level of inducements
that it was proposed to offer recruits. Not only was the cost too
great in general terms, but it seemed foolish to attract large
numbers of soldiers in this way if funds to train them would subsequently be unavailable after the impositions of budgetary
restrictions in August. [24] The 'special class' simply added to the
cost. It was estimated that a recruit would cost £44 per annum as
opposed to £19 for a member of the Army Reserve. In effect the
War Office would be competing with itself through higher
bounties for the same men, at least in the short term. Until
Regular soldiers completed their engagements and moved into
the Regular Reserve, there would be a shortage of man-power on
which to draw for the Reserve, the 'special class' of the
Territorial Force, and the Territorial Force as a whole. [25] This was
hardly a 'single, simple and inexpensive organization'.

Scarbrough was, however, correct in claiming that a
Territorial Force reconstituted along these lines would have a
'recognized position as a genuine second line of the Army'. It
would be confirmed as a means of expanding the regular forces
of the nation in an emergency, it would be assimilated in every
way to the Regular Army, and it could therefore call for
financial support that would be denied if it was raised merely as a
home defence force.

The scheme was by no means ideal, but it satisfied the main requirements both of Churchill and his military advisers. Even though Wilson still hesitated, he had at least been able to secure the means of supplying the Regular Army with reinforcements - at an apparently exorbitant cost; while Churchill was at last approaching long-overdue agreement on the terms that had been promised by the end of September. Yet as the work on finalising the conditions of service drew nearer completion, Churchill hesitated. On 1 December he wrote to the Cabinet, emphasising the urgency of reaching a swift agreement, and sought permission to publish a pamphlet outling the War Office proposals — despite the widespread feeling in the War Office that no preliminary announcements should be made until the Government itself had come to a firm decision. Churchill admitted that he had reservations about imposing a general service obligation, but added that his advisers had assured him that the attractive pay and bounties would more than offset any injury the new burden might do to recruitment. In any case, he warned, the psychological moment for capturing the interest in part-time soldiering was rapidly passing; immediate action was needed. [26] The next day Churchill revealed his doubts to the Army Council. An exasperated Wilson recorded in his diary:

We have been months at this, with Winston's knowledge and approval. This morning he suddenly and unexpectedly ran out. He said he would get no more recruits, there would be a complete frost, etc., etc., and he wanted to revert to the Territorial Force of pre-war days. I said that I could not agree to 6-10 millions being spent on a sham. [27]

Churchill thereupon agreed that two schemes should be put to the Cabinet, which would have to choose where the War Office had been unable to make up its mind. The difference between the alternatives hinged on the nature of the general service obligation; that much at least Wilson had managed to secure from Churchill. One scheme envisaged the Territorials' liability for overseas service only coming into force after the passing of a general conscription act; the other made the Territorials liable for overseas service after the Regular Army Reserve had been called out by Royal Proclamation. In both cases the 'special class', supernumerary to the Territorial establishment, would also be created.[28] The second alternative was clearly much more in line with the thinking of the military members of the War Office, for it made possible the embodiment of the Territorial Force for use in a moderate or even small war that would not warrant general conscription.

The delay in reaching a final agreement had long since become an embarrassment to the War Office. Eight months had passed since Churchill had summoned the Territorial representatives to hear his general proposals, yet it seemed that little progress had been made. The Army Committee of the House of Commons was restive, and had already passed a resolution condemning the delay. [29] Field Marshal Lord Haig had urged a speedy decision; [30] so too had Lord Esher, in his capacity as Chairman of the County of London Territorial Association. [31] Questions were asked in Parliament,[32] letters were written to *The Times* (the plaintive cry, 'When, Sir, will this operation be completed?' [33] was typical). These pressures and growing doubts made it necessary for the War Office to reassure the Territorial supporters that it fully intended to re-establish the Force. [34] Widespread fears that the War Office was less than enthusiastic about the Territorials were not calmed by a spate of reports in *The Times* to the effect that the Government was unable to make up its mind. [35] Most important of all, perhaps, were the growing signs of discontent in the Territorial Associations. A resolution from the City of Glasgow Association roundly criticising the Government's delay received the firm support of several Associations; others passed similar resolutions.[36]

Churchill in particular was hesitant. He was keenly aware of the damaging effects of the continual delay, and he therefore suggested to his military advisers that a 'loophole of escape' could be found by opening recruiting at once on the basis of tentative conditions of service, including an overseas obligation – thereby quelling the rumbles of discontent over the Government's delay, and introducing in March the necessary legislation to amend the Territorial Act. If, in the intervening months, it was found that recruiting had been gravely affected by the inclusion of a general service obligation, the legislation could be dropped and recruiting could proceed on the basis of the pre-war conditions. [37] The response to this proposal was cool, nor was the Army Committee prepared to accept the opening of recruiting before the final conditions of service had been published, and it further insisted that until general conscription had been imposed Territorial service abroad could only be in units that were maintained intact.[38]

Blocked on these avenues Churchill appealed to the Cabinet for a decision. He admitted that though the advantages of the second alternative were 'overwhelming' from a military point of view, he thought it 'essentially unfair to ask men who are not soldiers to take on a liability to be sent away ... for long periods while the mass of their fellow-countrymen pursue their ordinary avocations and bear no part whatever of the national burden'. Furthermore he had told the Territorial representatives in April that the Territorial Force would not be embodied and despatched abroad unless the emergency was sufficiently grave to warrant the introduction of general conscription. If the Government went ahead and imposed a general service obligation as the War Office wanted, Churchill feared that charges of bad faith might arise and that public opinion might turn against the Territorial Force, with serious effects on recruiting. The proposal could be dropped and the Territorial Force could carry on along pre-war lines, but such an open admission of mismanagement and War Office disagreement would hardly commend the Force to the nation. Churchill therefore specifically asked the Cabinet to solve his dilemma.[39]

When the Cabinet met on 7 January 1920, Churchill reminded them again that the government was pledged to reconstitute the Territorial Force and that little time was available to arrive at a decision, since a public meeting had been announced for 15 January. But the Cabinet was no more able than the War Office to reach an agreement on the conditions of service. The proposals were deceptively simple, the implications of their decision far--reaching. There were strong arguments on both sides. In support of a general service obligation there was the opinion of those who were closely in touch with the Territorial movement; they had made it clear that if the Force was reconstituted on pre-war lines, and not made liable for overseas service, it would not be taken seriously and recruiting would be poor. Those who hesitated for fear that Territorial units would be broken up and used as drafts for the Regular Army would be reassured by the creation of the 'special class' beyond the normal Territorial establishments. Against this argument was the assertion that a foreign service obligation would deter men from enlisting because of the dangers it posed to their security of employment. Consequently the stable, responsible class that it was hoped would join the new citizen army would hold back, and the Territorials would be drawn from the elements who had previously filled the ranks of the Militia, mainly young or un-employed labourers. There was also a political consideration. If a foreign service obligation was to be imposed, amending legislation would have to be introduced in Parliament, giving the Government's opponents an opportunity to charge that the Force was being raised for intervention in Russia. Political dangers attended one course of action, the possibility of the scheme's failure the other.

Various alternative proposals were put forward: that foreign service be confined within the bounds of the Empire; that Territorials be given a choice of liabilities; that the foreign service obligation run for the first two years of a four-year engagement (it was hoped this would satisfy the employment objections, though exactly how is not clear); that the Territorials be liable for overseas service only after Parliament had passed a resolution approving that action; and that the Territorials be sent overseas only after general conscription had been introduced. Each of these suggestions had its short-comings. The first un-necessarily restricted the area within which the Territorials could be used. The second created administrative nightmares and destroyed the integrity of units, as would the third, for it would establish two classes within each unit. The fourth would not satisfy those who mistrusted the Government, for it seemed clear that no Government would risk introducing such a motion unless it was certain of success; while the fifth did not meet the War Office requirements for a moderate war, and in any case committed the Government to conscription in emergency situations, which, although it was agreed might be inevitable, was not a course the Government wished to state publicly. With objections at every turn the Cabinet made the obvious choice: it appointed a sub-committee to wrestle with the problem and recommend action.[40]

When the Cabinet sub-committee first met it made little headway towards settling the central issue. Two of its members, Churchill and F.G. Kellaway, Deputy Minister of Munitions, were reluctant to recommend a general service obligation. The others, Auckland Geddes, President of the Board of Trade, and Lord Lee, Minister of Agriculture and Fisheries, were, in Henry Wilson's eyes, 'quite sound and good'.[41] *The Times* quickly became aware of a 'serious hitch', and reported that from a position of virtual agreement in the Government, there had been a 'violent change' as the old fears about a general service obligation surfaced once more. In view of the widespread Territorial willingness to accept such an obligation, *The Times'* reporter castigated the Government for its lack of political courage, and warned that unless it took the obvious course, the Territorials would be nothing but a 'sham factor in national defence'.[42] The following day it announced that the War Office had postponed until 23 January the meeting between the Secretary of State for War and the Territorial Associations that had been set previously for 15 January. This had been brought about, it said, by the 'marked divergence of opinion' that had emerged in Cabinet and which the sub-committee had so far been unable to resolve.[43]

In fact the sub-committee was approaching agreement, as the pressures on Churchill mounted. On 13 January he met a group of Territorial Association representatives, Territorial divisional commanders, and Territorial officers who had commanded Territorial brigades during the war. When the question of a general service obligation was put to them individually, there was overwhelming support for it: twenty-nine voted in favour and only three against.[44] Shortly afterwards Auckland Geddes wrote to Churchill, saying that from discussions he had held with interested parties, he had reached the unshakeable conclusion that to reconstitute the Territorials on the basis of home defence without a foreign service commitment 'would be regarded as simply playing with the Force'.[45]

Churchill was not yet convinced, and in the absence of any decision, his meeting with the Territorial Associations, already postponed once, was further put off until 30 January. *The Times* claimed that there had been a significant hardening of opinion in favour of general service,[46] but Churchill still held out. He was supported by the Duke of Rutland, who wrote to him to say that the difficulties of imposing a foreign service obligation could be avoided if it was made voluntary, since 'the *vast* majority of the men would volunteer for such General Service the moment the urgent necessity of their services was announced'. Churchill was delighted, and had a copy of Rutland's letter sent to Wilson:[47] he remained unimpressed. A further meeting of the sub-committee confirmed Geddes' and Lee's support of the general service obligation, but again no decision was reached. Wilson wrote gloomily in his diary: '... Winston is heading for Home Service obligation which will be his ruin'.[48] Three days later, just before the Cabinet was due to consider the matter in time for the Government's decision to be announced on the 30th, Churchill conceded defeat. He told a relieved Wilson that he accepted the need for a general service obligation that would come into effect after an Act had been passed by Parliament authorising the despatch of Territorial troops overseas.[49]

A meeting of Cabinet ministers was held on the 27th, and Churchill told them that a decision had to be reached that morning. He admitted that his conversion to a general service obligation had been a recent one, but now he was convinced that it was impossible to reconstitute the Territorials for home defence only. He thought it best to make an unequivocal statement of the Government's policy, to ask recruits to accept an obligation for overseas service, and to offer them, by way of protection, a guarantee that they would not be sent out of the country until Parliament had passed an Act declaring a state of emergency. Furthermore, to allay the most widespread of all Territorial fears, the Government should undertake to send them abroad only in their units. To prevaricate on the Government's position would risk giving rise to suspicions that the Force was being raised for internal strike breaking purposes, and that, foreign liability or not, the Government would send the Territorials abroad if it so wished. The vexatious question of supplying drafts for the Regular Army would be solved, not by creating a 'special class' of Territorials, but by raising seventy four battalions of the old Special Reserve, renaming them the Militia, and attaching them to the Regular Army. The Territorial Force could be reconstituted along these lines, assured of its place as the second line of the British Army, and confirmed as the sole basis for the expansion of the nation's military power – all within the budgetary limits laid down by the Cabinet the previous August. It would be necessary to recast the role of the Yeomanry, to reduce some of its units and to convert others, but the essential details that were so urgently needed had been worked out. All that was left was for those present to give their approval. The meeting was no doubt relieved to hear this, and after a short discussion decided to accept in principle the proposals Churchill had presented.[50]

Three days later, on 30 January, Churchill unveiled the Government's plans. He emphasised the responsibilities that were to be placed on the Territorial Force — 'the purpose of the Territorial Army shall be Imperial Defence, including our obligations to France and Flanders' — and balanced against them the inducements and safeguards that recruits would enjoy. If a Territorial with military experience completed the maximum of fifty drills in a year, passed the musketry course, and attended the annual fifteen days' camp, he could earn a bounty of £5; a recruit would join under slightly different conditions and could earn up to £4. These financial rewards were in addition to the pay, at Regular rates, that he would earn during camp. An overseas obligation would be imposed, but would come into operation only under stringent conditions. Not merely would a proclamation calling out the Army Reserve be required, but Parliament would have to pass an Act specifically authorising the despatch overseas of the Territorial Force. Furthermore, to meet the most strongly felt objection, Churchill promised that not only would Territorial units go abroad as units, but that as soon as their efficiency made it possible, they would fight in Territorial brigades and divisions. In every sense the Territorial Force was to be a self-contained, second line Army.[51]

These were welcome words to the Territorial representatives who had been waiting for a year to learn the Government's intentions. Criticism of the Government, however, for the delays, the confusion, and for the final form of the conditions of service, was not so easily silenced. Public recriminations and charges of bad faith undermined the recruiting campaign. Though the War Office had reached a decision on the most important conditions of service, there were still essential questions that remained to be answered, at least to the satisfaction of many of the Associations.

Recruiting officially opened on 1 February. Progress was disappointingly slow. Apart from the obvious war weariness that beset the nation as a whole, there were other factors that held down enlistment. Notwithstanding Churchill's commendation of the bounties and rates of pay to be offered Territorials,[52] the inducement was not quite as attractive as he suggested. In the post-war boom wages were very high, so that for the steadily employed man — the type that the War Office wanted to recruit

– service in the Territorial Army was not necessarily financially advantageous.[53] Indeed, enlistment in the Territorial Force could be positively harmful, or so many feared. They worried that employers would not be willing to grant them leave with pay to attend camp (or at least to make up the difference between military and civil pay scales), and especially that they would not grant them extra leave so that they could spend at least part of their annual holidays with their families. Some Associations thought that the answer to this was to impose a legal obligation on employers as a means of sharing the national burden of defence. Sir George Milne's sub-committee recommended this in March 1919, and there was some support for the proposal, but on closer examination it was thought to be impracticable. If employers were required to give special holiday and pay privileges to members of the Territorial Force they might refuse to employ them in the first place. If they did employ them and allowed them extra holidays and pay, there might be opposition from the foremen and other workers arising out of resentment over this preferential treatment. There was also the possibility that the granting of employment privileges to Territorial soldiers would be construed as a none-too-subtle form of pressure to get men into the Force. Small employers in particular would find it difficult to make the concessions that were relatively easy for large firms and government departments. In general, then, the employers' obligations – legally imposed as distinct from those that were the fruits of a patriotic conscience – opened up so many other problems that it was not pursued further. Instead the Government relied upon the goodwill and co-operation of employers, and encouraged the Territorial Associations to do the same. This avoided antagonism between government and industry, but it was of little help to those Territorials, or would-be recruits, who worked for unco-operative firms.[54]

The Labour movement was suspicious of the Territorial Force, despite the argument that a strong volunteer citizen army was the best safeguard against the reintroduction of conscription. Apart from its broad objections to military expenditure and to the continuing militarisation of the nation, Labour remained wary of the Government's intentions on the use of the Territorials for internal purposes. In April the Secretary of the City of Dundee Territorial Association sought clarification on this point. He wrote that recruiting was suffering badly because there was a feeling of uncertainty over the Territorial liability to be used in aid of the civil power, especially to break up strikes. [55] This was a complex question. The Territorial conditions of service stated that members of the Territorial Force were not liable to be used in aid of the civil power – which seemed a sufficiently firm pledge to calm fears – but went on to say that 'when embodied they are in the same position as officers and men with regard to their being ordered on duties of this nature'. The Force could be embodied once the Regular Reserve had been called up by Royal Proclamation, and the Reserve, unlike the Territorials, could be used to support the civil authority. Thus, as Scarbrough explained to Viscount Peel, Under-Secretary of State, it was possible to argue that the Territorials could be called out and likewise employed. What was needed was some safeguard – much as with the foreign service liability – that would prevent this extreme power from being abused and the Force being employed merely to break up strikes. He suggested that in addition to a proclamation calling on the Reserve, there should also be a proclamation by Parliament authorising the embodiment of the Territorials. [56] Peel agreed, adding to Churchill that the uncertainty on this question was 'giving rise to suspicion'. [57] Churchill would have none of it, insisting that the Government's intentions were perfectly clear: the Territorials could not be called out 'in the suppression of civil disturbances or labour disputes', but they were liable to be embodied 'in the event of a grave national emergency such as an attempted revolution endangering the fundamental peace and safety of the entire country'. [58]

The distinction was not as clear as Churchill thought. The difficulty was the same as that which surrounded the controversy over the general service obligation: what constituted a 'grave national emergency'? The violent upheaval of the war, coming on top of the decade of unrest and agitation prior to 1914, shattered the comfortable stability that Britain seemed to have enjoyed for so long. The example of a Communist revolution in Russia, the spreading of doctrines that challenged commonly held beliefs, radical demands by Britain's Labour movement – in this sort of atmosphere the myriad revolutionary groups that were formed in Britain after the war (many of them simply vehicles for the airing of demobilised soldiers' grievances) all too easily appeared as a real threat to the nation. The Volunteers clearly understood the nature of the enemy they were to fight – foreign forces landing on the shores of Britain. By 1918 the spectre of revolution in Britain made it much more difficult to distinguish between genuine internal threats and the inevitable readjustment to the strains in society that the war had magnified. Throughout 1918 and 1919 the Home Office Intelligence Department produced monthly assessments of revolutionary activity in the United Kingdom; it was not entirely successful in delineating where political agitation became a threat to the nation. In these circumstances it was not unreasonable for Labour sympathisers among Territorial recruits to worry that they might be called out to uphold a system that in their minds had outlived its time. The weapon of a general strike was the most powerful in the labour arsenal: did it constitute that 'grave national emergency' of which Churchill spoke? (Certainly the Cabinet decided so in 1921,[59] as did Baldwin in 1926, with unfortunate consequences for the Territorial Force.) In the face of Churchill's refusal to provide additional guarantees there remained a lingering suspicion that the Territorials might be called out to suppress political and industrial unrest, even though, as Peel noted, the ultimate safeguard against embodiment was that no Government would call out the Force 'unless it was sure that the feeling of the country justified so grave a step'.[60]

Nor was the final form of the overseas service obligation greeted with unanimous approval. While most Associations agreed to accept the liability, some still argued that there was insufficient protection for the Territorials, that they should not be liable to be sent overseas until general conscription had been introduced. There were even doubts cast on the reliability of the War Office pledge to respect the integrity of Territorial units, a further sign of the distrust that existed.[61]

These anxieties, dissatisfactions and suspicions were given public expression in *The Times*, which reported that at a meeting of the West Riding Territorial Association in April, several speakers had charged that the War Office was deliberately sabotaging the recruiting campaign because it did not want the Territorial Force to succeed: having failed to kill it off at once, it was withholding the information and support that was needed if the required numbers of recruits were to be obtained.[62] A *Times* leader doubted that the Government was ill-disposed towards the Force, but did think that 'as regards the War Office, there may be some ground for the persistent notion that the success of the

Territorial Army is not desired'.[63] Churchill's vehement denial of the charge, his defence of the delay in announcing the reconstitution terms,[64] and an appeal by the King to the Lords Lieutenant and Lord Mayors for their support,[65] did not quell the rumours or satisfy the critics.[66]

The Territorial Force had got off to a shaky start, and not the least of its handicaps was the mistrust between the War Office and the Territorial Associations (especially on the part of the Associations) that poisoned relations for many years. In part it arose over the difficulty of assessing the nature of Britain's military requirements in the unsettled circumstances of the post-war world. Even more was it a reflection of the fundamental dilemma of how to incorporate part-time volunteer forces within a regular military organisation so that the prime requirements of military efficiency and utility did not make excessive demands on the spirit of patriotism and sacrifice (among others) that animated citizens to become soldiers.

The War Office tried to find an answer to this problem. The consequent — and perhaps inevitable — delays in producing a set of proposals allowed to escape that psychological moment when an appeal to the Territorial spirit would have been most productive. The scheme that was finally launched satisfied no one completely, and contained compromises whose resolution was to give rise to further bad feeling. In explaining his proposals to the House of Commons, Churchill had warned that if the day came when Britain's war reserves ran out, and that coincided with the revival of Germany's military power, the arrangements upon which the Territorial Force was to be organised would require 'drastic and timely revison'.[67] Apart from its predictive insight, that was a telling comment on the inherent shortcomings of the 1920 reconstitution scheme.

Notes

I wish to thank for their support The Royal Military College of Canada. The University of Western Ontario, and the Canada Council. Quotations from Crown Copyright material held in the Public Record Office are by permission of the Controller of HM Stationery Office. I am indebted also to the Directors and Archivists of the Museums, Libraries, and County Record Offices for granting me access to the papers in their care.
  1. Hugh Cunningham, The Volunteer Force: A Social and Political History, 1859-1908 (London, 1975), p. 4; Michael Howard, *The Continental Commitment: The dilemma of British defence policy in the era of the two world wars* (London, 1972),

chapters 1, 2.

2. Cunningham, *The Volunteer Force,* chapter 7: Howard, *Lord Haldane and the Territorial Army* (London, 1966).

3. During the war the Territorial Force lost over 122,000 (all ranks) killed, with a further 432,500 wounded or missing. Seventy-one Territorials won the Victoria Cross. Great Britain, *Parliamentary Debates (House of Commons),* Fifth Series, 114, c. 1691 [Hereafter cited as 5 *Parl. Debs. H.c.];* *The Times,* 3 April 1919.

4. See, for example, the warning of the Chiefs of Staff, 'Note on Emergency Measures', 12 April 1939. Annex to COS 288th meeting, CAB 53/11.

5. Chiefs of Staff Annual Review of Defence Policy, 12 October 1933. COS 310, CAB 53/23. This led to the appointment of the Defence Requirements Committee which drew up a rearmament programme designed primarily to confront a European threat.

6. When discussing reconstitution proposals, the Surrey Territorial Association agreed that grievances over service in India would seriously affect recruiting, and unanimously passed a resolution condemning the 'shabby' War Office treatment of those who had volunteered for imperial duty, had been sent to India, and had been kept there after conscripts in Europe had been demobilised. Surrey Record Office, Surrey Territorial and Auxiliary Force Association Records, Acc. 976/2, Association meeting, 7 April 1919. See also F.G. Stone's comment: '[The] Territorials who were kept [in India] long after their engagements had terminated are not likely to be good recruiting agents for the Force.' 'The Great Vital Question of National Defence', *Nineteenth Century,* LXXXVII (January-May 1920), pp. 236-53.

7. In answer to a question from Brigadier-General H. Page Croft, a member of the Hertfordshire Association, a government spokesman admitted that 'a great many more Territorials have seen active service in India than is thought by public opinion'. 5 *Parl Debs. H.C.,* 114, c. 1052. 1 April 1919.

8. 'Reconstruction of the Territorial Force', 24 February 1919. WO 32/11246.

9. 5 *Parl. Debs. H.C.,* 113, c. 104.

10. *Ibid.,* c. 78, 3 March 1919.

11. See minutes by the Adjutant-General (1 and 24 March 1919), Deputy Director of Military Operations [Walter Kirke, Director-General of the Territorial Army, 1936-9] (12 March 1919), Deputy Chief of the General Staff (21 March 1919). WO 32/11246.

12. 'The Pledge', as it was always called, bedevilled relations between the War Office and the Territorial Army for almost twenty years. When the War Office tried to eliminate it in 1932, the moment was inauspicious. Annual camps had been suspended that year as an economy measure, and charges of bad faith and a high-handed lack of consultation were levelled against the War Office. The Territorial Associations tried to use their power to extract a promise of the resumption of camps in return for giving up the pledge; unable to commit itself the War Office dropped the matter. The pledge still applied in 1939 despite efforts to abolish it. See WO 32/2678, which contains a lengthy correspondence between the Under-Secretary of State for War, the Earl of Stanhope, and the Earl of Derby, President of the Council of County Territorial Associations, on the abortive 1932 attempt; also the Derby Papers (Liverpool Record Office, 920 920 Der (17)), War Office (1932) file.

13. Adjutant-General to Secretary of State, 31 March 1919. WO 32/11246.

14. *The Times,* 3 April 1919.

15. *Ibid.,* 3 May 1919.

16. See minutes by the Quartermaster-General (10 June 1919), Director of Organization (13 June 1919), Director-General of Mobilization (17 June 1919). WO 32/11246.

17. War Cabinet 616, 15 August 1919. CAB 23/12.

18. Imperial War Museum, Wilson Papers, Correspondence Files 18 B/17, 6 October 1919. Quotations from the Wilson Papers are by permission of Major C.J. Wilson.
19. Minute, 10 June 1919. WO 32/11246.
20. Scarbrough to DPS, 30 September 1919. WO 32/2677.
21. 4 *Parl. Debs. H.C.*, 193, c. 856, 27 July 1908. Haldane, however implied that this pledge did not necessarily hold when the Territorials had been embodied and under military law – which begged the whole question.
22. 30 September 1919. WO 32/2677.
23. 'Organisation of the Territorial Force', 21 November 1919. WO 32/2681. This was subsequently incorporated into Churchill's Cabinet paper on the reconstruction of the Territorial Force. C.P. 371, CAB 24/95.
24. Harris to Under-Secretary of State, 20 October 1919. WO 32/11247. These criticisms of the pay scales were echoed by the Master-General of the Ordnance, who said that Wilson agreed with him. 1 December 1919. WO 32/2681.
25. Scarbrough to Churchill, 6 January 1920; Adjutant-General to Churchill, 7 January 1920. WO 32/2681.
26. WO 32/2681.
27. Wilson Papers, diary entry for 2 December 1919.
28. Army Council minutes, 259th meeting, 2 December 1919. WO 163/24.
29. *The Times*, 29 October 1919.
30. 'My message [on receiving the Freedom of the City of London] ...is to urge you...to set up forthwith the organization of a strong Citizen Army on Territorial lines. . . .' *Ibid.*, 13 June 1919.
31. *Ibid.*, 7 July 1919.
32. e.g. 5 *Parl. Debs. H.C.*, 120, c. 300, 27 October 1919.
33. *The Times*, 9 October 1919.
34. Statements by the Deputy Chief of the General Staff, *The Times*, 15 August 1919; by Churchill, 6 December 1919.
35. See *The Times*, 15 and 21 November: 6, 17 and 18 December 1919.
36. For support of the City of Glasgow resolution see: East Sussex Record Office, Sussex Territorial Army Association Records, D 912/7, Association meeting, 24 November 1919; Northumberland Record Office, Northumberland Territorial Force Association Records, NRO 408/6, Association meeting, 12 December 1919. For similar resolutions see: Central Library, Manchester (Archives Department), East Lancashire Territorial and Auxiliary Forces Association Records, M 73, Association meeting, 6 June 1919; Gwent County Archives, Monmouthshire Territorial Army Association Records, D 766.1, Association meeting, 23 October 1919; Greater London Record Office (London Records), County of London Territorial Army and Air Force Association Records, A/TA/2, Association meeting, 30 October 1919. On 6 January 1920 the City of London Association also passed a resolution supporting the Glasgow protest: Guildhall Library, City of London Territorial and Auxiliary Force Association Records, 12,606/2.
37. Churchill to CIGS, AG, DGTF, 8 December 1919. WO 32/2681.
38. *The Times*, 19 December 1919.
39. C.P. 388, CAB 24/95. 'Liability of Territorial Force for General Service', 5 January 1920. Churchill had again advised the Cabinet on 23 December of the urgency of reaching a decision, the more so since he was due to meet the Territorial Associations on 15 January to announce the Government's proposals. Cab 19(19)5, CAB 23/18.
40. Cab 2(20)2, CAB 23/20.
41. Wilson Papers, diary entry for 9 January 1920.
42. 9 January 1920.
43. 10 January 1920.
44. Scarbrough to Wilson, 13 January 1920. WO 32/2681. Wilson's tally was slightly

different; he recorded three dissenting votes. Wilson Papers, diary entry for 13 January 1920. Churchill later told the Cabinet of this vote, but said of those who favoured a general service obligation, 'their views perhaps were somewhat vitiated by the fact that their wish was father to the thought'. 27 January 1920. Cab 8(20), Appendix III (4), CAB 23/20.

45. Geddes to sub-committee secretary, 17 January 1920. WO 32/2681.

46. 21 January 1920.

47. Rutland to Churchill, 21 January 1920; minute by Churchill, 25 January 1920. WO 32/2681.

48. Wilson Papers, diary entry for 23 January 1920.

49. *Ibid.*, 26 January 1920.

50. Cab 8(20), Appendix III(4), CAB 23/20. The meeting was not one of the Cabinet but a 'Conference of Ministers'.

51. *The Times*, 31 January 1920.

52. The bounty was also criticised for being *too* liberal. Sir Francis Acland, who as Financial Secretary to the War Office, 1908-10, had worked closely with Haldane on the creation of the original Territorial Force, complained that 'instead of the Territorials being a real civilian force depending upon the goodwill and patriotism of the masses of the citizens they are going to become pinchbeck regulars dependent on money and organised on a purely military basis'. 5 *Parl. Debs. H.C.*, 125, c. 1374, 23 February 1920.

53. This was Churchill's explanation of the poor recruiting response in South Wales, where, by the middle of May, three battalions had enlisted only eighty-two men. 5 *Parl. Debs. H.C.*, 130, c. 2018, 22 June 1920.

54. For discussions of employers' obligations, see: Greater London Record Office (Middlesex Records), Middlesex Territorial and Auxiliary Forces Association Records, Acc. 994/4, General Purposes Committee meeting, 7 April 1919; Kent County Archives, Kent Territorial and Auxiliary Forces Association Records, MD/TA 1/3, Association meeting, 7 April 1919; Monmouthshire Territorial Army Association Records, D 766.1, Association meeting, 24 April 1919; Sussex Territorial Army Association Records, D 912/7, Association meeting, 14 July 1919; Gloucestershire County Record Office, Gloucestershire Territorial Army Association Records, Acc. D 2388, Association meeting, 9 February 1920; report of Army Committee meeting with Churchill and Scarbrough, *The Times*, 5 March 1920; City of Leeds Archives Department, West Riding Territorial Army and Air Force Association Records, Acc. 1469/3, Association meeting, 26 April 1920; Cumbria Record Office, Cumberland and Westmorland Territorial Army Associations Records, vol. 3, Joint Committee meeting, 30 April 1920; East Lancashire Territorial Association Records, M 73/3/26, Recruiting and Discharge Committee, 21 May 1920.

55. 16 April 1920. WO 32/2676.

56. 30 March 1920. WO 32/2676. The need for some form of additional guarantee seemed to be underlined by a ruling from the Judge-Advocate General that once all men of the first class of the Army Reserve had been called, the Army Council was obliged to embody the whole Territorial Army within a month unless Parliament decided otherwise. JAG to DGTF, 6 May 1920. WO 32/2676.

57. 28 April 1920. WO 32/2676.

58. 29 April 1920. WO 32/2676.

59. In April 1921, to counter the threat of a crippling strike, the Cabinet decided to create a special Defence Force. Although it was legally separate from the Territorial Army, no one could fail to observe that recruiting was carried out at Territorial drill halls and that service with the Defence Force counted towards Territorial engagements. Thus the Territorial Force was associated with strike breaking.

60. 31 May 1920. WO 32/2676.

61. See: Liverpool Record Office, West Lancashire Territorial Army Association Records, Acc. 2074, Minute Book 1908-22, Association meeting, 12 February 1920; Monmouthshire Territorial Army Association Records, D 766.1, Association meeting, 18 February 1920; Kent Territorial Army Association Records, MD/TA 3/4, General Purposes Committee meeting, 30 July 1920; Duke of York's Headquarters, Council of TA & VR Associations Secretariat, Council of County Territorial Associations Records, Association meeting, 21 July 1920; CCTA Executive Committee meeting, 1 December 1920.
62. West Riding Territorial Army Association Records, Acc. 1469/3, Association meeting, 26 April 1920; *The Times*, 27 April 1920.
63. 29 April 1920.
64. 5 *Parl. Debs. H.C.*, 128, cc. 1876-7, 4 May 1920.
65. *The Times*, 17 May 1920.
66. Although one correspondent (3 May 1920) complained that it was 'pernicious' to suggest that the War Office was unenthusiastic, *The Times* returned to the charge on May 15. The King's interest, it wrote, came 'opportunely at a time when official dilatoriness has brought the fortunes of the force to a low ebb,... .[The] Government launched the new scheme in February in so half-hearted a fashion that the results...have been disastrous'.
67. 5 *Parl. Debs. H.C.*, 125, c. 1360, 23 February 1920.

Civil-Military Relations in Nazi Germany's Shadow: the Case of Hungary, 1939-1941

N.F. DREISZIGER

In examining the early phases of the Second World War in Eastern Europe, most historians have concentrated on diplomatic and military developments. Although this has been a useful approach, it does not explain completely Hitler's success in reducing much of this area to vassalage very early during the war. Part of the reason for the Führer's triumph is, of course, simple: the *Wehrmacht* conquered Poland in 1939 and Yugoslavia in 1941. Diplomacy also played a significant role in the Nazis' success. Hitler and his diplomats had been quite effective in playing off one East European state against the other. But there is more to the story of Eastern Europe's fall than military weakness and the lack of international co-operation. The nations of Eastern Europe were divided not only among themselves but, in some cases, they also lacked internal cohesion.

Among the states which succumbed to the Third Reich without armed resistance, Hungary is probably the best example of a country divided internally. One of the more pronounced divisions within contemporary Hungarian society was the rift between the country's civilian leadership and its military establishment. It is the purpose of this study to examine this rift and its effects, during the first two years of the war, on Hungarian decision-making concerning the vital questions of alliances and strategy.

I

The state of Hungarian politics and the country's international position on the eve of the Second World War cannot be understood without a brief reference to the traumatic events of 1918-20 which had given birth to the Hungary of the interwar period. The Great War and its turbulent aftermath had profound effects on the country. When the dust had settled after the storm, gone was the 'thousand year old' Empire of the Holy Crown of St Stephen. The peace-makers had reduced Hungary to less than

30 per cent of her former size and left her with about a third of her population.[1] These enormous losses, when added to the scars left by the war and its troubled aftermath, caused severe and lasting dislocations in the country's economic and political life.

The war and the peace settlement had brought an end to the influential role Hungary had played in international affairs before 1918. From the position of being one of the ruling nations within the Habsburg Empire, Hungary plummeted to the status of a land-locked small nation, reduced to economic and military impotence. The new Hungary, moreover, was isolated. Both Czechoslovakia and Yugoslavia, countries born out of the maelstrom of 1918-20, and the much enlarged Rumania, had a vital interest in preserving the new territorial order established in East Europe. And the cornerstone of this order was a weak Hungary.

The years 1918-20 in Hungary witnessed a great deal of internal strife which caused further setbacks in national development. In the autumn of 1918 the country was swept by revolution which brought to power a group of men imbued with the spirit of pacifism and reform. But the tide of revolution continued to surge, and the spring of 1919 saw the transfer of power to radicals dedicated to the ideas of the dictatorship of the proletariat and the building of a Socialist society. In the summer a reaction set in against the long months of impatient experimentation in leftist politics. Unlike Russia, where the forces of Bolshevism emerged victorious after a bitter civil war, in Hungary fate in the end entrusted the task of re-building the country from the ruins of war and revolution, not to the Reds, but to their enemies, the Whites.

The tumultuous events of 1918-20 had left their indelible marks on Hungary. Many of the country's provinces had been lost during the 'democratic' revolution in 1918; consequently, liberalism and pacifism stood discredited in Hungarian society between the wars. The Western democracies, France, in particular, for whom a portion of Hungary's intelligentsia had a great deal of respect earlier, were considered to be the authors of the peace settlement and, as such, they came to be seen as Hungary's enemies. The hatred of the left and the distrust of Western Europe permeated Hungarian society to the core during the interwar period. The resentment against what had transpired in 1918-20 came to focus with great vehemence and heavy concentration on the peace settlement which was imposed on Hungary in the Treaty of

Trianon. The facts that Hungary had not been consulted in the deliberations which had led to the drawing up of this treaty, and that she was compelled to accept it under duress, enabled many Hungarians to disregard the circumstance that the disintegration of historic Hungary had been basically the consequence of a malaise that had ailed the country for generations and for which Hungary's successive governments had failed to find a lasting and effective cure: the nationalities question.[2]

Hatred of the peace settlement virtually became the *raison d'être* of Hungarian society after 1920, and the open and avowed aim of national policy became the revision of this settlement. On this aim there was no disagreement in the diverse groupings and classes making up the nation, least of all between the civilian leaders and the military. What these two groups disagreed on often, was the means of attaining this national aim.

II

Hungary's policy aiming at the revision of the Treaty of Trianon had not met any significant success for many years after 1920. The dislocations that the rise of the Axis powers caused in European international affairs during the late 1930s increased the prospects for the alteration of the East European *status quo*. Contrary to what might be expected, this turn of events did not unite the influential elements of Hungarian society behind the Government's policy of revision. In fact, it was precisely during these years of approaching crisis that dissension grew within the leading circles of the country, and a serious rift developed between the civilians and the military. It was also during this very same period that Hungary, much against the will of some of her leaders, drifted into the Axis fold.

For an understanding of the causes of this rift it is necessary to give a brief description of Hungary's civilian leadership and military establishment on the eve of the Second World War. This is not a simple task, for both the country's civilian government and its armed forces were made up of diverse elements.

At the risk of perpetrating an oversimplification, it may be said that the Government of Hungary on the eve of the war was dominated by a group of aristocrats dedicated to the preservation of the *status quo* at home and its destruction in the international affairs of Eastern Europe. Perhaps the most outstanding figure of this group was Count Pál Teleki, the country's Premier in 1939.[3] While Teleki and his aristocratic associates were keen to revise the provisions of the Treaty of Trianon, their approach to revision was more cautious than that of many other groups in the country. While they realised that Italy and Germany were more interested in a revision of the peace settlements than were France and Britain, and that friendship with the Axis powers was the most useful tool of Hungarian foreign policy, men like Teleki were always reluctant to risk involvement in a European war to attain their aims. Accordingly, co-operation with Italy and Germany short of participating in Axis military ventures became the cornerstone of Hungarian foreign policy up to 1941. This approach was plainly defined as early as November of 1937 when another of Hungary's aristocratic statesmen, Kálmán Kánya de Kánya (Minister of External Affairs, 1933-8) told Hitler that 'Hungary had no intention of achieving her revisionist aims by force of arms and thereby possibly unleashing a European war'.[4] The policy was upheld in August of 1938 when the Hungarian leaders refused to promise co-operation in Hitler's planned invasion of Czechoslovakia.[5] It must be stated that neither in 1937-8, nor during the subsequent period, did all or even most of Hungary's civilian leaders share Kánya's and Teleki's caution, just as decision-making at the highest level was not always and never completely dominated by the aristrocratic element within the country's leadership. But what made it even more difficult for Teleki to conduct a cautious foreign policy aimed at the peaceful revision of the Treaty of Trianon was the growing influence that the Hungarian military wielded by 1939.

The military establishment of interwar Hungary was small. The country's forces had been limited by the Treaty of Trianon to a professional army of 35,000. Aeroplanes, tanks and other modern weapons were outlawed. Like many other small forces, Hungary's army, known as the *honvéd*, had a relatively large officer corps. Nearly all of its officers were veterans of the Great War. Most of them had received their training and had started their careers in the Imperial forces of the Habsburg Empire. Two facts are worthy of special mention concerning the social composition of the *honvéd's* officer corps. Unlike the country's diplomatic service and political leadership, which tended to recruit most of its members from the upper classes, the officers were predominantly middle- and lower-class in origin. The second noteworthy characteristic is the fact that a disproportionately large percentage of the *honvéd's* officers were of non-Hungarian background, but of German (more precisely, Swabian) descent. [6]

Although, as has been mentioned, Hungary's interwar military establishment was small, it possessed an influence in the country's political life that was out of all proportion to its size. The explanation for this fact is not simple. In the history of most nations, periods following wars and civil wars usually witness an increased influence of military men. Hungary of the post-1919 years was certainly no exception. [7] Even the country's head-of-state, Regent Miklós Horthy, was a military man. As such, he had an understanding for the ideas and sympathy for the aspirations of fellow officers. The fact that he was a naval officer, however, tended to weaken the bond of identity between him and Hungary's numerous colonels and generals. [8] The interests of the military were usually kept in view by Horthy, but having the ex-admiral as the country's Regent was not quite the same as having an army officer as the head of the Government. It is not surprising that in the pre-1938 days the influence of Hungary's military did not grow as much as it did during the years of General Gyula Gömbös's premiership (1932-6). [9]

Another factor which contributed to the strength of the Hungarian military in the interwar period was the fact that during the Great War the officer class of the *honvéd* developed a strong *esprit de corps* and, at the end of the war, the degree of its cohesion was unrivalled in Hungarian society. More importantly, this officer class acted as the 'saviour' of the country in the civil war of 1919. The officer class's *esprit de corps* was reinforced by the feeling of outrage caused by the peace settlement, while its cohesion was maintained through the establishment of secret societies. The idea of the military being the saviour of the country was perpetuated by those Hungarians (military men and civilians alike) who regarded the *honvéd* as the best instrument of revising the Treaty of Trianon.

III

During the 1920s the chances of attaining 'revision' by force of arms were next to non-existent. But the mid-thirties brought a number of developments, both inside and outside of Hungary, which must have heightened the hopes of many Hungarian officers. The appointment of Gömbös as Premier in 1932 was the first of this encouraging turn of events. Gömbös was determined to emulate the Italian pattern of politics. While in office, he promoted many officers of the rightist outlook to high positions within the *honvéd* and the civil service. Illness and death kept Gömbös from realising his aim, while his aristocratic and liberal opponents prevented the continuation of his policies beyond his departure from the ranks of the living. But this setback for his followers and sympathisers was compensated for by the rise in European international politics of the Rome-Berlin Axis. [10]

It was the rise of Italian and, especially, German strength in Central Europe which accentuated the differences of outlook between Hungary's civilian and military leaders. Most members of the former group looked askance on Hitler's and Mussolini's radical domestic policies and adventurous foreign policy moves. The latter, on the other hand, were impressed by the success of Italian and German rearmament and admired the way Hitler gradually and deftly freed Germany from the fetters imposed at Versailles. German economic and military strength and the effectiveness of Hitler's diplomacy contrasted sharply with the weakness of Hungary and the fruitless foreign policy manoeuvrings of her leaders. Feelings between the country's civilian leaders and its more impatient military men became particularly tense during the late summer and autumn of 1938, when the Hungarian Government refused to participate in the planned German invasion of Czechoslovakia. The invasion did not take place in 1938: the Munich 'surrender' deprived Hitler of the strategic reason as well as the diplomatic excuse for his planned military adventure. Although Hitler was cheated out of what he expected to be another triumphant march into another of Central Europe's ancient capitals, Munich appeared to have been a great victory for German diplomacy. But as far as Hungary was concerned, Munich was a disaster. Once the international crisis was over and German and even Polish demands satisfied, there was no reason why the Czechs and Slovaks should yield to further demands on their territory. At Munich, Hungarian aspirations for revision were not considered. After Munich, the conditions for the realisation of these aspirations were no longer favourable. In the end, in an arbitral award decided on by the German and Italian Foreign Ministers in Vienna, Hungary was given back a part of the territory she had lost to Czechoslovakia in 1919. But the so-called First Vienna Award did not satisfy the Hungarian military who continued to blame their country's 'timid' civilian leadership for missing the boat in September when a bolder policy may have led to a more drastic revision of Hungary's northern boundaries. [11]

In 1939 recriminations between the civilians and the military diminished in intensity. In September of 1938 the soldiers had been angry at the civilians for getting nothing for Hungary during the Munich crisis; in subsequent months, however, they also became resentful against the Germans for failing to give adequate support to Hungary's territorial claims during the negotiations which preceded the First Vienna Award. Especially disappointing was the German decision not to return to Hungary Subcarpathia, a mountainous region with a large Ruthenian (Ukrainian) population. At the time Hitler had planned to use this area as a pawn in diplomatic manoeuvrings *vis-à-vis* Poland and even possibly Russia. Early in 1939, however, the Führer decided that the interest of Germany was best served not through the creation of some kind of a Ruthenian state in Subcarpathia, but by the annexation of the region to Hungary. [12] Accordingly, the Hungarian Government was given the green light, and the *honvéd* occupied the region during the second half of March. In Budapest the impression was maintained that the occupation had been executed entirely on Hungarian initiative. As a result, the Government's popularity greatly increased. The 'impatient revisionists' were impressed by the boldness of the move, while those who resented or feared Germany, lauded the Government's audacity in defying, as they believed, Hitler's will.

The popularity of the Government with certain factions of the right and the military continued through the crisis-filled summer and autumn of 1939. The sudden announcement in late August of the Nazi-Soviet Non-Aggression Pact, could hardly have pleased Hungarian officers whose anti-Bolshevism was usually strong and genuine. The German attack on Poland probably also disappointed many. The majority of Hungarians had a great deal of sympathy for the Poles. It is well known that the Hungarian Government refused to co-operate in any way with the Germans in September of 1939 and even opened the country's northeastern borders to Polish refugees. There can be little doubt that the Government's stand was whole-heartedly approved by most of the country's soldiers. But the *détente* between the more cautious elements of the Government on the one hand and the radical right and the military on the other, was not destined to last very long. Neither the internal political situation nor the evolution of international events in Eastern Europe favoured its prolongation.

IV

The crises of 1938-9 had not passed without leaving their indelible marks on Hungarian politics. The international upheavals of these two fateful years were accompanied by internal changes, many of which strengthened the influence of the military in national affairs. In particular, the year 1938 witnessed the long-awaited start of a rearmament programme. [13] Even more important was the passage in 1939 of the Home Defence Act (*Honvédelmi Törvény*). This law re-introduced the principle of universal liability for military service, restricted certain political freedoms (such as the freedom of assembly and association), provided for the supervision by the military of the press and, more importantly, of industries involved in the production of a wide range of war materials. The act created a new decision-making body in Hungary, the Supreme Council of Home Defence, made up of the Regent, the members of the Ministerial Council, the Chief-of-Staff and the Commander-in-Chief of the Army. The Council's establishment meant that in the vital question of war and peace there was now a body above the civilian government, a body in which the soldiers had direct representation. Another general effect of the new legislation was the fact that, from 1939 on, the country's military played an important role in the supervision of the part of the national economy related to the production of all war materials. [14] But the significance of the rearmament programme and the new home defence act was surpassed by the changes which had taken place in this period, particularly during the autumn of 1938, in the composition of Hungary's civilian and military leadership.

Perhaps the most important of these changes, as far as Hungary's relation to the Axis was concerned, was the dismissal of Kánya from the Ministerial Council. He had been one of Hungary's most assertive and most influential Ministers of External Affairs during the interwar period. He was always a cautious man who distrusted the Axis leaders as he distrusted the Hungarian right-radicals and the military. Prior to Munich, he had been the most adamant opponent of the idea of Hungary's collaboration in a German invasion of Czechoslovakia. Not surprisingly, he had earned the hatred of Hitler and his right-hand man in foreign affairs, Ribbentrop. Whether Kánya was dismissed because of his superiors' desire to appease Berlin, is not certain,[15] but soon after the First Vienna Award he was no longer a desirable figure to have in the Cabinet and he was deprived of his portfolio in a re-shuffle of the Ministerial Council. His successor was Count István Csáky, a vain, impressionable, talented but somewhat inexperienced politician. Although a member of Hungary's circle of aristocratic statesmen, Csáky shared neither his predecessor's caution nor his distrust of the Axis. Kánya's departure from national politics was counter-balanced a few months later by the replacement of Béla Imrédy as Premier. During the Sudeten Crisis, Imrédy had become a convert to the Axis cause and for some five months he sponsored measures that were designed to bring Hungary's internal and external policies more in line with those of Germany and Italy. But his efforts alarmed Hungary's conservatives and liberals alike and he was manoeuvred into resigning from office.[16] His successor was Teleki who made every effort to prevent or delay the implementation of Imrédy's pro-Axis programme.

Another important change in Hungarian leadership during the autumn of 1938 was the appointment of General Henrik Werth as Chief-of-Staff. Werth was still another of the high-ranking officers of the General Staff with a German ethnic background. Moreoever, he spoke perfect German and had married a citizen of the Third Reich. There is no evidence that the above factors had played a significant role in Werth's selection, nor that there had been representations from Berlin asking for his appointment.[17] But once established in his new post, Werth became one of the most persistent advocates of aligning Hungarian foreign and military policies with those of the Axis powers.

V

The international developments of the first year of the Second World War had further unsettling impact on Hungarian politics and, especially, on civil-military relations. The war, first in Eastern Europe and then also in the West, witnessed the crumbling away of a greater and greater portion of the international order established by the Paris peace settlements. This step-by-step process increased most Hungarian leaders' expectations about new and more extensive revisions of the territorial settlement in East Central Europe. But a further revision of the country's northern boundary was not possible: after Czechoslovakia's total dismemberment in 1939, Slovakia became a German satellite. Its territorial integrity was assured by Germany. Nor was there much prospect for revision in the foreseeable future in the south. A significant element within Hungary's leadership was reluctant to pick a quarrel with Yugoslavia. There remained the question of revision in the East and it was in this direction that most eyes in Budapest turned after the outbreak of the war.

There can be little doubt, that, for Hungarians, the most painful of all territorial losses during 1919-20 had been the lost of Transylvania. That land had been an historic part of Hungary. During the centuries when the Habsburgs ruled the western and northern parts of the country and the Turks kept ravaging the southern and the central portions, Transylvania often served as the focal point of Hungarian national feelings and political strength. Although a land of mixed population, its political and cultural life had always been dominated by the Hungarians who comprised much of its upper and middle classes. Even during the beginning of the twentieth century, by which time the local Rumanian population began to have an increased demographic and economic weight, many of Transylvania's counties remained predominantly Hungarian and its cities often had large Hungarian majorities. The transfer of all of this area, as well as of other Hungarian lands, to Rumania in 1919 seemed particularly cruel and unjustified.[18] Accordingly, as soon as the international situation indicated the likelihood of further erosion of the post-1919 *status quo* in Eastern Europe, Hungarians began scheming in earnest for the regaining of the lands that had been lost to Rumania.

Most Hungarian leaders were confident that the long-awaited opportunity to solve the Transylvanian question would soon present itself. They had every reason to think so. Rumania's international position kept deteriorating after September of 1939. Hungary was not the only country eager to press her territorial

demands against her. In the wake of the Great War, Rumania
had also gained lands from Bulgaria and Russia. The Bulgarian
claim to Dobruja did not alarm Bucharest unduly, but much
more threatening was the desire of the Soviet Union to regain
Bessarabia. Soviet calls for the return of this region started in
November of 1939 and continued during the winter. But
Rumania was also a possible target for an attack from still another
quarter: Germany. The Ploesti oil-fields were one of the most
important sources of energy in Europe, and Hitler could not afford to allow them to fall into hostile hands. Against these
dangers the Rumanians had no defences. France and Britain were
hardly in a position to offer serious help. The British had issued a
guarantee to Rumania earlier, but this was a guarantee of that
country's independence and not of her territorial integrity.

Rumania's increasing difficulties after the autumn of 1939 gave
rise to various plans in Budapest all designed to solve the Transylvanian question in a manner satisfactory to Hungary's interests. How differently Hungary's civilian and military leaders
approached this issue is illustrated by the plans that were advanced by ex-Premier Count István Bethlen and General Werth.
The scheme of the former, outlined in a long, secret memorandum to the Government, started with the premise that Germany
would lose the war against the West European democracies. Accordingly, Bethlen argued, Hungary should remain neutral in the
European struggle and preserve her strength for the attainment of
her national aims at the end of the war. Bethlen hoped, that by
participating in some kind of a security arrangement for post-war
Europe, and by not annexing Transylvania but allowing it to
become an autonomous member of a loose East European federa-
tion, Hungary could obtain Western diplomatic support for her
plans.[19]

Werth's plans for Transylvania were quite different. The
Chief-of-Staff was not willing to wait until the outcome of the
war was settled. When the Russian threat against Rumania
became acute in the winter of 1939-40, Werth urged his government to prepare for the recovery of Transylvania by force should
an armed conflict develop between Moscow and Bucharest.[20] In
April of 1940 Werth returned to this subject in a memorandum
addressed to Horthy and the leading members of the Government. The Chief-of-Staff discussed at length the probable outcome of the war. Unlike Bethlen, he concluded that Germany

would more than likely emerge as the victor, but even if she did not, a complete German defeat was impossible because of the superior strength of the *Wehrmacht*. Werth, who had just held discussions with representatives of the German General Staff, informed his civilian superiors that the Germans had offered their co-operation against Rumania. But simple military co-operation was not sufficient according to Werth. Hungary should abandon her neutrality and formally become an ally of Berlin so that she could regain the lands she had lost in the wake of the First World War. Knowing that certain members of his audience were still not convinced of Germany's invincibility, Werth added that even if Germany did not win the war, Hungary could retain her conquests because at the end of an exhausting struggle the Allied Powers would be 'too weak to send large forces in the Danube Valley'.[21]

To Werth's disappointment, a Hungarian-German alliance against Rumania never came about. From the late spring of 1940 on, Hitler was preoccupied with the Western front and, for the time being, did not wish to undertake any military ventures in the East. Interestingly enough, Hitler's desire to maintain peace in Eastern Europe and the Balkans nearly gave Hungary an opportunity to achieve revision in Transylvania on her own terms. That, in the end, the solution of the Transylvanian question in 1940 was made on terms dictated not from Budapest but from Berlin, seems to have been in a large part the result of a conflict between the Hungarian Government and the military, in particular, a clash between Teleki and Werth.

VI

The approach that the Hungarian leadership after some delay adopted towards the question of Transylvania differed appreciably from that advocated by Werth. Teleki, who was still largely responsible for the formulation of Hungary's foreign policy in the summer of 1940, was repelled by the idea of abandoning the country's neutrality and joining Germany, not only in a military action against Rumania, but also in the war against the West. Unlike Werth, Teleki was doubtful about the prospects of a German victory. He felt that the superiority of moral strength and physical resources was on the Allied side. He could not accept Werth's suggestion that Hungary should become an ally of Germany in the war. He rejected the Chief-of-Staff's proposals in a letter to Horthy. He stressed to the Regent that Germany's victory was not a foregone conclusion and, therefore, it was not advantageous for Hungary to side with her completely. Werth, the Premier argued, did not see the problem of Hungary's interests from the point of view of a Hungarian. Teleki also asked Horthy to see to it that the soldiers did not meddle in politics. [22]

Although Teleki rejected Werth's plan of regaining Transylvania with Germany military help, he did not give up hope of attaining a revision of his country's eastern boundaries through some other means. The opportunity seemed to have presented itself in the summer of 1940. At the time Hitler was still hoping to force Britain to her knees and thereby to end the war in Western Europe. To do this Hitler needed peace elsewhere in Europe, especially in the south-east, from where came many of the foodstuffs, fuel and raw materials needed by the *Wehrmacht*. In the meantime, the Russians had decided to act. At the end of June they confronted Rumania with an ultimatum demanding the return of Bessarabia. The Soviet move caused much hectic activity in Hungary. [23] The *honvéd* was mobilised and frantic efforts were made to ascertain Rome's and Berlin's attitudes to a Hungarian occupation of Transylvania in case of a Russo-Rumanian conflict. But that conflict never came about. Rumania surrendered Bessarabia without a fight. And from Berlin came word that Germany would be most unhappy about any disruption of the peace in Eastern Europe. [24] Even though the best opportunity for regaining Transylvania was now gone, the Hungarians continued their threatening attitude towards Rumania, demanding at the same time that the dispute be submitted to a conference attended by the statesmen of Germany, Italy, Hungary and Rumania. Teleki's aim was evident: threatened by a Hungarian-Rumanian conflict at the time when Germany's interest demanded peace in Eastern Europe, the Axis powers would be forced to support the Hungarian claims in any negotiations on the issue. [25] But, for the time being, Hitler did not wish to act as a mediator in a territorial dispute between Hungary and Rumania. At a meeting of the German, Italian and Hungarian leaders in Munich during mid-July, he rejected the idea of a four-power conference and told Teleki and Csáky to negotiate with the Rumanians alone. [26]

As could be expected, the Hungarian-Rumanian discussions did not get started for weeks and then achieved nothing. There was no real reason why Bucharest had to make substantial concessions. By this time Rumania had renounced the British guarantee and embarked on a pro-Axis policy. As a result of these changes she acquired a new friend: Germany. The Hungarians could do no more than continue their threats against Rumania and hope that Hitler would change his mind, and for the sake of peace in south-eastern Europe, would intervene in the dispute.

At the end of July Hitler changed his policy on this question. Almost overnight it seems, he decided to see to it that all outstanding international disputes were settled in Eastern Europe. The reason for this complete turnabout in German policy lay in international developments. In July, the Nazis' efforts to force Britain to come to terms with them were not having their desired effects. To deprive the British of their last ray of hope in the European struggle, Hitler decided to smash the Soviet Union in one huge campaign next spring. With Russia under German rule, Japan would be free to turn against the US, and Britain would have no hope of holding out against Germany. To prepare this bold venture, Hitler needed tranquillity in Eastern Europe, and to achieve this he had to settle the question of Hungarian-Rumanian relations. This was exactly what the Hungarians desired in August of 1940. But they wanted Hitler to act as a mediator in the dispute and not as an arbiter. They did not want to see another Vienna Award announced in which Germany and Italy imposed a settlement favourable first and foremost to German interests. If everything else failed, Teleki was prepared to accept arbitration, but he wanted the Rumanians to ask for it: if Bucharest called for arbitral award, Budapest could insist on certain pre--conditions. Moreover, if the revision of the boundaries came about through arbitration requested by Rumania, the settlement would have greater legitimacy in the eyes of the West, and Hungary would have a better chance to retain the territories gained at the end of the war, even if the Axis were defeated.

This was Teleki's plan. Its essential feature was to threaten war in south-eastern Europe and compel the Rumanians to request Hitler's diplomatic intervention. But in this plan Teleki was double-crossed. At the critical moment, Werth informed the Germans that, as a final measure, Hungary was willing to accept arbitration rather than go to war. [27] After such a disclosure, it was not difficult for Berlin to call Teleki's bluff. In the end the fate of Transylvania was settled by another German-Italian *dictum*. The region was divided between Rumania and Hungary in a way which left both sides bitterly dissatisfied. [28]

Werth's indiscretion, which had greatly helped to destroy Teleki's delicate web of plans spun for the solution of the Transylvanian question in accordance with Hungarian interests, deeply perturbed the sensitive and even depressive Premier. He decided to resign and announced his decision in a letter to Horthy. Teleki disclaimed any personal antipathy towards Werth. He complained of not being able to 'prevail against the military'. He accepted part of the blame for this unfortunate state of affairs: he had allowed the soldiers to become 'too powerful'. As a result, he no longer felt suitable to carry out the demanding task of leading the country in such difficult times. Someone else would have to be appointed who would end the division between the Government and the military. 'I have said and am still saying that in the interest of the country matters should be put into one single hand.' [29]

Teleki's letter had been written in a great hurry. The Premier was occupied with the settling up of the administration of the northern counties of Transylvania which had been returned by the Second Vienna Award. Consequently, on the following day he felt obliged to return to the subject in another, much longer letter. In this memorandum, which has many of the trappings of an academic paper, Teleki outlined in great detail the problem of civil-military relations in Hungary. He began by saying that he did not want any constitutional changes in the relations of the Government and the military: he considered the existing legal framework of these relations satisfactory. The problem was, he argued, that there had been a departure from the legal basis, and Hungary was drifting towards a sort of 'military dictatorship' imposed from 'below' rather than 'from above'. 'In Hungary', he continued, there were 'two governmental machineries'. One was the legal government, the other was the military establishment which extended to 'all branches of civil administration' and whose activities the 'lawful governmental system' was unable to supervise. What was needed, was to appoint a new premier who could end this state of affairs by gathering in his hands the highest executive powers.

In particular, Teleki continued, it was necessary to make clear that soldiers assigned to the various branches of the civil administration should become responsible to the civil authorities while personally they would continue to answer to their superior officers. This practice of assigning soldiers to the various government departments had been started by Premier Göbös and was expanded subsequently. Particularly strong was the military's control over the Ministry of Industry. In this department over one hundred soldiers had been given positions. Moreover, the ministry became subordinated to the head of the Ministry of Defence. The demarcation of authority between the two ministries became blurred. The resulting confusion caused serious blunders. On one occasion, Teleki recounted, Ministry of Industry officials negotiated and signed an export-import agreement in arms with Germany without informing the Minister of Commerce and the Minister of External Affairs. And the soldiers of this ministry were sources of trouble in internal affairs as well. They had interfered in labour disputes and had called for higher wages at a time when the Government was pursuing a policy of wage restraint. On still other occasions, officers assigned to factories and mines interfered with work regulations or began issuing their own directives regarding work discipline. To remedy this situation, Teleki recommended the delimitation of the respective spheres of authority of the Ministry of Defence and the Ministry of Industry in the matter of war production. He also called for the restriction, or, in some cases, the elimination of the influence of officers in the country's mines and factories.

Next, Teleki turned to fiscal matters. He complained that the Government had difficulty in supervising and controlling expenditures by the military, that certain officers had interfered with the investment policy of a state-owned company and that, in one city, the soldiers tried to have the tax-rate changed. The military also tried to interfere with social policy, according to Teleki. In the draft of the regulations enforcing the Home Defence Act of 1939, a group of officers called for the supervision of local school authorities by the leaders of a para-military youth corps, the *levente*. Fortunately, Teleki admitted, the undesirable portion of the draft regulations had been omitted before they were adopted. Still, on numerous occasions, *levente* instructors had violated school customs and regulations. Teleki also deplored the attitude of many members of the military towards the civil government and their disregard for the law of the land. He cited the example of the military's arrest of several priests in re-occupied Slovak areas, arrests which had been made without the knowledge of the civil authorities. This type of interference in home politics by the military had to be strictly suppressed, the Premier argued.

In the last part of the memorandum, Teleki discussed the role of the military in foreign affairs. He admitted that the soldiers had to gather information abroad and had to have their own staff for this purpose, but this task had to be done in harmony with the intentions and policies of the Government. In Hungary, much was lacking in the co-ordination of the activities of diplomats and soldiers abroad. He, as Premier, and the Minister of External Affairs, were not receiving all the reports Hungarian military attachés sent home from abroad. It was imperative, he stressed, that he should at least see the instructions that the Chief-of-Staff despatched to military attachés. If this had been done, many unpleasant misunderstandings could have been avoided. On his part, Teleki continued, he had always informed Werth of the Government's foreign policy line. Still, the Chief-of-Staff had done great harm when, during the crisis over Transylvania, he informed the Germans that Hungary wanted arbitration. In concluding his memorandum, Teleki asked Horthy to convey to the military his request for the separation of civil and military authority in Hungary and the subordination of the latter to the former in all cases not exclusively military in nature. [30]

In response to Teleki's strong protest against Hungary's military establishment, Horthy agreed to see to it that several of the grievances, especially the lack of government control over military expenditures, were remedied; but he refused to accept the Premier's resignation. [31] Thus, Teleki remained at the helm of the Hungarian ship of state for another six months, only to see his country drift still closer toward the Axis camp.

VII

The half year which separated the Second Vienna Award from Hungary's involvement in the German invasion of Yugoslavia, witnessed the further, stage-by-stage erosion of the country's neutrality. There is no need to tell the story of this process here. Its two milestones are familiar to students of war-time history: Budapest's consent to the transit through Hungary of German troops destined for pro-Axis Rumania, and Hungary's accession to the Tripartite Pact. [32] Civil-military relations in the country did not seem to have improved appreciably, in spite of Teleki's disclosures to the Regent. That these relations remained tense, became evident during the next crisis in Hungary's external relations: the German-Yugoslav confrontation in the early spring of 1941.

The last months of 1940 saw a diplomatic *rapprochement* between Hungary and Yugoslavia. There is no conclusive evidence that Budapest's efforts to seek friendship with Belgrade were not sincere. Although the issue of the Hungarian *irredenta* in Yugoslavia remained unsolved, the need for a neutral friend in a sea of Axis neighbours was a real consideration in the minds of Hungary's best statesmen. The *rapprochement* led to the signing, in December, of a peace and friendship pact between the two countries. [33]

Although better relations with Yugoslavia were seen by Teleki and like-minded Hungarian leaders as a means of reinforcing, through closer association with a neutral state, their country's neutrality, stronger friendship between Budapest and Belgrade was viewed with satisfaction in Berlin. The Hungarian-Yugoslav Pact of Peace was seen by Hitler as a stabilising factor in south-eastern Europe, and stability there was essential because of the approaching conflict with Russia. But Hitler's expectations were dashed by developments in Yugoslavia. In March of 1941 that country's government was overthrown by anti-German elements of its military. Hitler, in his rage, decided to crush Yugoslavia. To do this, he needed the co-operation of Hungary. Accordingly, he despatched a message to Horthy, promising to return to Hungary large areas which had been awarded to Yugoslavia by the peace-makers in 1919. Hitler's price was permission for the *Wehrmacht* to march through Hungary as well as Hungarian participation in the hostilities.

Hitler's message precipitated several days of frantic activity in Budapest. There is no need to give a detailed account of this here. It should suffice to say that the final Hungarian decision on the German request was taken at a meeting of the Supreme Defence Council on the first of April, almost a week after Hitler's plan had been brought to the Hungarian Government's knowledge. It is revealing of the state of politics in Budapest that, prior to the convening of the Council, Horthy had replied to Hitler's message in a letter whose tone was quite affirmative, [34] and that a tentative but complete agreement had been drawn up between Generals Paulus and Werth on the details of Hungarian-German military co-operation in the coming campaign. [35] At the meeting itself, Werth, supported by several ministers including General Károly Bartha, the Minister of Defence, called for Hungary's unconditional participation in the German invasion of Yugoslavia. But Werth and his supporters were out-voted by those ministers who felt that, for the sake of the country's reputation in the West, participation in the German campaign had to be limited and had to be tied to certain definite conditions. [36] In insisting on these conditions, Teleki and his associates had hoped to retain a semblance of Hungary's neutrality, save the nation's honour and, particularly, retain the goodwill of Britain. The next day, when Teleki learned that the imposition of the conditions on Hungary's participation in the invasion would not be enough to achieve the last of these objectives and might not even forestall a British declaration of war on Hungary, the Premier committed suicide. [37]

The Yugoslav crisis of the spring of 1941 brought to a close still another phase of Hungary's descent to the status of an Axis ally and satellite. It did not prove to be a final stage: the consequences of the crisis were not as drastic as some Hungarian leaders had expected. The *Wehrmacht* quickly crushed any effective Yugoslav resistance and the south-Slav state disintegrated. In the north-west, the Croatian Republic was formed under German protection. Hungary regained some of her former territories in the south, but her gains fell far short of what had been promised to her by Hitler. What was more important as far as Hungarian external relations were concerned, was the fact that the crisis had not brought a British declaration of war. With military activities in the Yugoslav lands having come to an early end for the time being, Hungary returned to the state of precarious *de jure* neutrality in the European conflict. But this state of affairs was not to last long, for the next crisis in Eastern Europe, Hitler's invasion of the USSR in June of 1941, was to bring about Hungary's irreversible involvement in the war on Germany's side.

VIII

The story of the diplomatic and political developments which preceded Hungary's involvement in the German invasion of Russia need not be repeated here.[38] It should suffice to say that Hungarian participation in the preparations for the attack was not envisaged by Hitler: the Führer distrusted the Hungarians. Nor did Hungary receive an official invitation to join the war even after the outbreak of the German-Russian conflict. While German pressure for Hungary to join was there, the decision to do so was made in Budapest. And in this decision the country's military, in particular, Generals Werth and Bartha, played a significant role.

While diplomatic relations between the German and Hungarian governments were cool, as illustrated by Hitler's refusal to inform Budapest of his planned campaign against Russia, contacts between the two countries' military were frequent and close. Contrary to what may be expected, these contacts were not sought by the Hungarians alone. In the months before the start of Operation Barbarossa, the German High Command had to take certain precautionary measures from which the Hungarians could not be left out. The German military wished to be assured that Hungarian defence works on the Russo-Hungarian border were adequate against any possible Soviet incursion. Accordingly, they sent one of their staff officers to Hungary and, with the consent of the Hungarian command, had him inspect the new defence works in Subcarpathia.[39] The Germans were also concerned with what they considered to be the inadequate equipment and training of the honvéd in certain areas, for example, in communications. As a result, they pressed for and obtained an increase in the number of German military advisers and training officers attached to Hungarian units. They also succeeded in reaching an agreement regarding the use of Hungary's military communications network. Close collaboration came to be maintained between the two countries' forces in the field of military intelligence operations also.[40]

In addition to the contacts that the execution of these agreements and co-operative ventures created, there were direct, secret discussions between high-ranking German and Hungarian generals on several occasions during the many months that were spent by the *Wehrmacht* in preparing for the invasion of Russia.

Whether these discussions had resulted in the Hungarian military being informed about Operation Barbarossa is an open question. Communist historians in Hungary claim that certain German generals informed their Hungarian counterparts of Germany's true intentions as early as the autumn of 1940 and repeated their warnings about the imminence of a Russo-German war during the Yugoslav crisis. [41] This claim, based upon evidence presented at the Nuremberg trials by the Soviet prosecutor, is not born out by other, more reliable sources. Indeed, if any German officer informed the Hungarians, he did so in contravention of Hitler's orders. We have it on the authority of Field-Marshals Keitel and Paulus that any reference to Operation Barbarossa was forbidden to German officers holding discussions with the Hungarians. [42]

Whether Hungary's military leaders were informed about Hitler's plans by their German counterparts, or they guessed the Führer's intentions from the all-too-obvious preparations that the *Wehrmacht* was making, is irrelevant. The fact is that by early May, General Werth seems to have been in full knowledge of the German plans. [43] And he did not remain silent. On the 6th of the month he approached the country's new Premier, Lászlo Bárdossy, with a memorandum. He argued that the need for new resources would soon drive Germany into a conflict with Russia, and in this war the Germans would expect Hungary to co-operate with them. He urged that the Hungarian Government should anticipate the outbreak of the Russo-German war by offering a military alliance to Germany. Bárdossy answered Werth by questioning the imminence of war between the Reich and the USSR, and by expressing doubt about Germany being willing to come to a military agreement with a small country like Hungary. [44]

Not satisfied with the Premier's reply, on the 31st the Chief-of-Staff approached Bárdossy with another plea for a Hungarian-German military pact. Arguing in the same vein as before, he asked for permission to take up this matter with German military leaders. Having not received a reply to his latest proposal, on 14 June Werth again submitted a memorandum to the Premier. In this long document the Chief-of-Staff predicted that the question of war between Germany and Soviet Russia would be decided 'very soon'. He also assured Bárdossy that, in view of the *Wehrmacht*'s past record and the doubtful strength of the Red Army, it was certain that the Germans would achieve victory in a short time. Hungary's participation in the war would last for a very short while. The reserves could be demobilised by harvest time. Werth suggested that any possible popular discontent which could result from mobilisation (the fifth in three years), should be headed off by the introduction of some social reforms.

It is interesting to note why Werth felt that Hungary had to participate in the expected German invasion of Russia. There is no doubt that he, like most experienced memorialists, listed every possible argument in support of his own point of view. Hungary was already committed to the Axis. Her Christian and nationalist ideology and anti-Bolshevik outlook obliged her to participate. The preservation of the country's territorial integrity and of its social and economic order also argued for the elimination of the Soviet Union, a potentially dangerous neighbour. But there were other reasons as well, ones which Werth argued at length and stressed with particular vehemence. One was the military situation. The Chief-of-Staff found it unlikely that the Germans would tolerate a large gap in their front against the Russians. If they did, the Red Army might drive into Hungarian territory through a poorly defended border. If the Germans refused to accept the existence of this gap, they would occupy it, a move which Hungary could not prevent, and which would still bring down on the country the displeasure and wrath of the Soviets. The other reason for participation, Werth stressed, was the question of Hungarian territorial aggrandisement. The Chief-of-Staff believed that Hungary's expansion depended on her participation in the German campaign. He explained that an Axis-orientated policy had netted Hungary substantial territorial gains. A continuation of this policy would no doubt bring about the restoration to the country of all its ancient territories. The situation was critical, according to Werth. Rumania had already committed herself to participation in the German war against Russia. If Hungary refused to join, the Chief-of-Staff argued, she would not only have to give up hopes of regaining more of Transylvania, but would have to face the prospect of losing the areas she had obtained in 1940. In sum, Werth's arguments amounted to saying that Hungarian participation carried no risks and was bound to result in further gains for the country, while non-participation could have unfortunate consequences. Accordingly, Werth again implored Bárdossy to take a speedy decision on this question and make a formal offer of Hungary's participation in the forthcoming German-Russian conflict. [45]

Werth's latest memorandum was discussed by Hungary's civilian leaders at a meeting of the Ministerial Council on 15 June. Here the Chief-of-Staff's request for a voluntary offer of Hungarian participation in a German war against Russia was rejected. Instead, the ministers decided to ascertain the true intentions of the Germans in the East. But before a feeler could have been put out in Berlin, the message came from Ribbentrop informing the Hungarian Government that German-Russian relations would be 'clarified' by the first week of July at the latest. [46] The note from Berlin did not mention the question of Hungary's role in the coming showdown. Evidently, Hungarian participation in the opening phase of the attack on Russia was not desired. What was more ominous was that the Germans announced the planned visit to Budapest of a member of their General Staff for the purpose of conducting discussions with the Hungarian military command. In anticipation of these talks, Bárdossy felt obliged to remind Werth of the Government's position on the question of the country's participation in the war. But the Premier's warning proved unnecessary, for the German emissary, General Franz Halder, came to Budapest a few days later with the aim of obtaining Hungarian co-operation in minor matters only. [47]

Prior to the beginning of Hitler's attack on Russia, then, no demand had been made by Berlin on either the Hungarian Government or the military to effect the country's involvement in the war. Nor did this situation change on 22 June, the day of the launching of Operation Barbarossa. It was only on the following day that an ominous change took place in the attitude of the Germans. On that morning General Kurt Himer, the *Wehrmacht's* special representative in Hungary, visited Werth to convey the view of the German High Command that support by Hungary would be most welcome. This support, however, would have to be offered voluntarily: Germany would make no formal requests. [48]

Himer's message to Werth introduced a new factor into the growing clash of views within Hungary's leadership on the question of participation in the war. Up to this time it was only the Hungarian military command which demanded involvement. Now it became known that this was Germany's wish also. The civilian government was still opposed; in fact, the Ministerial

Council had once more rejected the idea at a meeting held on the morning of the 23rd.[49] But the Cabinet does not seem to have been firm in its decision. A few of its members undoubtedly favoured participation in the war, while many others, including Bárdossy himself, felt increasingly uneasy about Hungarian inaction. To mollify those who demanded a demonstration of Hungarian solidarity with Hitler's 'crusade against Bolshevism', and to satisfy that subconscious desire for concrete action which seems to have possessed many of the ministers, at the above-mentioned meeting of the Council it was decided to break diplomatic relations with Moscow. This move may have given some relief to those who wished to avoid tackling the larger question of the day: the issue of Hungary's role in the German war. But it was temporary relief only, for the question of participation in the conflict was to return very soon to haunt Hungary's leaders.

When Bárdossy was informed of the contents of Hitner's message, he summoned Otto von Erdmannsdorff, Germany's Minister to Hungary, for an interview. At this meeting the Premier emphatically stated that the question of his country's participation in the war was up to the civilian authorities to decide. His government would be willing to review the question, but only if it was asked to do so through diplomatic channels. Communist historians usually claim that Bárdossy refused voluntary participation in the war because he wanted to exact a price for Hungarian help. It is more likely, however, that he was still in favour of staying out of the conflagration but did not want to admit this before the Germans. Accordingly, he tried to avoid Hungarian involvement by insisting on what the Germans were not willing to provide: a formal request for Hungarian assistance.[50] But the pressure on Bárdossy to yield continued to grow during the next forty-eight hours. On the 25th a message arrived from Rome bringing Mussolini's warning that continued Hungarian inaction could have unfortunate consequences for the country. Later that day came the news of Slovakia's entry into the war. The Axis front was now almost complete, only Hungary was missing. And, on the next day, an incident occurred which resulted in the entry into the war of that country as well: the air-raid on the city of Kassa (Kosice) and other points in north-eastern Hungary.

Much has been written on this perplexing incident of modern Hungarian history and yet next to nothing is known as to who carried out the attack and why. The raid, which in Kassa resulted in about sixty casualties and much material damage, was perpetrated by a small number of planes in broad daylight, in full view of Hungarian military authorities. Still, no positive identification of the aircraft was made, and commentators on the incident have been left guessing as to the nationality and motive of the attackers. The Hungarian military blamed the attack on the Russians, a view which became the official explanation of the incident at the time. Yet, already during the war, rumours circulated in Hungary that the bombing was the work of the Germans who wanted to drag the country into the war. This version was accepted after the war by Horthy and his supporters as the true explanation. Communist historians have consistently blamed German and Hungarian 'fascists' and 'militarists' for the incident, while a life-time student of Hungarian history, Professor C.A. Macartney, endorsed still another contemporary rumour, according to which the raid was carried out by Czech or Slovak deserters flying German planes, on their way to Russia. [51] In 1972 the argument came around a full circle when this writer argued in an article that neither the 'German' nor the 'Slovak' version stood the test of evidence and that the most likely explanation of the riddle was that Russian planes bombed Kassa by mistake. [52] Recently an American historian re-opened the debate by presenting some circumstantial evidence indicating that the raid may have been masterminded by one or more members of Hungary's officer corps. [53]

Who bombed Kassa and why may never be known. [54] And it does not really matter. What is more important is that the bombing precipitated a number of decisions in Budapest which ended in Hungary's entry into the war. The report of the attack was first received by Werth who, accompanied by Defence Minister Bartha, hurried to consult with Horthy. On hearing the news, the Regent became agitated and called for retaliation against Russia. By the time Bárdossy arrived at the meeting, a decision had been arrived at in favour of immediate action. Bárdossy insisted that before any steps were taken, the Ministerial Council had to be summoned. This was agreed to and the fateful meeting of Horthy, Werth, Bartha and Bárdossy came to a hasty end. By the time the ministers assembled the Premier had already made up his mind. The Hungarian military had wanted war all along. The Germans, whom he instinctively believed to be the real

perpetrators of the air-raid, wanted Hungarian participation badly enough to resort to such vile means to achieve their ends,
while the Regent clamoured for retaliation against Russia. In
view of this situation, Bárdossy believed that there was only one
course for him to follow: to obtain the Cabinet's consent to a
declaration of a state of hostilities between Hungary and the
USSR. And Cabinet consented without much disagreement. It is
ironic that Bárdossy may have been mistaken on two counts in
his analysis of the situation. The Kassa raid may not have been a
German 'plot', and it is not certain that by calling for a reply to
the attack Horthy meant a declaration of hostilities or only
reprisals against a selected Soviet target. [55] But before matters
could be clarified, the decisions had been taken and there was to
be no retreat. And so it came to pass that on the morning of 27
June 1941, Hungary's involvement in the war was announced in
Budapest.

The events of 26 June 1941 at first glance appear to have constituted a major departure in the history of Hungary during the
so-called Horthy Era. The country's government had for years
opposed involvement in a European war but on that day it
suddenly abandoned its former policy and entered the conflict on
Germany's side. When viewed in the context of Hungarian
civil-military relations in this same period, however, the
developments of that fateful day do not come as a surprise. On
the contrary, they seem to have been a logical outcome of a trend
in Hungarian politics which had its beginnings in the years
before the outbreak of the Second World War. Ever since the
premiership of General Gömbös, the influence of Hungary's
military had been growing in the country's affairs. As war approached in Europe, this increased strength of the military
resulted in a tug of war between the country's civilian leaders
and its generals on the question of strategy in a rapidly evolving
international situation. The country's soldiers, with few exceptions, favoured closer association with the Axis and a more
energetic programme of 'gathering in' the lands that Hungary
had lost in 1919-20. The civilian government was often divided
on these questions. Its best elements wished to follow a cautious
approach: they wanted to avoid an irreversible commitment to
Germany and involvement in a European war.

The division within the Hungarian Government was not the
only factor which worked to the advantage of the country's

officer corps. The international situation was increasingly conducive to a pro-Axis orientation. The fact that more and more of
East Central Europe came under Nazi control, undoubtedly
enhanced the influence of Hungarian officers advocating closer
co-operation with Germany; and Hitler's stunning victories in
1939 and 1940 helped to confirm the wisdom of their arguments.
It should be kept in mind that one of the lessons Hungarians had
drawn from the First World War was that a small nation could
not afford to be on the losing side in a European conflagration. In
the mid and late 'thirties it was still possible to argue that
Hungary had much to risk by tying her fate to a Germany bent
on trouble, but after the spring of 1940 such arguments carried
little weight.

Still another factor which had helped the growth of the
military's influence in Hungary had been the increasing
radicalisation of the country's politics after the mid 'thirties.
Fuelled by the discontent caused by the Depression and the
slowness of social reform, right-radical groups and movements
mushroomed in many segments of Hungarian society. They often
drew their inspiration from the success of German economic
recovery and rearmament as well as an effective German foreign
policy. Attempts to stem the rising rightist tide in Hungary
brought only temporary relief. The country's conservative and
liberal elements could fight only a rear-guard action against the
rightist onslaught. Since the time of Gömbös, every Hungarian
premier had come into office with the intention to reverse or at
least to slow down this trend, but not one of them succeeded.
Some, like Imrédy, became converts to the rightist cause, while
others collapsed or gave up under the strains and frustrations of
the struggle. The most obvious victim of this process was Teleki,
but there were others as well. And the departure of such men
from the top leadership of the country as Teleki, Kánya and
Bethlen had drastic consequences for Hungarian policy-making.
In their own time these men counterbalanced the influence of the
radical right and the military. They restrained the Regent, this
septuagenarian gentleman-soldier (or, more accurately, sailor)
who was given to fits of temper and over-enthusiasm in times of
crisis. Kánya had helped to restrain the old man in 1938 when
Hitler proposed a joint attack on Czechoslovakia. Teleki
dampened his enthusiasm in March of 1941 when the Führer
promised to return some rich Hungarian provinces in the south in

exchange for Hungarian co-operation against Yugoslavia. In June of 1941, however, Bárdossy, the only man who could have restrained Horthy, lacked the moral courage to do so. Bárdossy was an opportunist; he held out against involvement in the war as long as it was not overly inconvenient for him to do so. He did resist the pressure of the pro-German generals for some time, but when both the Germans and the Regent expressed their wish for Hungarian action against Russia, the Premier quickly abandoned his former position. The Kassa incident was a welcome excuse for him to do so.[56]

The real tragedy of 26 June was that the two men who broke the news of the air-raid to Horthy happened to be two pro-German generals. By the time Bárdossy arrived at the meeting, the ex-admiral was in agreement with the soldiers on the need for immediate, emphatic action. As head of state, Horthy should have been more circumspect and exercised more caution; while Bárdossy should have protested the haste of the soldiers. Unfortunately, he seems to have lacked the resolve to resist when confronted by an emphatic and unanimous demand. Under the circumstances the Cabinet could do very little. A few of its members voiced their disapproval, but they were voted down. Only a statesman of much wisdom, foresight and high moral scruples could have saved the country from the decision to join the German war. Hungary had several such statesmen during the Horthy Era. But in June of 1941 not one of them could be found among the top leaders of the country. They had fallen victims to the power struggles of the previous three years.

It is unlikely whether an absence of these conflicts within the bosom of the Hungarian state and, in particular, the absence of the struggle between Hungary's civilians and military, could have saved the country from becoming, sooner or later, one of Germany's satellites. It must be kept in mind that the influence the Germans came to wield over the economic and political life of all Central European small nations was enormous. But the lack of internal cohesion served only to strengthen the Germans' influence in Hungary and to wear down the ability of the nation to resist German pressure.

The weakness in Hungarian leadership which had manifested itself so strongly in June of 1941 proved to be temporary. In the months that followed, wiser counsel prevailed. It was realised, even before the German disasters at El Alamein and Stalingrad, that a complete commitment on Germany's side was not in the interest of the nation. The perpetrators of this commitment: Werth, Bartha and even Bárdossy, were replaced by men who were more cautious and responsible or, at least, less pro-German. But the decision of 26 June could not be reversed without inviting retaliation by the vengeful Führer. Even when German military fortunes began to near their nadir in 1944, Hungary's leaders found it impossible to effect their country's defection from the Axis camp.[57] Only total defeat brought an end to the alliance that was undertaken so hastily in June of 1941. And when defeat came, nothing was left of Hungary's war-time government and army. Her former leaders, military and civilian alike, were either dead or found themselves in Hungarian or Allied prisons, while the country was prostrated before new and more powerful masters.

Notes

Abbreviations

DGFP   R.J. Sontag *et al.* (eds.), *Documents on German Foreign Policy, 1918-1945* (Washington, 1949-63).

DIMK   László Zsigmond (gen. ed.), *Diplomáciai iratok Magyarország külpolitikájához, 1936-1945 [Diplomatic Documents on Hungary's Foreign Policy, 1936–1945]* (Budapest, 1962).

HK   *Hadtörténelmi Közlemények [Military History Communications].*

Horthy Papers   Miklósp Szinai and Lázló Scücs (eds.), *Horthy Miklós titkos iratai [The Secret Papers of Miklós Horthy]* (Budapest, Kossuth Könyvkiadó, 1965).

MMV   László Zsigmond *et al,* (eds.), *Magyarország és a második világháboru: titkos diplomáciai okmányok a hábooru elözményeihez és történetéhez [Hungary and the Second World War: Secret diplomatic documents on the origins and history of the war]* (Budapest, Kossuth Könyvkiadó, 3rd ed. 1966).

TMWC   *Trial of the Major War Criminals before the International Military Tribunal,* 42 vols. (Nuremberg, 1946-50).

1. C.A. Macartney, *October Fifteenth: A History of Modern Hungary, 1929-1945* (Edinburgh, University of Edinburgh Press, 1956), vol. 1, p. 4.
2. According to the Hungarian census of 1910 only 54.5 per cent of the population of Hungary proper (not including Croatia-Slovenia) admitted Hungarian as their

mother-tongue. Persons speaking other languages were: Rumanian, 16.1 per cent; Slovak, 10.7 per cent. German, 10.4 per cent; Ruthenian, 2.5 per cent. (C.A. Macartney, *Hungary and Her Successors* (London, Oxford University Press, 1937). p. 2.)

3. Other important aristocratic statesmen in the history of interwar Hungary were Count Albert Apponyi, Count Gyula Károlyi and Count István Bethlen. The latter two often acted in the role of confidential advisers to Horthy long after their departure from the limelight of national politics.

4. *DGFP* Ser. D. vol. V. doc. no. 149. Communist historians in Hungary avoid reference to this statement of Kánya. The exception is a more than thousand page collection of German documents relating to Hungary which gives a Hungarian translation of the memorandum containing Kánya's words. György Ránki et al. (eds.), *A Wilhelmstrasse és Magyarország: német diplomáciai iratok Magyarországról, 1933-1944 [The Wilhelmstrasse and Hungary: German Diplomatic Documents on Hungary, 1933-44]* (Budapest, Kissuth Könyvkiadó, 1968), doc. no. 104.

5. Thomas L. Sakmyster, 'Hungary and the Munich Crisis: The Revisionist Dilemma', *Slavic Review*, vol. 32, no. 4 (December 1973), pp. 734-9. Also by the same author, 'The Hungarian State Visit to Germany of August, 1938: Some New Evidence on Hungary in Hitler's Pre-Munich Policy', *Canadian Slavic Studies*, vol. 3, no. 4 (Winter 1969), pp. 677-91.

6. The unusually high percentage of non-Hungarian officers in the *honvéd* had its origins in the pre-1919 period. In the Imperial forces of Austria-Hungary advancement was on the basis of merit rather than birth or nationality, a fact which prompted sons of lower-middle-class families and minority groups to enter military service rather than the more exclusive world of the public service or the professions. Another factor which made for the enlistment of many ethnic Germans was the fact that soldiers with a command of German held an advantage over unilingual Hungarian recruits. An important reason for the existence of numerous officers of Slav descent in the *honvéd* after World War I was the fact that many Slav officers of the Imperial forces found themselves outcasts in their own countries at the end of the war because they had remained loyal to the Empire. Eventually, some of these officers ended up in the *honvéd* of post-1919 Hungary. For further details see Lajos Veress de Dálnok (gen. ed.), *Magyarország honvédelme a II. világháboru elött és alatt, 1920-1945 [Hungary's Defence before and during World War II, 1920-45]* (Munich, 1972) vol. I, p. 37f. Also Jenö Czebe and Tibor Pethö, *Hungary in World War II: A Military History of the Years of War* (Budapest, New Hungary, 1946), pp. 15f.

7. Another East European country where soldiers played a predominant role in politics in the interwar years was Poland. In Rumania the influence of Marshal Averescu was temporary, while soldiers did not play a significant role in the politics of Yugoslavia and especially, Czechoslovakia. The latter of these two states did not have an established military caste of its own at the outset of the interwar period.

8. Horthy believed that it was navies and not armies that decided the outcome of modern wars. His lack of enthusiasm for armies was known among Hungary's officers.

9. On Gömbös see Macartney, *October Fifteenth*, vol. I., chs. 7 and 8. N.F. Dreisziger, *Hungary's Way to World War II* (Toronto, Helikon, 1968), part III.

10. Gömbös had been the first advocate of the Rome-Berlin Axis, and promoted friendly relations between Germany and Italy throughout his term of office. Ironically, he died a short time before his expectations became a reality.

11. Sakmyster, 'Hungary and the Munich Crisis', p. 740; Dreisziger, *Hungary's Way*, pp. 94-9.

12. *DGFP* Ser. D. vol. IV, doc. no. 198. Also, Galeazzo Ciano, *The Ciano Diaries, 1939-1943* (New York, Doubleday, 1945), p. 42.

13. For details see Macartney, *October Fifteenth*, vol. I, pp. 212-19. Also, Thomas L. Sakmyster, 'Army Officers and Foreign Policy in Interwar Hungary, 1918-1941', *Journal of Contemporary History*, vol. 10, no. I (January 1975), pp. 26f.
14. Gyula Juhász, *A Teleki kormány külpolitikája, 1939-1941 [The Foreign Policy of the Teleki Government, 1939-1941]* (Budapest, Akadémiai Kjadó, 1964). pp. 15-16; György Ránki, *Emlékiratok és valóság Magyarország második világháborus szerepéről [Memoris and the Truth about Hungary's Role in the Second World War]* (Budapest, Kossuth, 1964), pp. 180-1).
15. According to Professor Macartney, Kánya may have been dismissed because he had offended Mme Imrédy, the wife of Premier Béla Imrédy. (*October Fifteenth*, vol. I, pp. 305f. and 315f.)
16. *Ibid.*, ch. 15.
17. *Ibid.*, p. 274. Vilmos Nagy de Nagybaczon, *Végzetes Esztendök, 1938-1945 [Fateful Years, 1938-1945]* (Budapest, Körmendy, c. 1946), p. 30.
18. For a recent treatment of the question of Transylvania's transfer to Rumania in 1919 see Peter Pastor, 'Franco-Rumanian Intervention in Russia and the *Vix Ultimatum:* Background to Hungary's Loss of Transylvania', *Canadian-American Review of Hungarian Studies*, vol. I, nos. 1 and 2 (Spring-Fall 1974), pp. 12-27. Professor Pastor's thesis is that early in 1919 the French government pushed for the cession of Transylvania to Rumania because it needed Rumanian support for French interventionist forces in the Ukraine which were hard pressed by the Bolsheviks.
19. *DIMK*, vol. IV, doc. no. 577. Also, N.F. Dreisziger, 'Count István Bethlen's Secret Plan for the Restoration of the Empire of Transylvania', *East European Quarterly*, vol. 8, no. 4 (January 1975), pp. 413-23.
20. Macartney, *October Fifteenth*, vol. I, pp. 388-9.
21. Juhász, *op. cit.*, pp. 103f.
22. *Ibid.*, p. 106.
23. *Ibid.*, pp. 121-4.
24. *Ibid.*, pp. 122-4, András Hory, *Még egy barázdát sem [Not even one furrow]* (Vienna, published by the author, 1967). p. 38.
25. Dreisziger, *Hungary's Way*, pp. 129-31. For a different interpretation of Teleki's aims see Juhász, *op. cit.*, pp. 150f.
26. Juhász, *op. cit.*, pp. 144-9.
27. The evidence on Werth's indiscretion is a memorandum by Teleki to Horthy (see footnote 29 below). Historians have generally accepted this evidence.
28. The Award transferred about a million Rumanians to Hungary and left almost half a million Hungarians within the new boundaries of Rumania. But a settlement which would have been satisfactory to both sides was probably impossible. For further details on the terms of the Award see Macartney, *October Fifteenth*, vol I, pp. 422-4.
29. Memorandum by Teleki addressed to Horthy, 1 September 1940. Horthy Papers, doc. no. 49 (pp. 233-9).
30. Appendix I to the above document. *Ibid.*, pp. 239-51.
31. Macartney, *October Fifteenth*, vol. I, p. 433.
32. *Ibid.*, ch. 21.
33. *Ibid.*, ch. 22. Dreisziger, *Hungary's Way*, pp. 146-8.
34. Horthy acknowledged the existence of Hungarian territorial claims against Yugoslavia and welcomed the proposed discussions between the German and Hungarian general staffs. *MMV*, doc. no. 127. also, Nagy, *op. cit.*, pp. 61f. For an English translation of Horthy's letter see Macartney, *October Fifteenth*, vol. 1, pp. 475ff.
35. Juhász, *op. cit.*, pp. 301-2. *MMV*, doc. no. 130.
36. Basically, these conditions were that Hungary would not cross the frontier until after the disintegration of the Yugoslav state and that Hungarian forces would

enter only certain territories that had formerly belonged to Hungary. (Dreisziger, *Hungary's Way*, p. 151.)

37. On Teleki's death see Macartney, *October Fifteenth*, vol. I, pp. 486ff; Dreisziger, *Hungary's Way*, pp. 152-5. Also, Loránt Tilkovszky, *Teleki Pál: legenda és valóság [Pál Teleki: The Legend and the Truth]* (Budapest, Kossuth, 1969 ch.) 1 and pp. 151f.

38. C.A. Macartney, 'Hungary's Declaration of War on the U.S.S.R. in 1941', in A.O. Sarkissian (ed.), *Studies in Diplomatic History and Historiography* (London, Longmans, 1961), pp. 153-65. Juhász, *op. cit.*, pp. 157-67.

39. The testimony of Lieutenant-General Gunther Krappe. *TMWC*, vol. VII, pp. 336f.

40. Joseph Kun, 'Magyarország második világháboruba való belépésének katonapolotikai vonatkozásai' *[The Military-Political Aspects of Hungary's Entry into the Second World War]*, HK 1952, no. 1, pp. 21-2.

41. György Ránki, 'Magyarország belépése a második világháboruba' *[Hungary's Entry into the Second World War]*, HK 6, no. 2 (1959), p. 40. Kun, *op. cit.*, p. 21.

42. W. Keitel, *The Memoirs of Field-Marshal Keitel* (New York, Stein and Day, 1966), p. 13. The memoirs of Ernst Alexander Paulus are cited by Mario D. Fenyo, *Hitler, Horthy, and Hungary: German-Hungarian Relations, 1941-1944* (New Haven and London, Yale University Press, 1972), p. 13.

43. András Zako, 'Egy emlékezetes évforduló, [A Memorable Anniversary] *Hadak Utján*, vol. XIII, no. [6] (June 1961), p. 8. Also, Macartney, *October Fifteenth*, vol. II, p. 18.

44. Macartney, *October Fifteenth*, vol. II, p. 18.

45. *MMV*, doc. no. 141.

46. *DGFP*, Ser. D. vol. XII, doc. no. 631.

47. Juhász, *op. cit.*, pp. 343f.

48. *DGFP*, Ser. D. vol. XIII, doc. no. 54. The German High Command had favoured Hungarian involvement in the war all along; however, Hitler had forbidden it to express this view to the Hungarians until after the start of the invasion.

49. Juhász, *op. cit.*, p. 346.

50. N.F. Dreisziger, 'New Twist to an Old Riddle: The Bombing of Kassa (Košice) June 26, 1941', *Journal of Modern History*, vol. 44, no. 2 (June 1972), p. 235. For a Marxist interpretation see Juhász, *op. cit.*, pp. 351-2.

51. Macartney, 'Hungary's Declaration', p. 165.

52. Dreisziger, 'New Twist', p. 242.

53. Sakmyster, 'Army Officers', p. 36.

54. I am presently gathering evidence of still another, completely unexpected explanation of the raid.

55. On this question of a possible misunderstanding between the Regent and the Premier see Macartney, *October Fifteenth*, vol. II, p. 26, especially note 1.

56. During the thirties Horthy had often sought the advice of Bethlen; but on this occasion, however, the old statesman was not consulted. But in June of 1941 who would have been interested in the views of a man who in late 1939 had forecast the defeat of Germany by France and Britain?

57. For the most recent study of the Hungarian attempt of 1944 to defect from the war see Peter Gosztony, 'Horthy, Hitler and the Hungary of 1944', *Canadian-American Review of Hungarian Studies*, vol. II, no. 1 (Spring 1975), pp. 43-58.

Notes on Contributors

George F. G. Stanley was Rhodes Scholar for Alberta in 1930. During World War II, he was Deputy Director of the Historical Section (General Staff) at NDHQ in the rank of Lieutenant-Colonel. From 1949 to 1968, he was Head of the History Department, and from 1959 Dean and Chairman of the Arts Division at the Royal Military College of Canada. From 1968 until his retirement in 1975 he was Curator of the Davidson Collection and Director of Canadian Studies, Mount Allison University, New Brunswick. He has published, among many other books, *The Birth of Western Canada* (London, 1936); *Canada's Soldiers* (Toronto, 1954); *Louis Riel* (Toronto, 1963); *New France: The Last Phase 1744-60* (Toronto, 1968); *Canada Invaded, 1775-76* (Toronto, 1973).

Commander W. A. B. Douglas, RCN (Rtd.), Director, Directorate of History, National Defence Headquarters, Ottawa. From 1964 to 1967 Naval Staff Officer and Associate Professor of Military Studies, RMC. B.A. (Toronto) 1951, M.A. (Dalhousie) 1961, Ph.D. (Queen's) 1973.

Desmond Morton is Professor of History and Associate Dean of Humanities at Erindale College, University of Toronto. He was RMC's first Rhodes Scholar (1959) and read for his Doctorate at the University of London, England. Among his numerous books are *Ministers and Generals: Politics and the Canadian Militia 1868-1904* (Toronto, 1970), *The Canadian General: Sir William Otter* (Toronto, 1975), *The last War Drum: the North West Campaign of 1885* (Toronto, 1972).

Adrian Preston was educated at RMC, University of British Columbia, University of Toronto and University of London, King's College. Since 1965 he has been Associate Professor of History at RMC. In 1971-2 he held the Chair of Military and Strategic Studies at Acadia University, N.S. He has published *In Relief of Gordon* (London, 1967), *The South African Diaries of Sir Garnet Wolseley 1875* (Cape Town, 1971), *The South*

African Journals of Sir Garnet Wolseley 1879-80 (Cape Town, 1973) and over thirty articles in military and learned journals world-wide. He is the co-editor, with Peter Dennis, of *Soldiers as Statesmen* (London, 1976).

W. Murray Hogben received his Ph.D. for his dissertation, 'The Foreign and Political Department of the Government of India, 1876-1919, a study in imperial careers and attitudes' (University of Toronto, 1973). He has subsequently published several articles on the North-West Frontier of India, and on the early Indianisation of the Indian Political Service, and is revising his thesis for the purpose of publication. He has been teaching British and European history at RMC since 1973, and has also wide interests in European expansion and non-European reactions to this movement.

A.M.J. Hyatt is Associate Professor of History at the University of Western Ontario, London, Ontario. He was educated at RMC and Duke University and is the author of numerous articles on Canadian military history as well as editor of *Dreadnought to Polaris: Maritime Strategy in the 20th Century* (Toronto, 1973).

G. William Hines was educated at Queen's University, Kingston and Duke University. In 1973-4 he was a Research Associate in the Department of History at RMC. He is now employed by the Canadian Imperial Bank of Commerce and is currently preparing a book on British amphibious doctrine in the nineteenth century.

Peter Dennis was born in Adelaide, South Australia, and educated at the University of Adelaide and Duke University, North Carolina. Since 1969 he has been a member of the RMC History Department. In 1973-4 he held the Chair of Military and Strategic Studies at The University of Western Ontario. He is the author of *Decision by Default: Peacetime Conscription and British Defence, 1919–1939* (London and Durham, N.C., 1972), and co-editor, with Adrian Preston, of *Soldiers as Statesmen* (London, 1976).

N.F. Dreisziger, Assistant Professor in the Department of History at the Royal Military College of Canada, earned his Diploma in Russian and East European Studies and his M.A. and Ph.D. degrees at the University of Toronto. He is the author of *Hungary's Way to World War II*; the editor and co-author of a forthcoming monograph on Hungarians in Canada in the *History of the Peoples of Canada* series; and the editor of the *Canadian-American Review of Hungarian Studies*. He has also published articles on East Central European and North American subjects in such journals as the *Journal of Modern History*, *East European Quarterly*, *New York History* and the *Canadian Historical Papers*. Dr Dreisziger has been teaching courses in Canada, Russian and European history at RMC since 1970.

Index